'The voice of wine'   *Sunday Telegraph*

Matthew Jukes is the wine buyer for Bibendum restaurant and The Crescent wine bar, both on London's Fulham Road. He had his own weekly radio feature on the BBC for five years, presented Channel 4's TV series *Wine Hunt* and is a regular guest on BBC One's prime-time Saturday night programme *Friends Like These*. Writing a weekly column for the *Daily Mail* and an on-line newsletter www.expertwine.com, Matthew is also the author of *Wine* and the number one bestselling guide *The Wine List 2002*, both published by Headline. He has been awarded the International Wine and Spirit Competition's trophy for **Communicator of the Year 2002**.

First published in 2002 by
HEADLINE BOOK PUBLISHING

10 9 8 7 6 5 4 3 2 1

A CIP catalogue record for this title is available from the British Library

ISBN 0 7472 4423 5

Printed and bound in Great Britain by Butler & Tanner Ltd, Frome

Designed by Fiona Pike, Pike Design

Headline Book Publishing
A division of Hodder Headline
338 Euston Road
London NW1 3BH

www.headline.co.uk
www.hodderheadline.com

THE WINE LIST 2003

MATTHEW JUKES

THE TOP 250 WINES OF THE YEAR

headline

To Elspeth

I would like to thank everyone I have met in the last year for their time, energy, enthusiasm and, crucially, wine. There are too many of you to name individually, but you know who you are. This is an immensely enjoyable book to put together and I look forward to doing it all again next year. Special thanks must go to Nathalie, Isadora, Elspeth, Ma and Pa, Robert Kirby, and the team at Headline, especially Jo Roberts-Miller, for bringing this opus to life. It is now your turn to decide what to drink, as I'm having a few weeks off.

CONTENTS

INTRODUCTION

Before I kick off this year's edition, I would like to thank everyone who bought last year's. I was absolutely delighted to see it make the Times Book Chart and, by the close of play, it had notched up enough sales to make it the number one wine book in the UK.

I have kept the exact same recipe this year, apart from a few subtle design tweaks and the jazzy new red livery. The Wine List 2003 is the only book you'll ever need to track down the best wines in the world. The main chapter in the book, as the title suggests, is a list of my favourite 250 wines. There are a lot of dreary bottles out there, but if you follow my suggestions, you'll never drink a dull bottle of wine again. I have included all of the peripheral information you need to track these wines down and also what to serve with them. Your task is simply to grab a corkscrew, some glasses and relax.

This book is split into four main sections.

The **A-Z of food and wine** covers all of the ingredients and dishes you'll come across in the course of eating out and entertaining at home. Just find your dish and discover what style of wine is best suited to bringing out the full flavour of your cooking without losing any of the subtleties in the wine. This year I have a few new entries – frogs' legs and haggis spring to mind. Goodness knows what I will be adding to this ever-expanding section next year!

The top 250 is a distillation of my 26,000 tasting notes into a shorter list of around 600. Once completed, I ruthlessly cull this longish list into a hard core of 250. Fifty weeks non-stop tasting ends and two weeks intense writing takes over. But what makes a wine worthy of listing? Apart from fantastic flavour, cutting-edge winemaking and great value for money, I have made sure that each of the wines is ready to drink. This means you can uncork a bottle the second you get home. But be aware that there is only a finite quantity of each of my wines on the shelves. Last year, some wines sold at light speed, so if you want to grab some of the rarer bottles, you'll have to get in quick. Others, with larger stocks, last for ages. Six months into the life of TWL02, over 200 wines were still available. As I write every word of this book myself (apparently an odd concept in the realm of annual guides) and don't use other people's tasting notes (heaven forbid) or industry databases, the research is all mine. This also means that any errors are mine also. I have endeavoured to list each wine's average retail price. Some shops may sell a little over this, others under. Some of the wines are available in supermarkets, others in small independent outfits. Just because a merchant is not on your doorstep, don't let this stop you buying their wines. Get together with some friends and order a case over the phone. Every merchant in this book delivers nationwide and the charge should only work out to fifty or so pence a bottle. I have issued a few merchants with stickers to let you know which wines on their shelves have made my Top 250 – keep your eyes peeled.

So, who did well this year? Australia and New Zealand combined have over 70 entries. South Africa also did well, with 19, and South America has a worthy 18. Only California disappoints with a poor 6, but value for money always dents this region's chances. This year Europe has fought back. France has over 60, but the surprise must be the brilliant performance of Italy, Spain and Portugal, who have totted up a massive total of 66 wines. Canada, Hungary, England, Greece and Germany all make it, but lack the firepower to influence the overall outcome. The Old World wins the battle with 135 to the New World's 115 wines, almost an exact reversal of last year's tally.

As an aside, this past year has seen the welcome emergence of Stelvin closures, otherwise known as screwcaps. The idea of putting dry, fresh white wines under screwcap is not a new one. In the past inexpensive wines huddled under these twist tops. How times have changed. Some of the smartest wineries in the world (and a number of wines in my Top 250) have had enough of rogue, bacteria-infected corks tainting their wines and making them taste dull and musty. These perfectionist estates want you to taste their wine in tip-top condition and a screwcap is the ideal closure, despite often costing more to produce than a cork. Plastic corks fulfil the same job. They may not be as aesthetically pleasing as a real cork, but who wants to drink shoddy wine? I encounter corked wines every day, from the cheapest house wines, all the way up to Grand Cru Burgundies. Somehow this problem must be stopped. Screwcaps and plastic corks eliminate the problem, so embrace these innovations and drink these wines safe in the knowledge that they are at the top of their game.

The **Gazetteer** is a comprehensive list of the finest wineries in the world. This is the ultimate wine who's who. Add this information to my Top 250 and you've cracked it. Use this list when you're shopping for fine wine, when you're on holiday to track down the best estates, or when you're in a restaurant with an unfamiliar wine list.

The **Directory** is the essential list of the top independent wine merchants in the UK, plus their hometown or postcode, telephone number and, new for this year, email address. I have also included the HQ hot lines for each of the major supermarket and specialist wine retail chains. Use this service – it is the best way to track down and order any wine you are after.

A–Z OF FOOD
AND WINE
COMBINATIONS

FOOD AND WINE

INTRODUCTION

The following list of dishes and ingredients is designed to point you in the direction of some great food and wine matches. I have been working in the restaurant business for over fifteen years, writing wine lists and training wine waiters, and during this time I have discovered some superb food and wine combinations. Now I know that wine and, for that matter, food appreciation is very much a matter of personal taste. Not everyone loves everything, and tastes do differ. This is, of course, good news, because if we were all alike there would be no point in making the thousands of different wines, or cooking the innumerable dishes the world has to offer. And while I recognise and celebrate this diversity, for each of the following listings, I have endeavoured to guide you to a group of wines, styles or grape varieties that should suit the food in question well. Your task is to make the final selection. You could do this by using my Top 250, the Gazetteer section, or by just going 'off piste' and searching for good matches yourself. You will see some wine styles popping up more often than others. These are multipurpose, multitalented styles like Sauvignon Blanc or New World Merlot – try to keep a few bottles of these wines at home, in readiness for unexpected guests or impromptu cooking. Surprisingly, Beaujolais, one of the most derided styles of wine, is incredibly versatile – it pops up over 20 times in this section! One thing is for certain, if there is a wicked food and wine combo, you'll find it here.

And just to prove it works – I was recently challenged to match a wine to Shakuti, an Indian masala lamb shank dish with an intense sauce containing twenty-six spices. After considering the challenge, and mentally breaking down the dish into its component flavours and textures, I tried to come up with a complementary wine. In the end, I plumped for a 1998 Gravello, Librandi from Calabria in southern Italy. Camellia Panjabi, a serious Indian food expert and restaurateur, exclaimed that the food and wine combination, which she previously thought to be impossible, was 'perfect, fantastic', and she smiled like a Cheshire cat. This strongly flavoured dish would have walked all over a huge number of red wines, let alone anything white, but I knew there was a good match somewhere, and this unlikely combination made the lamb sing, while the wine mellowed to unravel its full array of aromas and flavours. Who'd have thought that the rare red grape Gaglioppo would have found its perfect companion in India?

APÉRITIF WINE STYLES

Pre-dinner nibbles like *dry roasted almonds, bruschetta, cashews, canapés, crostini, crudités, olives* and *gougères* (glorious cheese puffs, served with alacrity in Burgundy and Chablis) are designed to give your palate a kick-start and get your juices flowing before a meal. It is crucial at this stage of proceedings not to swamp your taste buds with big, juicy, powerful wines. Save these for later and aim for refreshing, palate-teasing styles that set the scene, rather than hog the stage: Champagne is always a winner if you're feeling flush, if not, then sparkling wines from the Loire (Saumur), the south of France (Limoux) or Crémant de Bourgogne (Burgundy) would do. Italy offers up superb fizz in the form of Prosecco, from Veneto, or serious sparklers from Trentino or Alto Adige. I am not a Cava fan, but Spain has innumerable versions to sample. The real non-Champs fun comes from the New World – New Zealand, Australia and California are the places to go for superb value and awesome quality. Fino or manzanilla sherries are wonderful palate cleansers, ever so foody, and, although perpetually 'out of fashion', will ensure you are regarded as a purveyor of fine taste – whether it be refreshingly retro or light years ahead of your time. The least expensive (and often safest) option for an apéritif, though, is a zesty, uplifting, zingy dry white wine. There are thousands of these around and loads of first-class examples in this book. Stick with unoaked styles and keep the price down so that you can step up a level or two with the next bottle when the food hits the table. A neutral dry white can always be pepped up with a dash of Crème de Cassis to make a Kir (use dry sparkling wine or inexpensive Champagne to make a flashy Kir Royale).

STARTERS AND MAIN COURSES

Anchovies Strongly flavoured and fresh or cured, anchovies need dry, unoaked, tangy acidic whites or juicy, bone-dry rosés. Try Italy, Spain or France and keep to a low budget – a fiver should do it. There are a few worthy rosés from the New World, but tread carefully as they can be a little alcohol-rich. Dry sherry is also a banker.

Antipasti The classic Italian selection of *artichokes, prosciutto, bruschetta, olives, marinated peppers* and *aubergines* enjoys being serenaded with light Italian reds like Valpolicella and Bardolino, or clean, vibrant whites like Pinot Grigio, Est! Est!! Est!!!, Cataratto, Orvieto, Verdicchio or Pinot Bianco.

Artichokes Dry, unoaked whites are best here, especially if you are dipping the artichokes in *vinaigrette* (see 'Vinaigrette'). Alsatian Sylvaner or Pinot Blanc, Loire Sauvignon Blanc or Aligoté from Burgundy are perfect partners, as are the Italian whites listed above for 'Antipasti'.

Asparagus Because of its inbuilt asparagusy characteristics, Sauvignon Blanc is the obvious match here. Australian or New Zealand versions have tons of flavour and would be better suited to asparagus dishes that have *hollandaise*, *balsamic vinegar* or *olive oil* and *Parmesan*. Loire Sauvignon Blanc and Chenin Blanc are great if the dish is plainer. Northern Italian whites like Pinot Bianco or Pinot Grigio, as well as South African Sauvignon Blanc (in between New Zealand and Loire in style) would all do the job well.

Aubergines If served grilled, with *pesto* or with *olive oil*, *garlic* and *basil*, you must identify the most dominant flavours in the dish. In both of these cases they are the same – garlic and basil – so tackle them with dry Sauvignon Blanc (see 'Garlic'). Plain aubergine dishes are fairly thin on the ground as these glossy, black beauties are often used within veggie recipes (for example, *ratatouille* or *caponata*). If cheese or meat (*moussaka*) is involved those flavours take over from the aubergines, so light, youthful reds are required. Southern Italian or Sicilian, southern French Grenache-based blends, Chilean Carmenère or Argentinian Tempranillo are all good matches. Just make sure they are not too heavy. If the dish is hotter or spicier, or the aubergines are *stuffed*, you will need a more feisty red, but don't be tempted by anything too weighty (avoid Cabernet, Zinfandel, Shiraz etc.). *Imam bayildi*, the classic aubergine, onion, olive oil and tomato dish is a winner with juicy, slightly chilled New World Merlot, bright purple Valpolicella, glossy Sardinian Cannonau or black-fruit-imbued Montepulciano d'Abruzzo.

Avocado If the avocado is *undressed*, you need light, unoaked whites, in particular Sauvignon Blanc, Muscadet or Bourgogne Aligoté. If *dressed* with *vinaigrette* or with *Marie Rose sauce* for a prawn cocktail, richer Sauvignon Blancs or New World Verdelho are fine, as are white Rhônes and Alsatian Pinot Blanc. *Guacamole*, depending on its chilli content, needs cool, dry whites to quench the thirst.

Bacon This usually pops up as an ingredient in a dish and not often as the sole item, unless the shops are shut and your fridge is bare. But if you feel like a glass of wine to accompany a *full English breakfast* (I know I do), with black pudding and all the extras, then chilled red Côtes-du-Rhône or Beaujolais would be superb, as would sparkling Shiraz from down under. If, however, you are using grilled *pancetta* or *lardons* in a salad, remember that the salty flavour and/or the smoked taste could suggest a move away from a salady white wine to a juicy, fresh red. *Bacon and eggs* with red Burgundy is heavenly, if a bit decadent.

Barbecues The carefree, fun lovin', often haphazard nature of barbecues, combined with the spicy marinades and intense, smoky sauces, ensures an informal and flavour-packed occasion. Aim for New World gluggers, white or red, so long as they are assertive and juicy. Lightly oaked Chardonnay, Sémillon or blends for whites, or inexpensive Zinfandel, Merlot, Carmenère, Cabernet Sauvignon or Shiraz for reds, would all be a treat. Try Chile, Argentina, Australia, South Africa or New Zealand for likely candidates.

Beans With *baked beans* the tomato sauce takes over and you simply need fruit-driven reds to go with the tomato flavour. Any forward reds with fresh acidity, such as those from the Loire, Spain or Italy, should work well. Just try to keep the price down. Anything goes with *green beans* as they are hardly robust vegetables and you'd have to tiptoe with a fairy light white to let a green bean express itself. A *Tuscan bean salad* would demand a chilled light red, or a tart, zingy white. If you have beans in a stew, such as *cassoulet* or various Spanish dishes, then Grenache-dominant wines from the south of France (Fitou, Corbières, Faugères or Minervois), or Garnacha-based wines from Spain (Navarra, Terra Alta, Priorato or Tarragona) would deal easily with the beanie ballast. *Black bean sauce* requires a radical rethink. Any wines subjected to such sweetness and intensity of flavour must be huge, red and very smooth – Zinfandel is the only one with its hand up! *Refried beans*, either in tacos or other Mexican dishes, have a certain sludginess and earthy character that needs either rich whites like New World Chardonnay (Chile and Australia do the best value), or fresh, fruity reds. I would try Bonarda, Sangiovese or Tempranillo from Argentina as a starting point, then head to Chile if you have no joy. My favourite bean of the year is the noble cannellini, base of all great beany soups. But you'll have to wait with spoon and glass at the ready until the 'Soup' entry to see what works.

Beef There are so many beefy incarnations. The general rule must be that reds are the order of the day, but it is the size and shape of them that determines just how good the match will be. *Roast* (or *en croûte/Beef Wellington*) Sunday lunches invoke a degree of formality, perhaps even a modicum of decorum, and when you gather around the table do, by all means, push the boat out. It is at times like these when old-fashioned gentleman's claret (red Bordeaux) really makes sense. Don't ask me why, but fine wines such as claret, Bandol, erudite northern Rhônes – Hermitage, Cornas, St-Joseph or Côte-Rôtie – or even Italy's answer to an Aston Martin Vantage, the Super-Tuscans, are simply magnificent with this king of beef dishes. Of course, not one of these wines is cheap. Nowhere near, in fact, so if you are looking to shave a few pounds off the budget, I would recommend heading towards top Cabernets from Australia's Margaret River (Western Australia) or the Napa Valley in California. You've guessed it, again fairly dear, but these reds will give you the richness and complexity that you are yearning for. If you are on a strict budget, try to replicate the flavours of the aforementioned great wines by following clever selections.

Not all wines from the Bordeaux sub-regions are exorbitantly priced. The Côtes de Castillon, Bourg, Blaye and Francs, in a good year, can really hit the spot with roast beef, while Bergerac, Bordeaux's neighbour, or hearty Languedoc reds (copying the Rhône model) would also do very well. Most Aussie (try McLaren Vale in particular), South African, Chilean and Argentinian Cabernets or Cab/Shiraz blends, around the tenner mark, offer charm, complexity and excitement. It is at this price point that the New World leads the pack. Drop down to a fiver and you'll still have fun, but remember to stick to hotter climate wines, as claret at this price is usually dire.

Remember, if you like your beef *rare*, you can safely drink a younger, slightly more tannic wine, as harsh tannins balance well with juicy, rare meat. If you like your beef *well done*, then an older wine, smoother, more harmonious and at its peak of drinking, will work better. *Stews*, *casseroles* and *pies* require heavier, structured reds, particularly if meaty, stock-rich gravy is involved. Cabernet Sauvignon, Syrah (Shiraz), Piemontese (northern Italian) reds, Zinfandel and Malbec are but a few of the superb, hunky grapes to go for. Track down wines from South Africa, Australia, California and Argentina. Southern Rhônes like Gigondas, Lirac, Rasteau or Vacqueyras will be superb, as will Provençal or Languedoc reds made from a similar blend of swarthy red grapes. Portuguese wines are worth considering with rich beef dishes, as the red wines from Dão and the Douro Valley are woefully under-priced and impressive of late. The great, black wine from Cahors in southwest France also deserves a mention, as it is a gifted beef partner. *Bollito misto*, the Italian stew made from beef, and about everything else you could possibly think of, demands indigenous wines – Teroldego and Marzemino, from Trentino in northern Italy, would be a good place to kick off. *Boeuf bourguignon*, as the name suggests, usually enlists the help of red Burgundy. But don't cook with anything expensive. Save your money for the 'drinking' wine, and choose a more upmarket version of the wine you have used to cook with. *Steak and kidney pie* needs earthy, rustic reds with fresh acidity and pokey tannins, to slice through the gravy and sturdy kidneys; Madiran and Cahors from France, Malbec from Argentina and New World war-horses like South African Pinotage also enjoy this challenge. *Cottage pie*, with carrot, celery, onions and minced beef rarely requires anything more talented than a feisty, inexpensive red. You could even try Bulgaria or Hungary (although *I* didn't tell you this) or southern Italy or Sicily (a much safer bet) and wallow. Go mad, buy two bottles. *Beef stroganoff* also demands inbuilt rusticity, so search for southern Rhônes (Vacqueyras, Lirac, Cairanne or Gigondas); even Côtes-du-Rhône from the right domaines can be a joy (see the Gazetteer). *Hungarian goulash* would be all the more authentic if a Hungarian red wine joined it. Good luck, I have yet to find the dream date, so if you want to be in more familiar territory, head straight for Chilean Cabernet or Carmenère. Straight *steak* has a more directly meaty flavour than a stew, so finer wines can be dragged out of the cellar (or offie). Try Chianti, Brunello di Montalcino, Ribera del Duero, Californian Merlot, top-end Cru Beaujolais, Crozes-Hermitage, St-Joseph, and South African, Argentinian and New Zealand Cabernet Sauvignon. Watch out for *Béarnaise sauce* which, though great with steak, can be a bit of a passion killer for red wines. With *steak au poivre*, the pungent, pulverised peppercorns take over each mouthful, so look for meaty (peppery) wines like northern Rhône reds or their cousins from further afield – Shiraz from Australia or South Africa, or South African Pinotage. *Burgers*, one of my all time favourite dishes (at home!), often served with ketchup, bacon, cheese or relish, need fruit-driven, less expensive reds like Italian Dolcetto, Spanish Garnacha, young Rioja Crianza, Californian Zinfandel, Chilean or South African Merlot, and again the ever-versatile, meaty South African Pinotage. *Chilli con carne* is a funny dish to match with wine, but again, as with burgers, search for fruitier styles like Aussie Merlot, or Negroamaro or Nero d'Avola from southern Italy and Sicily. *Steak tartare* is a strange one, and I'm still not sure whether I really like it, but it works terrifically well with light reds and rosés – Tavel and other Grenache-based rosés are perfect, as are Pinot Noirs like Sancerre red or rosé. If you fancy splashing out, then rosé Champagne is the ultimate combo, but go easy on the capers, if served alongside. *Cold, rare roast beef salad,* and other cold beef dishes, need fresh reds with low tannins – Beaujolais, Valpolicella, red Loires (either Cabernet Franc or Gamay) or Argentinian Tempranillo or Bonarda would work. The only occasion you can break the red-wine-with-beef rule (there has to be one) is with *carpaccio* (raw/rare) or *bresaola* (air-dried). These wafer-thin sliced beef dishes can handle whites. Any dry Italian white or light Montepulciano-style red would be perfect.

Cajun – see 'Mexican'.

Capers Sauvignon Blanc from almost anywhere, or very dry Italian whites like Soave, or Greco from Campania, are good matches, as they can cut through the peculiar green, vinegary tanginess experienced when you munch on a caper.

Caviar Ridiculously decadent, but if you can afford caviar, you will no doubt be able to splash out on Champagne as well. Avoid rosés, though, and there is no need for prestige cuvées unless you're desperately trying to impress. If the caviar is in a sauce then consider the main ingredients in the dish. Sauvignon Blanc is always a safe bet, but poached sea bass (for example) with a Champagne and caviar sauce would, bankrupt you for a start, and would follow the sea bass more than the caviar in the wine-matching process, so read on for the 'Fish' section. Or, head for the nearest independent merchant and fork out for the best white Burgundy they can offer.

Charcuterie A selection of charcuterie (or *assiette de charcuterie* including *saucisson*, *salami*, *ham* etc.) often contains diverse flavours along a similar textural theme. Characterful rosés, top quality, slightly chilled, Beaujolais or Loire Gamay would be my first choices. Light to medium Italian reds, like Valpolicella, Morellino di Scansano, Montepulciano d'Abruzzo or Aglianico from the south would also be a good match. White wine lovers may prefer Riesling, which usually manages to harness at least as much flavour intensity as the reds anyway. Do watch out for pickles, gherkins/ cornichons or caperberries served alongside charcuterie, as vinegar is dangerous when it comes to wine. You'll not be able to taste the next mouthful! So tap the pickles first, to knock off as much vinegar as possible. (For *chorizo* and *spicy salami*, see 'Pork'.)

Cheese (cooked) There is an entire 'cheese-board' section at the end of this chapter, but here I have dealt with cheese in cooking. *Cauliflower cheese* (*Leek Mornays* etc.) and *cheese sauces*, depending on the strength of cheese used, needs medium- to full-bodied whites such as New World Chardonnays or Sémillons. For reds, the quest for fresh acidity and pure berry fruit leads to wines from the Loire, or even to Chilean or South African Merlot, Italian Dolcetto or Freisa, or youthful Rioja, Navarra, Toro or Campo de Borja reds from Spain. *Fondue*, not my favourite form of food fun, needs bone-dry whites to cut through the waxy, stringy, molten cheese. If you were to be a perfectionist you would head in search of the inoffensive but innocuous wines from Savoie; Chignin-Bergeron, Abymes, Crépy or Apremont would be so exact you would probably be offered a job in the V&A for attention to detail. However, if you are simply after pleasant tasting, effective wines, then well-balanced, fully ripe (as opposed to exasperatingly lean, teeth-strippingly acidic) styles like junior Alsatian Pinot Blanc, Riesling and Sylvaner and Loire Sauvignon Blanc would be accurate. As would dry Portuguese white and various northeastern Italian varietals. *Raclette*, the rather disappointingly one-dimensional fondue-and-potato-style dish, fancies light red Burgundies or Cru Beaujolais. With *cheese soufflé*, one of the masterpieces of the cooked cheese repertoire (my wife crafts a mean one), you can really go out on a limb. Argentinian Torrontés, or any aromatic dry whites like dry Muscat (Alsace), Riesling (from Clare Valley/Adelaide Hills/Eden Valley in Australia, or from Alsace) or even lighter Gewürztraminer (from anywhere decent, but try Alto Adige in Italy or even Chile or the Cape) would be delicious. If the soufflé has any other hidden ingredients remember to consider them before plumping for a bottle. *Mozzarella*, with its unusual near-milky flavour and spongy texture, is well suited to Italian Pinot Bianco, Pinot Grigio, good Vernaccia, Gavi and Verdicchio. All Italians, but what do you expect, a revolution? *Grilled goat's cheese* is equally at home with Sancerre (after all the best goat's cheese hails from Chavignol, Sancerre's leading village) and all other Sauvignon Blanc wines. Lighter reds also work, particularly if you are tucking into a salad with ham hitching a ride as well. Goat's cheese is pretty forgiving, just avoid oaked whites and heavy reds and consider the context in which it is being served.

Chicken Chicken loves whites and reds alike, but is a touch fussy when it comes to grape varieties. Chardonnay is its favourite white, with Riesling coming in second. Pinot Noir is a chook's favourite red, with Gamay claiming the silver medal. This means that a well-educated chicken loves every bit of my beloved Burgundy region, and who can blame it? Lighter dishes like *cold chicken* or *turkey* are fairly versatile, with picnic-style wines doing the job nicely (see 'Picnics'). Try red Beaujolais and white Mâcon for authentic harmony. *Cold chicken and ham pie* goes well with lighter reds and manly rosés from the southern Rhône, Beaujolais and the Loire. If you are feeling adventurous then try chilled Beaujolais-Villages; it's a super match. *Poached chicken* can handle the same sort of wines, but perhaps those with a little more volume – Old or New World Pinot Noirs, for example. White wine companions include lighter New World Chardonnay or French Country Viognier. Possibly my favourite dish of all time, *roast chicken*, once again follows this theme a stage further. Finer red and white Burgundy, elegant Australian or Californian Chardonnay and Pinot Noir, and top flight Beaujolais are all wonderful matches. *Coq au vin* also works well with red Burgundy, but you can scale the wine down to a Chalonnais, Bourgogne rouge (from one of my reputable producers, of course) or Hautes-Côtes level (ditto). *Chicken casserole/pot pie* ups the ante further, with a broader brief to play with. Medium-weight Rhône reds and New World Grenache, as well as mildly oaky Chardonnays, are all in with a chance. *Chicken and mushroom pie*, *fricassee* and *creamy sauces* call out beyond Chardonnay to other varieties such as dry Riesling (from Alsace, Australia and New Zealand), Alsatian Tokay-Pinot

Gris and funky Rhône whites. New World Pinot Noir (from California, New Zealand and Victoria in Oz) is the only token red variety to feel truly at home here. We now throw a few obstacles in front of the poor bird as *chicken Kiev* changes the rules completely. Full, rich, even oaked-aged Sauvignon Blanc is needed to take on the buttery/garlic onslaught – California does this well with Fumé Blanc. Not content with this hurdle, *coronation chicken*, depending on who is making it, can have a bit of a kick, so dry Riesling (from Clare Valley in Australia, or New Zealand) would be worth trying. Lastly, *barbecued chicken wings* can be nuclear-hot (my brother still holds the record for devouring an inordinate number of these), and in my experience beer is often the only saviour. If, for some reason, you're a mild-mannered person who would like to spare the palates of your guests, then a regular, inexpensive New World Chardonnay with a touch of oak would be acceptable. The only thing to watch out for with *roast turkey* is the essential cranberry sauce factor. Often a fresh, young Rioja or New World Pinot Noir or Merlot complements this invasive red-fruit flavour well. At Christmas, Rioja is again a winner as the abundance of cocktail sausages, bacon, sprouts and the rest take the flavour spotlight away from the turkey. If you are very brave (or totally ahead of your time), then sparkling Shiraz from Australia would be fantastic, celebratory and a touch zany at the same time.

Chilli *Enchiladas*, *chimichangas*, *fajitas* and any other nuclear Mexican dishes as well as *chilli con carne* and, of course, *diablo-style/dragon's breath pizzas*, are all enlivened with a liberal dose of chillies. So thirst-quenching, chillable reds like Italian

Primitivo, Nero d'Avola or juicy New World Merlot are needed to cool you down and reassemble your taste buds. If you favour whites, then New World Chardonnay, thoroughly chilled, will have enough texture and body to handle the heat.

Chinese The main problem when matching wine to Chinese food is that you invariably feel drawn to sample every dish on the table, thus mixing flavours wildly. Sweet-and-sour dishes ram-raid spicy ones, with poor old plain, stir-fried food struggling for a break in the palate action. Thus, Chinese-friendly wines must be multi-skilled, pure fruit-driven offerings with firm acidity; tannic, youthful reds and oaky, full-bodied whites are out of bounds. White grape varieties to consider, in unoaked form, are Sauvignon Blanc, Riesling, Sémillon, Pinot Gris, Verdelho and Gewürztraminer. Reds are a little more difficult, as there are only a few truly juicy varieties, but New World Merlot, Argentinian Bonarda and US Zinfandel are usually safe bets. It is no surprise that New Zealand and Australian wines work well with this style of cooking as Asia is on their doorstep. For an unexpected combo, try *crispy aromatic duck* with chilled Chambourcin from Australia, or lighter Californian Zinfandel – it is a dead-cert.

Chutney see 'Pâté' and 'Pork'.

Duck *Roast* or *pan-fried duck* is often served with fruit, or fruity sauces, so you need to counter this with fruity wine. Reds are essential here, with New World Pinot Noir, Beaujolais, Rioja, Italian Barbera or Negroamaro, Australian Chambourcin and any other super-juicy, berry-drenched wines doing the job. *À l'orange* changes the colour of wine needed, but full-flavoured, juicy wines are still required. Alsace or Clare Valley Riesling, or Alsatian Tokay-Pinot Gris have enough richness and oiliness to work, as do top-end northern Italian white blends. With *cherries*, mature Burgundian Pinot Noir, top notch Barbera from Piedmont, Reserva Rioja and medium-weight Zinfandels from California are excellent. The more robust dish of *confit de canard* demands meatier reds with backbone and grip, like those from Bandol in Provence, from Languedoc, Roussillon or from the southwest of France, for example Madiran or Cahors.

Eggs For *quiche*, *soufflés* or *light savoury tarts* think of the main ingredient in them and consider its impact on the dish. Also, think about what you are eating alongside. Once you have narrowed these flavours down, unoaked or lightly oaked Chardonnay would probably be a fair starting point. *Omelettes*, *frittata* or *savoury pancakes* follow the same rules, however for *oeufs en meurette* (poached eggs in red wine with lardons) a red wine is definitely called for – Beaujolais or red Burgundy would be perfect. For *fried eggs*, see 'Bacon', and for *poached eggs*, for example on a salad, again look at the other ingredients. If the salad includes stronger-flavoured elements, but you prefer not to have Beaujolais, then Alsatian Riesling or Pinot Blanc are winners. For *quails' eggs*, see 'Apéritif Wine Styles'. Finally, *eggs Benedict* has a lot going on, from the muffin base, via the bacon or ham and ending with the gloopy hollandaise. Youthful Côtes-du-Rhône is a classic combination and is so delicious that your guests will inevitably ask you to cook another round of eggs each, sorry!

Fish The flavour of fish depends not only on the sort of fish you are cooking, but also, crucially, on how it is cooked. The general rule is the milder the flavour, the lighter the white wine, the richer the flavour, the heavier the wine. Fish cooked in red wine is one of the exceptions to a white-dominated section, as here a light red would be preferable to a stronger white. From Bianco de Custoza, Austrian Grüner Veltliner, Menetou-Salon and Quincy (Loire), white Burgundy (Mâcon, Rully, Pouilly-Fuissé, Meursault and so on), Californian Chardonnay, Jurançon Sec, Australian Pinot Gris, Marsanne or Sémillon, any Riesling or Viognier, the opportunities are endless. Just remember that poaching and steaming are gentler, non-taste-altering ways of cooking, while grilling, searing, frying and roasting all impart distinctive charred or caramelised nuances to the fish. Also consider what you are cooking the fish with; check through the ingredients for strong flavours, such as lemon, capers, balsamic vinegar, flavoured olive oil and herbs.

The finer the piece of fish, often the more money you can chuck at the wine. *Dover sole*, *turbot* and *sea bass*, at the top of my fish-wish-list, are all pricey, but if you've gone that far, complete the picture by splashing out on a bottle of white Burgundy. Failing that, for a tenner, you could pick up a top South African Chardonnay, Australian Sémillon, Adelaide Hills/Eden Valley/Clare Valley Riesling or Chardonnay, Riesling from Alsace, Lugana or Gavi from Italy, dry white Graves (Bordeaux), white Rhône wines and trendy Spanish Albariño to go with these fish. *Halibut*, *John Dory*, *sea bream*, *skate* and *brill* all enjoy these styles of wine, too, while *swordfish*, *monkfish* and *hake* can take slightly weightier whites, or even a fresh light red, such as Beaujolais. *Salmon* (*poached* or *grilled*) also likes Chardonnay, whether it is from the Old or New

World, but steer clear of oaky styles. *Trout* likes Riesling, and add Chablis to the list as well. But for an especially wicked combo, try to track down the unusually scented French Country wine, Jurançon Sec. *Fish cakes*, especially high-salmon-content ones, go wonderfully with dry Riesling or Sémillon, particularly if you are partial to a generous spoonful of tartare sauce. *Red mullet* has enough character to handle rosé wines, making a pretty-in-pink partnership between plate and glass. *Kedgeree* is trickier as the smoked haddock, cayenne, parsley and egg may make you lean towards red. But don't, as rapier-like acidity is needed to slice through this dish and I'm sure you know which white grape does this best – Sauvignon Blanc. While we are on the subject, Sauvignon is the grape to enjoy with *fish 'n' chips* (*cod*, *haddock* or *plaice*) because it can handle the batter and vinegar (go easy). It also shines with *fish pie*. The poshest partnership would be Pouilly-Fumé or Sancerre, but if you fancy a trip to the New World, then Marlborough in New Zealand has to be the starting point for fans of this zesty grape. Or, for a change, try Chenin Blanc, Aligoté and unoaked Chardonnay. *Fish soups* and *stews* tend to need more weight in a wine, and one of the most accurate matches would be a white Rhône made from Marsanne and Roussanne, or Viognier. Aussie Marsanne or Pinot Gris would also be a great option. *Sardines* require perky acidity to cut through their oily flesh; once again Sauvignon Blanc is the winner, but Italian Pinot Grigio or Gavi, Spanish Albariño, French Aligoté and even light reds, like Gamay, would be smashing. *Canned tuna*, and its finer, paler version, *albacore*, just need unoaked, dry white wine. Albacore, however, is more delicately flavoured than ordinary tuna, so take care not to swamp it. The Italian duo, Bianco di Custoza and Soave, would do this job with style. For *salade niçoise*, see 'Salads'. *Fresh tuna*, seared and served rare, secretly likes juicy, fresh, light reds and chilled rosés. *Brandade* (*salt cod*), with its garlic and oil components, can stand up to whites with a little more poke. Albariño, from Galicia in Spain, is a perfect choice, however Penedès whites and even light rosés are all within its grasp. *Herring*, *kippers* and *rollmops* all have a more robust texture thanks to the curing process. Once again, dry whites and rosés work well, but steer clear of oaked whites, as the power of the barrel will overshadow the subtleties of the dish. *Smoked eel* is often served with crème fraîche, and cream is always a little problematic for wine, but look to Austrian Riesling or Grüner Veltliner, German Pinot Gris or bone-dry Riesling, and almost any dry wine from Alsace, and they should step up to the mark with aplomb. *Smoked salmon* is perfect with Gewürztraminer, whether it is from Alsace, Chile, or anywhere come to think of it; just make sure you buy a dry, not off-dry version. The scent and tropical nature of Gewürz works amazingly well, but so does Viognier and even Canadian Pinot Blanc. Don't forget Champagne or top-end New World sparkling wine, particularly if serving blinis topped with smoked salmon and caviar. *Smoked trout* or *mackerel pâté* is a challenge for wine – fishy, smoky and creamy flavours all in one dish. Southern French Viognier, McLaren Vale Sémillon, Adelaide Hills Sauvignon Blanc and Pinot Gris (all Aussies), Alsatian Riesling and Pinot Blanc are all perfect matches. Lastly, *curries* or *Asian* fish dishes often sport spices, turmeric, ginger and chilli, so turn back to our favourite white saviour grapes for a solution; New World Sauvignon Blanc's supreme confidence and Aussie and New Zealand Riesling's natural skill make this tricky challenge a walk in the park.

Frogs' legs Tasting nearer to chicken than any other beast I can think of, aim for smooth, mildly oaked Chardonnay from Burgundy, Australia, South Africa or New Zealand. Consider what you've cooked these cheeky blighters in and tweak your wine choice accordingly – if *garlic butter* is involved, stick to Sauvignon Blanc. Good Luck.

Game All flighted game, including *pheasant, quail, guinea fowl, woodcock, teal, grouse, snipe, wild duck* and *partridge* adore the noble grape Pinot Noir. So red Burgundy would always be my first choice, with California, New Zealand and Oregon somewhere in the pack behind the leader. The longer the bird is hung, the more mature the wine required. I have enjoyed mature red Bordeaux, Super-Tuscan, northern Rhône, Spanish wines from Ribera del Duero or Tarragona and many other top reds with this heady style of cuisine. But it is important to aim for complex reds with layers of fruit, and this inevitably means spending up. *Hare* in jugged form often uses port and/or redcurrant jelly in the recipe, so a red wine is needed, and a big one at that. New-style Piemontese reds made from Nebbiolo or Nebbiolo/Barbera blends would have the brawn, as would big Australian Shiraz (McLaren Vale or Barossa Valley), Zinfandel from California or South African Pinotage. One cheaper and worthy source is the Douro Valley in Portugal, which makes red wines alongside port. Not only would you have a beefy wine, but it would be in perfect synergy if you use port in the ingredients. *Rabbit*, as well as being a less athletic version of a hare, is also less pungent and has lighter-coloured flesh. This time big reds are essential but not quite as insanely powerful as those suggested for hare. The classic combo of *rabbit with mustard and bacon* has some mighty flavours on board, so aim for fairly swarthy numbers, with feisty tannins and a youthful purple hue. Chianti, Carmignano, Vino Nobile di Montepulciano (all from Tuscany), Bandol (from Provence), Lirac, Rasteau, Vacqueyras and Gigondas (from the southern Rhône), Argentinian Malbec, South African Shiraz and smarter Chilean Cabernet blends would be spot on. *Wild boar* again favours rich, brooding red wines. Depending on the dish, you could choose any of the aforementioned reds. But this time add to the list the two noblest of Italian wines, Brunello di Montalcino and Barolo. *Venison* again loves reds and any wine in this section would do, including top Australian Cabernet Sauvignon and some of the better New Zealand Hawke's Bay Cabernets. Finally *game pie*, served cold, behaves like chicken and ham pie (see 'Chicken'). If served hot, open any wine suggested for steak and kidney pie (see 'Beef').

Garlic *Roast* garlic tends to walk all over fine wines, so if you are partial to shoving a few bulbs in the oven keep the wine spend down and follow the main dish's lead. *Garlic prawns*, *mushrooms* and *snails* all need aromatic, bone-dry Sauvignon Blanc to save the day. *Aïoli* (garlic mayonnaise) can add excitement to chicken, potatoes, fish, soups and so on, but just watch out for it because you'll get a shock if your wine is not prepared. (For *chicken Kiev* see 'Chicken'.)

Goose The best wines for roast goose lie somewhere between those suited to game and those in the 'Chicken' section. This means that lighter red Burgundy, and Pinot Noirs in general, are the reds to choose, while big, rich Chardonnays and Rieslings make up the white team.

Greek see 'Mezze'.

Haggis This is a new entry that I inadvertently left out last year, but have had numerous requests to include. Haggis enjoys the company of rich, textural white wines – who doesn't? Depending on your palate you could choose, at the rich end, a plump New World Chardonnay or, at the lighter end, a white Côtes-du-Rhône. If you really want to go over the top, try a Grand Cru Alsace Riesling or Tokay-Pinot Gris.

Ham Beaujolais-Villages, Chilean Merlot, Crianza Navarra and Rioja, Italian Nero d'Avola or Negroamaro and youthful, inexpensive South African Merlot or Pinotage all have the essential juiciness to complement a glorious ham. The golden rule is to avoid any reds that are too tannic or acidic – mellow styles are required. *Parma ham (prosciutto)* and melon, *jamón serrano* and *pata negra* all like dry German Riesling, many of the aromatic Trentino and Alto Adige whites from northern Italy, and lightly oaked Spanish Viura. *Honey-roast ham* needs mouth-filling, oily, dry whites like dry Muscat, Viognier and Riesling. Search for these in Alsace, the Rhône Valley and from the vast array of terrific French Country wines (and grab some figs to eat alongside while you are at it). *Ham hock* with lentils or boiled Jersey potatoes, and beetroot or peas (my favourite combinations) is a treat with smart rosé, and there are a fair few out there, so head to Tavel in the southern Rhône or to richer examples of Sancerre rosé. *Smoked ham* has a fairly strong aroma and lingering flavour, so Tokay-Pinot Gris from Alsace would be exact, as would Aussie Verdelho. If you favour red wine then choose a Merlot from Australia or Chile, and chill it a degree or so to retain the freshness. *Gammon steak* (avoiding pineapple or peaches, please) makes a neat partnership with oily, unoaked whites. All Alsatian wines and most dry German Rieslings would be delicious, as would the world-class Rieslings from Australia's Clare Valley, Eden Valley and Adelaide Hills. Sémillon rarely gets the call up for a specific dish, but Aussie versions, and dry white Bordeaux (both with a smattering of oak) are stunning with gammon steak.

Indian I've had a full induction into matching Indian food with wine this year as I designed and wrote the wine list for the re-launch of top London Indian restaurant, Chutney Mary. After tasting twenty or thirty Indian dishes it became clear to me that unoaked or mildly oaked whites were to be the driving force in my selection. Smooth, juicy rosés were also essential, as were fruit-driven reds, avoiding any that were noticeably tannic. The surprise came when I made the final selection and found that Italy, Australia and New Zealand had claimed the lion's share of the list. There were a few wines from other countries, but virtually no classics like claret, Burgundy or Rhône wines. Shock horror! This just proves that, depending on the style of cuisine, a wine list can be balanced, eclectic and hopefully thoroughly exciting, without relying on France. Grape varieties or styles of wine that go particularly well with Indian food are: whites – Pinot Grigio, Verdicchio, Sauvignon Blanc, Pinot Bianco, Fiano, Torrontés, Riesling, Viognier, Verdelho, light Gewürztraminers and Albariño; reds – Valpolicella, Beaujolais (Gamay), Grenache (Spanish Garnacha), Negroamaro, Pinot Noir, Nero d'Avola, Zinfandel, Barbera, Lagrein and Merlot. Other styles that work well include rich rosé, Prosecco (Italian sparkling wine), Asti (with puddings), rosé Champagne, Aussie sparklers and good quality ruby port. Do let me know if you unearth any other top combinations.

Japanese *Sushi* is a strange one to drink wine with, as surely tea or saké would be more appropriate? However, sparkling wines and Champagne are a treat with the best sushi, and the ever-ready Sauvignon Blanc is there as a fully qualified stand-by. *Teriyaki* dishes are a nightmare to match wine to, as the sweetness and fruitiness in the glossy soy and saké glaze is particularly dominant on the palate. Zinfandel from California, super-ripe Chambourcin, lighter Shiraz or Merlot from South Australia, and Nero d'Avola or Negroamaro from Sicily would just about manage this huge challenge. Wasabi, I'm afraid, is a wine assassin; Wasabi 1, Wine 0.

Junk food What should you drink with a hamburger, cheeseburger, chicken nuggets, bargain bucket or any of the other palate-numbing, industrial, fast-food offerings? A fizzy soft drink, of course, for that all-consuming burpy, bilious feeling that you are looking forward to enjoying, ten minutes after racing this glorious cuisine down your trap. If you are seriously considering opening a bottle of wine, you'll no doubt return to an even-colder-than-normal burger in its neon poly-box by the time you've found a bottle and glasses and struggled with the cork. You should, of course, eat outside your front door (to avoid any unwanted aromas inside) and then wash your palate clean with a simple Chilean Carmenère, Aussie Shiraz, Kiwi Sauvignon Blanc or South African Chardonnay. After that, fill in a membership for 'Slow Food' and vow not to enter another fast-food joint... until the next time.

Kidneys Lambs' kidneys generally absorb the flavour of the ingredients in which they are cooked, and as mustard is often used, keep the reds firm and chunky – Chianti, Barbera (both Italian), Rioja, Navarra (both Spanish), Languedoc and the Rhône Valley (both French) would all be worthy of consideration. (For *steak and kidney pie* see 'Beef'.)

Lamb Classically speaking there is nothing more accurate than red Bordeaux for *roast lamb* or *lamb chops*. However, reds from Bergerac and Burgundy, South Africa's Pinotage and Shiraz, California's Merlot, Australia's Shiraz and Cabernet blends, Spain's Rioja and Argentina and Chile's Cabernets and Merlots are all in with a shout. In fact, if you keep the wine neither lightweight nor heavyweight, but somewhere in the middle you will do well. You can, of course, go bonkers on the price of the wine or stick within a tighter budget; lamb is less critical than, say, beef or game. The way it is cooked, though, should influence your final choice. If cooked *pink*, the range of suitable wines is enormous (any of the above). If *well done*, then a fruitier style of red should be served, so head to the New World countries listed above. Watch out for gravy and mint sauce, as an abundance of either could trip the wine up. *Shepherd's pie* is incredibly easy to match to red wine. In fact, just open whatever you feel like; if it is red and wet, it will probably be spot on. *Lamb pot roast* and *casserole* tend to be a little richer than a chop or roast lamb because of the gravy; again, don't spend too much on the wine, as rustic Languedoc or southern Rhône reds should be perfect. Plain *lamb shank* is another relatively easy dish to match to red wine, with European examples from Portugal, Spain, Italy and France all offering enough acidity and structure to cut through the juicy meat. *Moussaka*, with cheese, onion, oregano and aubergines thrown into the mix, is altogether different. Lighter, fruit-driven reds such as New World Pinot Noir, Primitivo or any other southern Italian red and inexpensive workhorses from Toro or Campo de Borja in Spain will work well. *Stews* like *navarin* (with vegetables), *Irish stew*, *cassoulet* or *hot pot* all have broader shoulders when it comes to reds. Beefier southern French examples from Fitou, Corbières, St. Chinian, Madiran, Faugères, Minervois or Collioure would be spot on. From further afield, Malbec from Argentina or Carmenère from Chile, as well as medium-weight, fragrant Aussie Shiraz (McLaren Vale or Yarra Valley), would suit these dishes. *Cold roast lamb* follows the same rules as beef, and to a certain extent ham, in that fruity, light reds and juicy medium to full-bodied whites can work well. Beaujolais is, again (!), a great partner here, while Chardonnay in any of its following guises would enliven the dish – medium-priced white Burgundy, Chardonnay from Margaret River, Adelaide Hills or Yarra Valley (Australia) or Nelson or Marlborough (New Zealand); lighter South African and Chilean styles. Lastly, we come to *kebabs*, one of lamb's noblest incarnations. You would struggle to wrestle with a kebab and a glass of wine while staggering down the street after a late night out. But on the off-chance that you make it home before tucking in, then a glass of Aussie Chardonnay or a Sémillon/Chardonnay blend from one of the reliable brands would be a useful thirst-quencher, and not something you'd regret opening the next morning.

Liver *Calves' liver with sage*, yum. The main rule here is to choose a red wine with firm acidity. Loire reds made from Cabernet Franc are the pick of the bunch; Saumur-Champigny, Chinon or Bourgueil are all relatively inexpensive and a perfect match. Northern Italian reds like Valpolicella, Trentino Teroldego, Lagrein, Marzemino or Cabernet (Franc or Sauv) all have the required fruit richness with balancing acidity, freshness and grip. *Liver and bacon* needs a touch more spice in a red wine, so move to a warmer part of France or Italy (i.e. head south). Red Bordeaux or Chianti will do, but this may push the budget up unnecessarily.

Meat As in *balls* (see 'Pasta'), *pies* (see 'Beef') and *loaf* (see 'Terrines').

Mexican Mexican food, like *fajitas*, *enchiladas*, *tortillas*, *quesadillas*, *tacos*, *burritos* and the like, all loaded with *salsa*, lead to the consumption of copious quantities of lime-stuffed beer, which has undeniable thirst-quenching properties, crucial for tangy, chilli-hot food. But if you fancy a glass of wine,you must go in search of juicy, fruity, chillable red grapes like Nero d'Avola, Negroamaro and Primitivo (from southern Italy), Carmenère and Merlot from Chile, and budget Zinfandel from California to cool you down and smooth out your war-torn palate. As for whites, inexpensive New World oaked Chardonnay or Sémillon (or a blend of the two), chilled down ice-cold, will allow you to taste the food and the wine in turn, without suffering from chilli or refried bean overload. Interestingly, Cajun cookery follows a similar pattern to Mexican food when it comes to wine styles, as cayenne, paprika, oregano, garlic and thyme all cook up a storm and need to be tempered with juicy whites and reds.

Mezze (or *Meze*) This is the chance for dry Greek whites to shine.

And there are enough out there, of sufficiently high quality, to really hit the mark. If you are unable to track them down, then try Muscat, Pinot Blanc or Sylvaner from Alsace, New Zealand Sauvignon Blanc or Argentinian Torrontés. Also try to find dry Muscat from Australia, another rarity but stunning with mezze. Greek reds, I believe, are lagging behind the whites in terms of quality. The cheapies are fine, but I would avoid spending more than £7 or £8, as you will be hard-pushed to justify it with so much competition out there; I'd rather look further afield, perhaps to Italy and Spain.

Mixed grill Hurrah, real food! You must uncork a feisty southern Rhône red or its New World counterpart, a 'GSM' blend (Grenache, Shiraz and Mourvèdre), from Australia. Awesome.

Moroccan/North African The most important factor when it comes to matching this style of food with wine is the particularly wide range of spices used and the outstanding aroma of each recipe. Counter this sensory bombardment with either aromatic wines, or choose closed, neutral ones to act as a backdrop to the food and let the dish capture your senses. Spain, Italy and France are the most obvious ports of call. And within these three great wine nations, my favourite aromatic white styles would be Albariño (from Galicia in western Spain), Viognier (south of France) and Ribolla Gialla, Erbaluce, Tocai, Lugana and good Pinot Grigio (northeast and northwest Italy). Reds that work well are Rioja or similar-style Tempranillo/Garnacha blends (Spain), chilled Côtes-du-Rhône (France) and Nero d'Avola, Aglianico or Primitivo (southern Italy and Sicily). If you want to go the neutral route, choose Beaujolais as a red, or Alsace Pinot Blanc as a white. If you feel the need to stray further from the Med, aim for Sauvignon Blanc from Stellenbosch (South Africa) for its herbal, lime-juice character, and Barossa Valley Bush Vine Grenache (South Australia) for its pure red-berry fruit and herbal, smoky nose.

Mushrooms I am a wholehearted, unapologetic carnivore, but I can happily cook an evening's dinner oblivious of the fact that I have forgotten to include any meat if mushrooms play a central role in my dish. It is strange, and I try to feel cheated while doing the washing up, but my body and palate are replete, so, hey, what's the problem? Clearly, veggies live a life of abstinence from many of the headings in this chapter, but can still experience 'meaty' food in terms of intensity and flavour when mushrooms (and other ingredients) are wielded correctly. So, when matching wine to mushrooms, ignore the fact that they are fungi and look at the task they are fulfilling in the dish. *Baked* or *grilled* mushrooms usually retain their essence and flavour, and cellar temperature reds (i.e. chilled a touch) should allow the dish to express itself. Make sure that you choose loose, open reds that are ready to drink, with less dominant flavours – Gamay and Pinot Noir, for example. Creamy sauces are always tricky; if you overdo the cream, a robust, oaked Chardonnay or Sémillon is needed, but if the cream features only in a supporting, swirly role, then refreshing red grapes like Merlot and Barbera would be superb. *Mushroom omelettes* and *mushroom tarts* are both classic examples of how a mushroom can hold its own in an eggy, creamy arena – here, again, light fruit-driven reds enter the fray! *Wild mushrooms* can be intensely gamey and foresty, so turn to the

'Game' section and trade down in terms of weight (and price). *Mushrooms on toast* are back in vogue as a *de rigueur* starter – good news, as there is nothing better for setting the palate up for a main (wintry/meaty) course. Wine-wise, look to the main dish and downsize the style a touch, leaving something bigger in reserve for later. If you are having a double serving, as a stand-alone, in-front-of-the-telly dinner, then try Barbera or Dolcetto from northern Italy, with their truffley, black cherry aromas and flavours. These two varieties are becoming more widely available and don't half kick this dish into the corner of the net. *Stuffed mushrooms* depend on what they are stuffed with. I know it is obvious, but cheesy, veggie ones work well with light reds. Lose the cheese, though, and rich whites are in with a shout; medium-sized Chardonnays and Rieslings are ideal. For *mushroom risotto* see 'Risotto'.

Mustard Turn up the volume on the wine that you are drinking, whether white or red, if you have a mustard sauce, dressing or an accompanying dish with a mustard theme. You do not need to go crazy, but a notch up on quality (a pound or two more in a similar-styled wine will do).

Olives See 'Apéritif Wine Styles' if you are nibbling them. But if cooking with olives, say in a lamb recipe, take care not to introduce too much of the liquor from the tin as the water, brine or oil is pungent and can cast too strong an influence over the final taste of the dish. This will, in turn, affect the wine's chances of survival. The usual rule is to look at the main ingredient in the recipe and make sure that your chosen wine can be enjoyed alongside an olive, prior to its involvement in the dish. *Tapenade* is a funny old thing. Vehemently unfriendly when it comes to wine (unless you love dry sherry) it is best to go for very dry whites from cooler-climate regions, for example Frascati, Soave, Lugana, Est! Est!! Est!!! and Vernaccia (all Italian), or Sauvignon de Touraine, Cheverny, Bergerac Sec, Jurançon Sec or Pacherenc de Vic Bihl from France.

Onion As a stand-alone dish, onion must be at its best in a classic *onion tart*, and Alsatian Riesling is the only wine to drink alongside this noble offering. If you stray from this advice, I am certain you will receive a knock at the door from the wine police. If you conform, you will be in no doubt about the virtues of food and wine matching. You may also see *caramelised* onions offered as a side dish; if so, tread carefully. The intense sweetness, albeit tempered by the rest of your food, can put a wine off. So eat and sip cautiously – I chickened out of this one!

Oysters see 'Seafood'.

Paella Not worthy of a listing really, except that it is such a mix of ingredients and often crops up in 'what do I drink with…' questions. The answer is chilled Cabernet Franc (red Loire), Albariño (Spanish white) or French or Spanish Grenache-based rosés. Delish!

Pasta In the greater scheme of things, naked pasta virtually tastes neutral. But it is never served on its own! So, the trick is to consider what you are serving over, under or around it. Stuffed styles like *cannelloni*, *agnolotti*, *cappelletti*, *tortellini* or *ravioli* can contain veg, cheese, meat and all sorts, so bear this in mind. *Spinach and Ricotta tortellini* soaks up juicy Italian reds like Barbera, from Piedmont, young, simple Chianti, Franciacorta, Bardolino and Valpolicella. *Seafood* pasta dishes, including *vongole* (clams), love serious Sauvignon Blanc, decent Frascati (over £5), Soave (again, break over the fiver barrier, for quality), Lugana and Vernaccia di San Gimignano. *Meatballs*, *spaghetti Bolognese*, *lasagne* and *meaty sauces* all respond to juicy reds. Keep the budget down and head for expressive, fruit-driven examples that work in tandem with the dish as opposed to trying to score points. Consider all of Italy, many New World regions, except for hugely alcoholic wines, and, although heretical, anything bright and juicy from Spain. *Roasted vegetables* often pop up in pasta dishes allowing you to choose between richer whites and lighter reds. Not only is this an attractive veg-friendly dish, it also suits all wine palates (a safe dinner party dish for first-time guests). *Pesto* is a classic pasta combo, but on the face of it is remarkably hostile on the wine front. Oil, pine nuts, Parmesan and basil seem innocent enough, but combine them and you are forced into dry whites. Go to Italian regions Friuli and the Alto Adige as your guide, and find any bone-dry whites. They grow Sauvignon Blanc up there, so at least you can rely on that stalwart grape, but otherwise Pinot Grigio, Tocai Friulano and Pinot Bianco are a good starting point. *Red pesto* is a different call. Here go for light red wines and keep their temperature down to focus fruit flavours. *Cheesy* and *creamy sauces* tend to be more dominant than the ingredients bound therein, so once again Bardolino, Valpol, Dolcetto and Barbera from Piedmont, Montepulciano from Marche and medium-weight

Chianti are sublime. If, for some reason, you want to stray from the hallowed shores of Italy in search of wine with pasta (I don't know why, as all of these wines are cheap and widely available) then there is plenty of choice; medium-weight reds and dry whites are everywhere. Just remember not to overshadow the dish, particularly with higher-alcohol New World reds. For *tomato sauce*, see 'Tomato'. For *mushroom sauces*, see 'Mushrooms'.

Pâté Confusingly, pâté, regardless of its ingredients, is keen on white wines. The only reds that work are featherweights (Beaujolais and the like). In the white world, you need to find fruity, aromatic wines from any decent estate, but they must have a degree of sweetness. All styles from technically dry (but still ripe and fruity – Riesling, Gewürztraminer, Muscat and so on) up to genuine sweet wines can be considered. Pâté is usually served as a starter, so pouring a sweet wine can seem a little about face. But if you are serving pudding or cheese later on in the proceedings you can happily open a bottle of sweet wine, serve a few small glasses for starters and finish it off during cheese or pud. (Many sweet wines are sold in half bottles, so if it's a small gathering, you'll not waste a drop.) *Chicken liver pâté* favours dry to medium German Riesling, Alsace Riesling or Pinot Blanc, or mildly sweet white Bordeaux. *Country pâté*, a catch-all term that often hints at a coarser texture of pâté of indeterminate origin, again likes light white wines of varying sweetness. If you are pushed into a short wine list, or a sparsely stocked off-licence, then play safe; buy dry whites and hope for the best. But if you have the luxury of choice, then Alsace is a great region to start with. Riesling and Tokay-Pinot Gris are the plum choices here.

Head to the New World and you'll find Riesling in abundance in South Australia, while Chilean Gewürztraminer seems to be doing well, too. *Duck pâté* is fine, but *foie gras* (goose liver) is the real thing. We are now firmly in sweet wine territory. Sauternes, Loire and Alsace sweeties, Aussie botrytised Riesling and Sémillon, and with a tighter budget on the go, Monbazillac, Ste-Croix du Mont, Loupiac, Cadillac and Saussignac, Sauternes' taste-alike neighbours, all perform admirably. *Parfait*, the smoother, creamier, whipped version of pâté, tends to reveal its secret brandy ingredient more than a coarse pâté, so make sure your sweet wine is rich enough to cope with this. If you don't want a sweet wine, then 'nearly-sweet' or rich whites from Alsace also work. Vendange Tardive (late-picked) wines can offer richness without cloying, sugary sweetness and will appease the non-sweet wine fans. Grapes to consider are Tokay-Pinot Gris, Gewürztraminer and Riesling. *Smoked salmon pâté* and other fishy incarnations are well served by aromatic whites (see 'Fish'). One thing to remember with pâté dishes is that occasionally cheeky *chutney* (or *onion confit*) is served alongside, giving an intense fruit or veg explosion of flavour which may confuse the wine. Not so Alsatian Vendange Tardive wines, mentioned above, whose spice and richness of fruit will welcome the added flavours. Dry wines will, I'm afraid, suffer. I have already talked about gherkins and the like in the 'Charcuterie' section, so do keep them well under control.

Peppers Raw peppers crackle with fresh, crunchy, zingy, juicy, healthy flavours. It is no surprise that Sauvignon Blanc (from almost anywhere) is the best grape for salads and raw peppers, as 'capsicum' is a classic tasting note for this variety. It is a marriage made in heaven, but if you want to try something different, then dry Chenin Blanc from South Africa or Italian Pinot Grigio would be splendid. *Piemontese peppers* are a favourite Saturday lunch dish of mine, and with the olive oil, garlic and tomato ingredients, dry whites are required, especially if the traditional anchovy fillets are added astride the glistening tomato hemispheres. Assertive Sauvignon Blanc is the best option, although Verdicchio, Orvieto and Gavi (or less expensive Cortese-based whites) from Piedmont would be appropriate. A *stuffed pepper* depends more on the stuffing than the pepper itself, so look to the filling for guidance. Generally speaking, meat or cheese stuffing goes well with light Italian reds. Peppers *marinated in olive oil* love any dry white wines; for consummate accuracy Italian is best, so find some Soave, Frascati or Friuli single varietals such as Pinot Grigio, Pinot Bianco, Traminer or Sauvignon Blanc. For *gazpacho* see 'Soup'.

Picnics Screw caps are perfect for picnics. There is no need for a corkscrew as you can seal the bottle between pourings and not worry about knocking it over. So search for these excellently sealed bottles. Rosé has to be the first port of call as it is multitalented when it comes to cold food matching and they should be chilled down ice cold for departure. It will drink like a white early on and as the day hots up (if it does!), will behave more like a red. Other varieties that enjoy al fresco food are Sauvignon Blanc for whites and Beaujolais for reds. Chill all your wines prior to departure and drink them in order from white, via rosé to red, to enjoy them all at their best.

Pigeon see 'Game', but spend less!

Pizza Heroic pizzas rarely allow white wines enough space to be heard. However, I suppose a girly vegetable or seafood pizza might need a feeble white wine. Assuming you have a tomato base and some cheese on top, the real point of a pizza is the unlimited number of palate-expanding toppings that you sling aloft; mushroom, onion, anchovy, caper, olive, beef, ham, egg, pepperoni and, crucially, chillies. A real man's pizza has these and more, so you will have to find a feisty red and chill it down. My all-Italian pizza wine line-up includes: whites – Arneis, Soave, Bianco di Custoza, Verdicchio, Pinot Bianco, Pinot Grigio and Orvieto; chillable reds – Sardinian Cannonau, Freisa, Barbera and Dolcetto from Piedmont, Marzemino and Teroldego from Trentino, Bardolino and Valpolicella from Veneto and Montepulciano d'Abruzzo, Sangiovese di Romagna, Primitivo, Nero d'Avola, Negroamaro and Aglianico from further south. If you insist on drinking non-Italian wines with pizza, you're on your own.

Pork Pork pops up in many different incarnations. I have given the noble *sausage* its own section, further on. And, no doubt, *pâté* and *terrine* lovers are delighted that these two dishes also warrant separate headings. I have also dealt with *charcuterie*, *cassoulet*, *bacon*, *full English breakfast* and *ham* in other sections. Here I endeavour to cover any other pig-derivative dishes not previously mentioned. So, first up the princely *pork pie* and its less exciting asteroid cousin, the *Scotch egg*. A good pork pie is a real treat, and while I'm sure that a pint of bitter is more than likely the ideal partner, a glass of red Cru Beaujolais or white Bourgogne Aligoté wouldn't go amiss. The Scotch egg somehow crops up in pubs and picnic more than at the dinner table, and real ale is the preferred drink of choice. But you won't put a foot wrong by ordering a juicy red wine either. If you like a dollop of Branston or Piccalilli on the plate with your pie, then be ready for the wine to be sent into a tailspin. *Chorizo* and *salami* fall into the aforementioned 'Charcuterie' section, but do remember that the spicier the salami, the greater the need for cool red wine. A plate of chorizo is excellent with dry sherry – manzanilla and fino are best. Next on the agenda, *spare ribs*. Whether drenched in barbecue sauce or not, they are prehistoric fare, so cave-man reds are needed to slake your thirst. Juice and texture are the essential ingredients, so head to the New World in search of Argentinian Sangiovese, Bonarda or Tempranillo, Chilean Carmenère or Australian Cabernet/Shiraz blends. Californian Zinfandel would also work well, although it can be a bit expensive. *Rillettes*, which can also be made from duck or rabbit, is one of pork's lighter sides. This mild, fondanty, savoury dish is often served as part of a plate of cold meats, when white wine is called for, with Pinot Blanc, Sylvaner and Riesling from Alsace all working well. I have left the big daddy to last, *roast pork*. There are a number of ways to roast pork, so when it comes to matching it to wine, the brief is fairly open. One thing is certain – if you are going to serve a red, make it light. Pork is far more excited, though, to be associated with white wine, particularly if there is apple sauce in a boat moored alongside. Classy, unoaked Chardonnay from Chablis or Burgundy would be exact, although New World Chardonnays can hack it as long as they are not too decadently oaked. Riesling (dry and luxurious), Condrieu (the super-dear northern Rhône Viognier), Vouvray (make sure it says 'sec' – dry – on the label), southern Rhône whites (thin on the ground but a lot of bang for your buck) are all worth a substantial sniff.

Quiche (and posh tarts?) see 'Eggs'.

Rabbit see 'Game', apart from *rillettes* which love a little more scent and exoticism in their wines than pork rillettes, so Marsanne, Roussanne and Viognier from anywhere in the world (Rhône is your starting point) or Pinot Blanc and Riesling (the richer styles from Alsace) would be mouth-wateringly spot on.

Risotto Generally the richness and texture of a risotto needs to be 'cut' with the acidity of a clean, dry white wine with good fruit and flavour. But what have you got in your risotto? Bear these magic ingredient(s) in mind when matching wine to the creamy, cheesy (if you whack in a spot of Parmesan and butter alongside the stock!) rice. Reds can work with *wild mushrooms*, but usually whites are better. *À la Milanese*, with saffron, can force a light, dry white into submission unless it has enough fruit and 'oomph' – Arneis or Gavi from Piedmont is worth a go, as is Riesling from a good Australian or Alsatian producer. *Chicken and mushroom* risotto likes Chardonnay and Pinot Noir, just as a non-risotto dish might. *Primavera* favours fresh, zingy, green whites – Sauvignon anyone? For *seafood* risotto see 'Seafood'.

Salads A huge subject, that more often than not just needs a spot of common sense. Basic *green* or *mixed* salad is virtually tasteless, as far as wine is concerned, without dressing, but dressing often contains vinegar so here the rules change and you must dress carefully. People will tell you that light whites are best; but you are hardly going to order a glass of white to accompany your *pousse and shallot* salad after having downed a rare steak and chips. Just chomp through the salad and then bring your beefy red back into view. Don't worry, the salad is a palate cleanser and knows that it is not the main show. *Seafood* salad enjoys the white wines that go well with seafood (see below); *niçoise* likes tangy Sauv Blanc and Sauv blends; *chicken* salad works well with Rhône whites and middle-weight Chardonnays; *feta* salad, not surprisingly, is perfect with dry Greek whites; *French bean and shallot* salad likes Alsace Tokay-Pinot Gris and Pinot Blanc; *tomato and basil* salad is best matched with rosé and all things fresh, dry, keenly acidic, white and Italian; *Caesar* salad, if made properly, is great with Sauvignon Blanc; *Waldorf* salad needs softer, calmer whites like Alsatian Pinot Blanc and Sylvaner, or South African Chenin Blanc; *pasta* salad can get a little stodgy, so uplifting, acidity-rich, dry whites are essential. Every country in the wine world makes salad-friendly wines, even the UK, where the better dry white grapes like Bacchus, Reichensteiner and Seyval Blanc can be a joy.

Sausages (meaty ones as opposed to fish or veggie!) Any sausage dish including *toad-in-the-hole* and *bangers and mash* need manly, robust, no messin' about reds. Cahors, Garnacha blends from Tarragona, Shiraz or Cabernet from Western Australian or McLaren Vale, Malbec from Argentina, any Languedoc or southern Rhône reds, Barbera from northern Italy, Primitivo from southern Italy, Chinon and other red Loires are all suitable. Zinfandel, Merlot and Cabernet from California would be awesome, as would a bottle of claret. Hurrah for sausages and their global compatibility with red wine. They're not fussy. My desert island luxury, if ever it came to it, would be G.M. & M. Johns' soss, Bibendum Restaurant's mash, my mother-in-law's baked beans and a magnum of serious Côte-Rôtie.

Seafood Muscadet, Cheverny, Menetou-Salon, Pouilly-Fumé, Sancerre (Loire), Chenin Blanc (South Africa) Albariño (Spain), Lugana, Verdicchio, Soave and Pinot Grigio (Italy) and any bone-dry, unoaked New World whites are all compatible with seafood. This is another huge section where thinking the dish through pays dividends. *Squid* and *octopus* both need very dry whites with aromatic fruit like Sauvignon Blanc, northern Italian or Penedès (Spain) whites – and resinous Greek whites if the dish is served in its ink. The curious, bouncy texture of both squid and octopus does not embrace wine in the same way fish does, so concentrate on the method of cooking and the other ingredients to help you make the final choice. *Crevettes grìses*, or the little grey/brown shrimps, eaten whole as a pre-dinner nibble, are stunning with Muscadet or Loire Sauvignon Blanc. *Crayfish* and *prawns* are a step up in terms of flavour, and dry English whites, simple, dry Riesling and Sauvignon or Sémillon/Sauvignon Blanc blends are all lovely. If you favour a *prawn cocktail* (and I certainly do), then smartish Sauvignon Blanc is dry and aromatic enough to wade through the Marie Rose sauce. *Lobster*, the smartest of all crustaceans, served cold or in a salad, should lead you into the deepest, darkest corners of your cellar to uncork the finest whites. Burgundy (no upper limit), Australian and New Zealand Chardonnay (only the best – not too oaky), Californian Chardonnay (elegant as opposed to blockbuster) and Viognier, from its spiritual birthplace in Condrieu, in the northern Rhône, will all set you back a fortune. But if you've bought lobster in the first place, then you can go the extra light year and finish the job properly with a great white. *Lobster thermidor* is not my favourite dish, as I feel that lobster loses its magical texture and elegant flavour when served hot, but you can easily uncork richer (but less expensive) whites like Aussie Sémillons or South American Chardonnays. If you feel like a slice of lobster class, but for a slightly reduced price, then *langoustines* (or Bugs if you're on hols in Australia) are the answer. Lobster-wines are perfect here, just adjust the prices downwards a few quid or more. *Dressed crab* is a fabulous dish and once again Loire whites, like Muscadet (only £4 to £5 for a good bottle), are spot on. Dry whites such as Ugni Blanc from Gascony, Jurançon and simple Chablis, are also good, but Sauvignon Blanc is again probably the pick of the grapes. Don't just look at the Loire, though, as the white wines from Bordeaux and Bergerac often have a fair slug of Sauvignon in them, and, of course, Sauvignon is grown all over the New World. *Mussels* probably do best in *gratin* or *marinière* form, when dry Riesling, Barossa Valley Sémillon, New Zealand Pinot Gris and New World Sauvignon Blanc are all worthy contenders. *Scallops* can take on a little more weight in a white wine (mildly oaked Sauvignon Blanc, for example). They can even handle a spot of light red. *Scallops sauté Provençal* (with tomatoes and garlic) and *scallops wrapped in bacon* are wicked with smart rosé. *Scallops Bercy* (with shallots, butter, thyme, white wine, parsley and lemon juice) are superb with top Sancerre or Pouilly-Fumé – spend up, it will be worth it. *Oysters* are traditionally matched with Champagne, but not by me – I prefer a simple dry white like Muscadet, with its salty tang, or a 'village' Chablis or Petit Chablis. And lastly a *plateau de fruits de mer* – all of the above, plus whelks (yuk), winkles (what's the point?) and other strange bits and pieces – really only needs a Sauvignon de Touraine or a bottle of good Muscadet. You'll thank me, because after you receive the bill for this bountiful platter of seafood you'll be delighted to spend a fraction of that on a bottle of gluggable wine. Finally *seafood risotto* – here dry Italian wines including decent Frascati, Vernaccia di San Gimignano, Verdicchio Classico, Greco and Fiano, along with South African Sauvignon Blanc and Chenin Blanc make a rather delicious combination. Remember that Chilean Sauvignon is often cheaper than both South African and New Zealand versions, so if you are having a big risotto party then look here for a volume purchase. For *clams*, see 'Pasta'.

Side dishes see 'Vegetables'.

Snails mmmm, see 'Garlic'.

Soups Dry sherry is often quoted as soup's saviour. But I am unlikely to crack open a fresh bottle of fino every time I fancy a bowl of soup. And what's more, it isn't the best wine for the job, as the soup family is a diverse collection of individuals and no one wine can cover it entirely. *Minestrone*, with its wonderful cannellini-bean base, or *ribollita* (the stunning, next-day minestrone incarnation, re-boiled with cabbage and bread thrown in for extra body) likes to keep things Italian, with Teroldego or Marzemino from Trentino being superb wine candidates. But, if you want to hop over the border to France, then southern Rhônes make a refreshing and accurate alternative. *Spinach and chickpea* soup goes well with bone-dry whites like Orvieto, Frascati, New Zealand, South African or Chilean Sauvignon Blanc. *Vichyssoise* (chilled leek and potato soup) needs creamy, floral whites, such as simple Alsatian Riesling, South American or French Viognier or light, white Rhône. *Lobster* or *crayfish bisque* also has a creamy texture coupled with a deceptive richness, so dry sherry could conceivably make an appearance here. If you don't fancy that, then white Burgundy is best. *Bouillabaisse with rouille*, the serious fish, garlic, tomatoes, onion and herb broth, with floating toasty crostinis topped with garlic, chilli and mayo, is a mighty dish and yet only needs tiddly little whites like our old favourites Muscadet and Sauvignon de Touraine. *Consommé* is a definite dry sherry dish (at last). *Gazpacho* (chilled tomato, cucumber, onion, pepper and garlic soup) likes nothing more than Spanish new-wave (unoaked) Viura. *Mushroom* soup is another dry sherry candidate, while *French onion* soup goes well with dry Riesling from Alsace or South Australia. *Oxtail* demands hearty reds – rustic, earthy inexpensive southern French bruisers are ideal. *Lentil and chestnut* soup and *lentil and bacon* both crave dry sherry (try an amontillado), while *clam chowder* is basically a fishy soup with cream (and possibly potato), so Sauvignon Blanc, Chenin Blanc and all seafood-friendly whites are perfect. *Vegetable* soup can be dull, but can also be excellent; either way, rustic reds at the bottom of the ladder are sound. *Tomato* soup is a strange one. Always avoid oak. I favour light reds or dry whites; Gamay (Beaujolais, Loire) or Sauvignon Blanc (Pays d'Oc, Loire, Chile) all do the job admirably.

Sweetbreads Classically cooked with *butter and sorrel*, *sauce ravigote* (mustard, red wine vinegar, capers and tarragon) or *sauce gribiche* (like ravigote but with chopped hard-boiled eggs and parsley as well), sweetbreads demand aromatic, richly textured, self-confident white wines. Alsatian or South Australian Riesling, with a bit of age, would be my first choices. If you can't find any, then try creamy, oily, nutmeg and white peach-scented Rhône whites. *Ris de veau aux morilles* (veal sweetbreads with an intensely creamy wild mushroom sauce) needs the most intense of all Rhône whites or Alsatian Rieslings.

Tapas Sherry and dry white wines (preferably Spanish and avoid oaky ones) are perfect partners for these tasty Spanish snacks.

Terrines A terrine is a more robust pâté, generally served in slices. So what is good for a pâté is often good enough for a terrine. One of the classics is *ham and chicken*, which loves white Burgundy, or elegant non-French Chardonnays. Another white Burgundy lover is *jambon persillé*, the sublime parsley, jelly and ham dish. Beaujolais, Alsatian Gewürztraminer, Riesling and Tokay-Pinot Gris love *rabbit*, *hare* and *game* terrines, particularly if there are prunes lurking within. *Fish* terrines follow the lead of fish pâtés and *mousses* with Sauvignon Blanc, Riesling, clean, fresh Chardonnays, like Chablis, and finally the enigmatic Spanish stunner, Albariño.

Thai Along the same lines as Vietnamese and other 'Asian, but not overly so' styles of cuisine, it is best to look to the main ingredient in each Thai dish and then to concentrate on appropriate southern hemisphere, fruit-driven wines. Likely candidates are: Australian and New Zealand Riesling, Sémillon, Verdelho, Pinot Gris and Sauvignon Blanc; New World sparkling wines in general; dry Muscat from Portugal; and Pinot Gris from Argentina.

Tomato Strangely, tomatoes are pretty fussy when it comes to wine matching (see 'Soup'). Pinot Noir works, but generally New World versions perform better than their Old World counterparts, as they often have more fruit and lower acidity. Other reds, like Sicilian Nero d'Avola, Puglian Primitivo (Italy) and any juicy, warm-climate Merlot or Zinfandel are accommodating. When raw, as in a salad, rosé is a good choice. A *tomato sauce* demands dry, light whites and Italy is the best place to look for these, as they are often ripe and cheap. Tomato ketchup, while delicious, is so sweet and vinegary that it gives wine a hard time, so use sparingly on your burger if drinking fine wine. Drench it if you are gunning down a cheap glugger.

Truffles Truffley, foresty, feral and musky – yum. You have a choice of similarly scented wines to match this unusual life form – Burgundian Pinot Noir, Piedmont's magnificent Nebbiolo and Syrah (French and posh, please). If you want to cook chicken or fish with truffles, then vintage Champagne or top Alsatian Riesling would be nothing short of spectacular.

Turkey see 'Chicken'.

Turkish I have already covered lamb kebabs (with chilli sauce) in the 'Lamb' section. But Turkish food is inevitably best with Greek wines (endeavouring to be non-controversial), as the cuisine styles are linked and the resinous whites and purple, scented reds are spot on.

Veal There are some mightily good dishes in this section, but there is no hard and fast rule as to what to follow on the wine front, so tread carefully. Veal does, however, like to be treated with respect when choosing wine, preferring to keep the company of senior white wines and lighter reds. *Saltimbocca*, the epic veal, sage and prosciutto dish, needs a wine to 'jump in the mouth'. Pinot Nero (Italian Pinot Noir) would be just right, but is hard to find; if your search is unsuccessful try another weirdo, Trincadeira from Portugal, which makes an inexpensive, inspirational substitute. *Vitello tonnato* (stunning) – the thinly sliced, braised veal dish, served cold and drizzled in a sauce made from marinated tuna, lemon juice, olive oil and capers, is one of the world's most sumptuous starters. Take the tuna and anchovy (used in the braising stage) as your lead. Fresh, sunny, seaside whites like Verdicchio and Vernaccia work especially well. *Wiener schnitzel*, fried veal in egg and breadcrumbs can often taste a little on the dry side, so what else is on the plate? If there is nothing of enormous character to deflect your mission, give it the kiss of life with a juicy, mildly oaked Chardonnay. *Blanquette de veau*, the French classic with a cream sauce, is definitely a white wine dish. Again Chardonnay (near or far) will do, but for perfection go for Viognier, Roussanne or Marsanne blends from the Rhône which would be pinpoint accurate. *Osso bucco*, veal shin with wine, tomatoes, parsley, garlic and zesty gremolata, is a lighter, more heady stew than most, and New Zealand, Tasmanian, Yarra Valley, Adelaide Hills (Aussie) or Oregon Pinot Noir would be great, as would huge, full-on Chardonnays from anywhere in my Gazetteer.

Vegetables Vegetables (and accompaniments) on the whole are relatively neutral tasting compared to the main dish. But depending on how they are cooked they can require a moment or two's thought. Any *gratin* (baked with cheese), or *dauphinoise* (potato with cream and garlic) dish needs light reds or self-confident whites on the table. *Beetroot* is a tad tricky, but Alsatian whites generally have the texture and flavour to make it through. *Cabbage*, *leeks*, *spinach*, *parsnips*, *cauliflower*, *sprouts*, *courgettes*, *carrots*, *peas* and *potatoes* are usually innocent, but *gnocchi*, whether plain or flavoured with spinach, needs juicy, fruit-driven wines to cut through their texture and lubricate the palate. *Marinated vegetables* and *polenta* not surprisingly love Italian whites – Pinot Grigio, Soave and so on. *Lentils* often dry the palate out and rustic, earthy reds are essential. Look to French Country wines or to Chile and Argentina. *Corn on the cob* is a dead ringer for New World Sauvignon Blanc. Open a bottle and, on some wines, you'll actually find a canned sweetcorn aroma!

Vegetarian If you are a strict vegetarian or vegan, look at the label on the wine bottle – many now advertise their credentials. If you are still unsure, ask your wine merchant.

Vinaigrette A passion killer for wine, as vinegar is so strong that it makes any wine taste flat for a few seconds. Dressing made with lemon juice and oil is more wine-friendly.

Vinegar See above! Balsamic vinegar seems to be more accommodating than most.

Welsh rarebit Always finish on a good note, and cheese on toast is a must for survival. Whether you make these for late-night nibbling or as a traditional savoury after pudding, you deserve a meaty little rustic red swimming alongside. Anything from the south of France, southern Italy or Spain would be a fantastic match.

PUDDINGS

A sweet wine is a glorious way to finish off a feast, so read on for a short list of my favourite puddings and their dream wines. There is only one rule when matching wine to sweet food. Make sure the wine is at least as sweet as the pudding, otherwise it will taste dry. Most wine shops have a few sweet wines lurking on the racks, but sadly not as many as one would like. They are often sold in half bottles, which is great as they can easily stretch to six people and there will be no wastage. You may have to find a decent independent merchant to get a good selection of sweeties (see the 'Directory' page 209). And check out my Top 250 for a comprehensive range of sweet wines that between them cover all the dishes in this section.

Almond tart Despite its luxurious ingredients and decadent texture this needs fairly careful handling on the wine front. Lighter sweeties like Muscat de Beaumes-de-Venise, Muscat de Rivesaltes, Moelleux (sweet) Loire whites and Jurançons would be spot on. For an almondy tart with fresh fruit on top go for similar wines. *Bakewell tart*, while perhaps not as elegant as a fresh fruit tart, will still revel in a gorgeous sweet wine.

Apple *Strudels*, *pies*, *fritters* and *crumbles* enjoy varying degrees of nutty, cinnamony, buttery pastry and brown-sugar-toffee flavours. But for all of the above a richer, heavier style of pudding wine is needed, without going too crazy. German Riesling, of at least Auslese status, late-picked Muscat or Riesling from Australia, classic French Sauternes or New World botrytised Sémillon and lighter Hungarian Tokaji are all runners. *Baked apples* need ice-cold, light, fresh German or Austrian Riesling (Spätlese or Auslese level) and clean, light Muscats. See below for *tarte tatin*.

Apricot A galactically awesome combo is Vendange Tardive (late-picked) Condrieu (from the northern Rhône) and *apricot crumble*. Unfortunately this wine is rare and exceedingly expensive, so where else should you look? The answer is sweet Jurançon, bursting with flavour, or Monbazillac, a budget Sauternes-style offering from the southwest of France.

Bananas *Raw*, surely it is breakfast or you are playing tennis, so put the corkscrew down. *Banoffee pie*, the hideous love-child of sticky toffee and frisky bananas, can only be tamed by the most outrageous of sweet wines – Hungarian Tokaji, Australian liqueur Muscat and Malmsey Madeira. With comedy *banana splits*, the toppings and ice cream flavours are more dominant than the perky banana, so tread carefully. Anyway, you shouldn't serve wine at children's parties.

Berries *Black, goose, blue, rasp, logan, huckle* (no joke), *straw, mul, dingle* (joke), *cran, bil* and his mate *damson* pop up in many different guises. But whether they are served *au naturel*, in a *compote*, for breakfast or cooked in a *summer pudding*, they all love the talented duo Sémillon and Muscat. Track down these grapes from France – Sauternes, Saussignac, Monbazillac, Loupiac and Cadillac all falling neatly into the Sémillon camp; Muscat de Rivesaltes, de Beaumes-de-Venise, de Frontignan and de Lunel all advertise Muscat on the label, so are easier to find. Aussie late-picked Muscats are all great, but watch out for liqueur Muscats, as they are wildly different and will stomp all over a *fruit purée*.

Biscuits/Biscotti (and proper shortbread) Vin Santo has to be the top choice, with heady sweet wines like Sauternes or New World botrytised Sémillon coming in a worthy second. Other, lighter biscuits enjoy the company of simpler sweet wines, but I would stick to Sémillon or Chenin Blanc-based French versions.

Brandy snaps A personal favourite, which is luckily not burdened with brandy. Try Australian liqueur Muscat, you'll love it – just try to stop when you've got through the first box and bottle.

Bread and butter pudding You need wines with a bit of clout for a traditional B&B pudding. Weightier Muscat is my favourite grape for the job – Moscatel de Setúbal from Portugal and Moscato or Passito di Pantelleria from the volcanic island off the south of Sicily, would both be a delight. A bottle of each guv'nor – 'night 'night.

Cakes What is wrong with a cup of tea? Well quite a lot, actually, when you could enjoy a teeny glass of cream sherry or a schooner of Aussie liqueur Muscat with *coffee cake*, demi-sec Champagne with *Victoria* or *lemon sponge* or Bual Madeira with *Dundee*, *Battenberg, brownies* or a traditional *fruitcake. Doughnuts*, by the way, love elephants.

Cheesecake My favourite is cherry, but to be honest it doesn't really matter what fruit you put in them; the cake, not the fruit, controls the choice of wine. Botrytised Sémillon and Riesling from the New World, Coteaux du Layon and other sweet Loire wines, Austrian Beerenauslese and Alsatian Vendange Tardive Riesling and Tokay all work. The trick is to keep the sweetness intense, without resorting to a heavyweight style of wine.

Cherries In *pie* form, cherries behave like berries and prefer the company of mid-weight sweet wines. Cherries served with *chocolate*, in a *marquise*, or *Black Forest gâteau* can handle a richer wine. Try Amarone, the wickedly intense red wine from Veneto in Italy, or Californian Zinfandel for a bizarre match. It works, honest.

Chocolate A deluxe *choccy cake* can, if it is not too intense, retreat into lighter Muscats and botrytised Rieslings. *Chocolate mousse*, *petits pots au chocolat* and *chocolate soufflé* all head towards Orange Muscat, with its pervading aroma and flavour of orange blossom. This is one of the finest food and wine combinations of all, as orange and chocolate are natural partners (just ask Terry). Australia and California make two examples that I know of, so well done Brown Bros. and Andrew Quady respectively, your culinary credentials are assured. *Chocolate pithiviers*, the single most decadent dish in the pudding repertoire, needs unctuous fortified wines. And while we are on the subject of top choccy, St-Emilion au Chocolat is no slouch. Match these ridiculously insane dishes with Passito di Pantelleria, Tokaji, black Muscat (space-age), liqueur Muscat, PX (short for Pedro Ximénez, the boozy, black, teeth-rottingly sweet turbo-sherry), botrytised Sémillon from the New World, Maury and Banyuls – the mega, port-like sweet Grenache wines from the south of France and, finally, tawny port.

Christmas pudding It is useful to have a wine that lasts well once opened. Liqueur Muscat from Australia and tawny port, as well as Malmsey Madeira, all fit the bill. You'll find that you can squeeze twelve glasses out of a bottle without short-changing anyone. Not bad, hey?

Cinnamon rolls A heavenly creation; however, eating one should be considered a criminal offence. You need sweetness and toffeed aromas in the wine to cope with the intensity of sugar. Vin Santo, Tokaji, liqueur Muscat and old oloroso sherry would warrant another five years in the slammer. *Lardy cakes* guarantee you repeat offender status, so be prepared.

Crème brûlée As I only like the top crunchy bit as opposed to the silky creamy bit, I can only make a stab at the best match. I reckon that somewhere between my almond tart and my cheesecake wines you'll find the perfect companion. Loire sweeties, made from Chenin Blanc, appear in both sections, so they must be spot on; Coteaux du Layon, Moelleux Vouvrays, Bonnezeaux (pronounced 'Bonzo'!) and Quarts de Chaume are your choices. You could always look for some South African Chenin sweet wines, as the grape is widely planted down there.

Crème caramel Another pud that you won't get me near, but I have it on good authority that light, delicate sweeties are required. German Auslese Rieslings from the Mosel, and fairy light, fresh Muscats would be ideal.

Crêpes Suzette Clairette de Die, the little-known sparkling wine from the Rhône, or Asti from Italy, would be the cheaper options, with demi-sec Champagne being the 'with knobs on' choice.

Custard As soon as you wade in with custard on, say, a jam roly-poly, you are giving the wine much more to think about. Creaminess in a dish needs acidity in a wine to counter it, so with custard being the ultimate in eggy creaminess, the big guns like Malmsey Madeira, liqueur Muscat and Tokaji must be released from their cages to run riot.

Doughnuts see 'Cakes'.

Fruit *Raw* fruit of any kind has a much lighter flavour than you would expect when pitted against a sweet wine. So stay dainty with Asti, German or Austrian Spätlese Rieslings, demi-sec Champagne, fresh Muscats, Italy's Recioto di Soave, Spain's Moscatel de Valencia or very light Sauternes. Oh, if you fancy a *lychee*, then sweet Gewürztraminer is a safe bet, as it has remarkable lychee characteristics on the nose and palate. *Poached* fruit, for example *peaches* and *apricots*, pick up sweetness from the added sugar and can be pretty intense, so tread carefully. You may need a rich Coteaux du Layon from the Loire to see you through. For *pies* see 'Berries'.

Fruitcake see 'Cakes'.

Gingerbread A wonderful creation which, along with *ginger cake* and *ginger biscuits*, is made even better when accompanied by a glass of old Malmsey Madeira.

Gooseberry fool This refreshing pud doesn't take to heavy sweet wines. Young, sweet Sémillon, like Sauternes, Saussignac,

Monbazillac or Loupiac would be delicious. Just try to keep the price down, as more expensive wines will usually be too intense. Otherwise grab some fresh young German Riesling for a fruit-cocktail-style flavour.

Ice cream I once did a tasting where rosé Sancerre ended up being the perfect partner for Chunky Monkey. So, as you may be able to guess, matching wine with ice cream is not always straightforward. My safest rule is that *vanilla*, *chocolate*, *rum and raisin*, *coffee*, *toffee* and *cookie-dough* ice creams love Pedro Ximénez (PX), the intensely coffee-and-raisin-drenched sweet sherry. You could always try sweet liqueur Muscats from Australia as well. If you have a *fruity ice cream* or *sorbet*, just leave it alone.

Jam tart Very sweet is the only rule, as you can't get sweeter than jam. Icewine (made from pressing grapes that have frozen on the vine) from Canada might be a relatively inexpensive way of tackling this dish. Other than that you are looking at a monstrous price tag, and you'd have to ask, is the tart worth it?

Jelly Light German or Austrian Rieslings should not interfere too much with the jelly. Otherwise you could recreate a kid's tea party and have a fizzy drink (Asti?).

Lemon meringue pie German Riesling or Loire Chenin Blanc handle the citrus theme well. The good thing is that these two styles of wine are relatively inexpensive, and there is, at last, a move back to German wines these days.

Meringue On their own, meringues are virtually tasteless, but when served with fruit (*pavlova*), it is the fruit that concerns you, so see 'Fruit'.

Mince pies I love to follow the Christmas cake and pudding idea of Madeira, tawny port and liqueur Muscats. It will save you another trip to the shops, and they are all big enough boys to wrestle with the brandy butter. They also go a very long way – twelve to fifteen glasses in one bottle.

Pastries These belong to the same school as tarts and cakes, in that you are not really expected to crack open a bottle of wine for one – *pain au chocolat* and liqueur Muscat anyone? However, if you are in the mood, then Coteaux du Layon, Muscat de Beaumes-de-Venise, Saussignac and Monbazillac are France's best efforts. Botrytised Riesling from Australia and New Zealand might also work well. Finally try German Spätlese Riesling, keeping the price down.

Peach melba Botrytised Riesling does the peachy thing well, so head down under, or to Germany. Alternatively a late-picked Viognier from the Rhône would be stunning, but they are hard to come by. For *poached peaches* see 'Fruit'.

Pecan pie A well-deserved entry for one of the all-time classic American dishes, which strangely needs to be drunk exclusively with Australian wine. Magill Tawny, from super-winery Penfold's, is the benchmark wine with these naughty, addictive slabs of pudding. Otherwise, Aussie liqueur Muscats or, if you fancy something a little posher, give the rest of the world a chance and try Malmsey Madeira.

Pineapple upside-down pudding Got to get a mention, as one of the most irresistible menu items of all time. The caramel and pineapple team up to form a fairly exotic partnership in this dish, and smart Sauternes would give a real result here. If you are cutting back, then Australian botrytised Sémillon would also work wonders.

Plum crumble Of the crumble family, plum is up there with blackberry and apple (both Ma Jukesy specialities) as one of the mightiest. A bit of concentration is needed (in the wine, not you reader) so head off to Canada for Riesling Icewines, or to Italy for heroic Vin Santo.

Rhubarb crumble A relative lightweight next to the plum above, rhubarb crumble likes to take it easy. Exotically sweet Riesling from just about anywhere has a rhubarby nose and palate. So this is the one grape that I would allow.

Rice pudding Cor, I haven't had rice pudding since school, and I'm not about to start, so I don't know. Sorry.

Rum baba By the very nature of the beast, a rum baba has a bit of a kick. Underneath the mild, genial exterior, a sweet-wine-bashing horror is waiting to get out. As rum baba is the Hannibal Lecter of the pud world, you have to go for fortified wine to stand a chance, so our front line soldiers, tawny port, Bual or Malmsey Madeira and liqueur Muscat are the best bet we've got. Go get 'em.

Sorbet see 'Ice cream'.

Steamed puddings It is quite simple. The greatest syrupy, toffeed, old-fashioned puddings (spotted dick, treacle sponge and suet pudding included) deserve the most regal sweet wines. And they have all been mentioned before – top-flight botrytised Sémillon, Bual or Malmsey Madeira, Tokaji, Vin Santo and liqueur Muscat.

Strawberries Top quality strawberries absolutely love Asti (Spumante) and Moscato d'Asti, demi-sec Champagne and Clairette de Die. Fizz with a touch of sweetness – perfect for a spot of tennis.

Tarte au citron see 'Lemon meringue pie'.

Tarte tatin Another spectacular dish, but one that doesn't quite fit into the 'Apple' section. By the way, pear tatin is perfectly acceptable, but pineapple is not! When cooked to perfection, honeyed Loire sweeties like Coteaux du Layon are right on the button. New World botrytised Sémillons would do, but could be a little clumsy.

Tiramisù A strangely unappetising dish in my opinion, as the coffee, mascarpone and chocolate, with the addition of brandy, never seem to knit together. It is best accompanied by Vin Santo (to blot out the flavour).

Toffee apple see 'Tarte tatin'.

Treacle sponge see 'Steamed puddings'.

Treacle tart Treacle tart, particularly if you have included lemon zest to lighten the mood, is not as stodgy as you might expect. You could try Sauternes, but if in any doubt, then Hungarian Tokaji or youthful liqueur Muscat would probably be safest.

Trifle The marvellous old English creation, adorning sideboards up and down the country, must be delighted to have so many options on the wine front. German Riesling Beerenauslese is my top choice, but any sweet Riesling would be lovely. Likewise, Sauternes and the family of worldwide sweet Sémillons all love this dish. If you are going to tip in a bit of booze, sherry is traditionally used, and good quality cream sherry is probably best.

Zabaglione Passito di Pantelleria, from the tiny volcanic island off Sicily, is the only wine to accompany this creamy concoction, unless the Marsala you use in the recipe is also drinkable.

CHEESE

The old red-wine-with-cheese law is downright wrong. When pondering which wine to drink with your cheese, keep an open mind, as surprisingly almost anything goes – white, red, sweet, dry and fortified. Try to keep your cheese board simple to limit the number of flavours and therefore wines needed, and watch out for chutney, as its pungent flavours tend to trip wines up. I have listed several categories of cheese and within each, some of my favourite styles.

Fresh cheese (*Cream cheese, feta, ricotta* and *mozzarella*)
Usually used in salads, or cooking, the flavours are not dominant, so drink what you fancy. See 'Cheese (cooked)'.

Natural rind cheese (*Crottin de Chavignol, Sainte-Maure de Touraine, Saint-Marcellin* and *Selles-sur-Cher*) Light Sauvignon Blanc or Chenin Blanc from the Loire are superb with goat's cheese, with Sancerre being the pick of the crop (Chavignol is one of the finest wine villages in Sancerre *and* the producer of the famous Crottin). However, any dry, fresh, unoaked white would be fine. If you feel like drinking red, then Loire Cabernet Franc or Gamay work perfectly well.

Soft white cheese (*Camembert, Brie de Meaux, Pavé d'Affinois, Chaource, Bonchester, Pencarreg, Explorateur, Boursault, Gratte-Paille* and *Brillat-Savarin*) Once again, Sauvignon Blanc works terrifically well here, although you may want some more 'oomph' in which case head to New Zealand, South Africa or Australia. Remember that the richer the cheese, the bigger the white, so Chardonnay can be considered, too. For reds try Pinot Noir (either red Sancerre or lighter red Burgundies), fresh young Rhône Syrah and rosé Champagne. Gratte-Paille and Brillat-Savarin traditionally go well with youthful, inexpensive claret – stick to my favoured châteaux in the Gazetteer section to avoid disappointment.

Washed rind cheese The milder examples like *Chaumes, Port Salut* and *Milleens* like nothing more than dry, fruity reds – light Loire red or Bordeaux, for example. The smellier cheeses, including *Epoisses, Chambertin* and *Langres*, really enjoy white Burgundy,

Alsace Riesling or Tokay and other controlled (not too oaky) Chardonnays from further afield. *Munster* loves Alsatian Gewürztraminer and *Vacherin Mont d'Or* loves red Burgundy, Beaujolais and lighter red Rhônes.

Semi-soft cheese This covers a huge selection of cheese. Try the following combinations: *Livarot* – Alsatian Tokay Pinot-Gris; *Maroilles* – Roussanne or Marsanne from the Rhône; *Pont-l'Evêque* – Viognier, also from the Rhône; *Raclette* – (assuming you are reading this on a skiing holiday, you lucky thing) likes anything from the Savoie region, red or white; *Gubbeen* – Pinot Blanc or Sylvaner from Alsace; *Edam* – whatever, it is not fussy and likes light whites and reds; *Morbier* – Rhône whites; *Fontina* – light, Alpine Gamay; *Reblochon* – this outstanding cheese likes much richer Gamay from Beaujolais and red Burgundy; *Saint-Nectaire* – another heroic cheese, likes the same again, plus Côtes-du-Rhône; *Tomme de Savoie* (we are in the zone here) – likes either Rhône whites or lighter reds; *Bel Paese* and *Taleggio* – Lombardy whites such as Lugana, and reds including Franciacorta; *Milleens* – needs gutsier whites or light fresh reds.

Hard cheese The largest category of all, ranging from mild, via medium to strong and extra-strong cheeses. As a starting point get an idea of the strength of your chosen cheese and this will help your wine selection. Cheeses in this group are, among others – *Cheddar, Gruyère, Cheshire, Parmigiano-Reggiano, Pecorino, Cornish Yarg, Double Gloucester, Lancashire, Caerphilly, Gouda, Beaufort, Manchego, Cantal, Etorki, Comté, Emmenthal, Jarlsberg* and *Mimolette*. From mild to extra strong, the wines to go for are: whites – Alsace Pinot Blanc, Chablis, Jurançon Sec, white Burgundy, white Rhônes, New World Chardonnays; reds – Loire reds, Chilean Merlot, Côtes-du-Rhône, spicy Italian reds like Primitivo, Old World Cabernet from Bordeaux or New World from Margaret River (Australia), Shiraz from Barossa Valley, McLaren Vale and Clare Valley (Australia), Vino Nobile di Montepulciano and Chianti (Italy) and Zinfandel (California); fortified – port (tawny, LBV and vintage), Madeira, Banyuls and Maury (both from France) and old oloroso sherries.

Blue cheese For *Stilton* look no further than Madeira, tawny port and LBV or vintage port; *Roquefort* and *Fourme d'Ambert*, in contrast, prefer sweet Sauternes, Monbazillac or Saussignac; *Dolcelatte* is a bit of a lightweight and because of its unusual sweet flavour and texture, I'd leave it alone; *Gorgonzola* likes Amarone della Valpolicella; *Chashel Blue* needs sweet whites; and *Beenleigh Blue* must, just must, have authentic scrumpy cider (I thought I should not end on a wine!).

THE TOP 250

£2.59   half bottle **Tesco Cava Brut, NV**, Penedès, Spain (**Tes**). Impressive, budget, sofa sipping for fizz fans.

£5.49   **Prosecco La Marca, NV**, Veneto, Italy (**Wai**). Mildly sparkling and wonderfully ripe, this is an afternoon wine, for uncorking and relaxing with at the weekend. It is smooth and gently fizzy and has a fair degree of ripe, grapey fruit on the finish. You could pep it up with a sploosh of peach juice and make yourself a perfect Bellini.

£6.99   **Omni, BRL Hardy, Australian Sparkling Wine, NV**, (**Sai**). This wine sells like mad in Australia, thanks to its teeny price tag and unrivalled value for money. I think it is a winner, too, despite a slightly odd label design and weird, un-winey name. Omni is bottle-fermented, like all great sparklers, and is blended by one of the world's top fizz experts, Ed Carr. While there is not an awful lot of excitement on the nose, the palate reveals creamy, slightly honeyed, peachy fruit and a crisp dry finish. It is clean and refreshing and a must for a party.

£7.99   **Banrock Station Sparkling Shiraz, NV**, South Australia (**Sai**, **Tes** and **Wai**). I adore this style of wine, but do not want to drink it everyday. The prime time to uncork this funky stunner is with super-spicy meat dishes, chargrilled or barbecued food. However, if you are searching for a wine to cope with the rich and varied tapestry that is the British Christmas dinner, then this wine will not only knock the lot into a cocked hat (with corks on), it will also lend a celebratory note to proceedings by virtue of its frothy bubbles. The rich, blackberry, plum, pepper and spice palate is intense, but not heavy. You must serve this fridge cold, because the bubbles lift the entire wine to a level hitherto unknown for the lusty, macho Shiraz grape.

£7.99 **Chapel Down Brut, NV**, England (**Boo**, **Fortnum & Mason**, **Saf**, **Sai** and **Selfridges**). After recently tasting Chapel Down's cracking fizz, and being mightily impressed, I have decided to save you a fortune and also encourage you to support one of the best wines made within our hallowed shores. The Brits are highly skilled at making fizz and over the last few years there has been a big leap in quality. Chapel Down is one of a band of fine producers, and here the nose, palate, texture and finish are in perfect harmony. At this price the Champenois should be quaking in their boots.

£9.99 **Brown Brothers Sparkling Pinot Noir & Chardonnay, NV**, King Valley, Victoria, Australia (**Peckham & Rye** and **Wai**). Brown Brothers are past masters at making fine pudding wines – see the sweet section. But they have now cracked another tricky style of winemaking – the sparkler. This wine uses the two best fizz grapes in the world, Pinot Noir and Chardonnay, which is the same noble combo that makes the greatest Champagnes. The biscuity nose, creamy palate and zesty acidity are in perfect balance. How appropriate that Champagne is often quoted as the 'king of wines and the wine of kings', as this New World pretender to the throne actually comes from the King Valley.

£9.99 **Chandon Australia, NV**, Victoria, Australia (**Saf**, **Unw** and **Wai**). Try as they might, fizz producers all over the world are finding it impossible to knock this mighty brand off the top of the tree. I have a few ten-pound sparklers in this book and they are all fabulous. What's cool about this one is that, for me, it is the most consistent wine in the company's global portfolio. Yes, that does include vintage Moët and Dom Pérignon, although, admittedly, their recent DP '95 is sublime. The problem is that for every 1995 there is a slack 1992 letting the side down. So, while the French worry about the weather, thousands of miles away in the Yarra Valley, their Ozzie cousins plod away making terrific, reliable, downright delicious wine. If you haven't already tasted this wine (there can't be many of you surely?), then it is a wonderfully creamy, rich style of fizz, made in the traditional (Champagne) method from Chardonnay and Pinot Noir. The grapes are sourced from far and wide and the result is the best value, crowd-pleaser on the market.

£10.99 **Bredon, NV**, Champagne, France (**Wai**). This is one of the best value of the current batch of supermarket Champagnes. Get ready to pounce if it is discounted near Christmas.

£11.99 **Green Point by Chandon, 1998**, Victoria, Australia (**Bot**, **Odd**, **Tes**, **Unw** and **WRa**). This is the second year in a row that Chandon Australia's big brother Green Point has made the Top 250. Last year's '97 was a blowsy, ripe, fruit cocktail of a wine, with rich mouth-filling flavours and a heady finish. The 1998 is a much tighter specimen. It seems that the powers that be have decided to give this wine more finesse and a longer, finer structure. This is a good move as it brings Green Point into direct competition with Champagne and, at this price, there is precious little going on in Reims or Epernay. As you can see from my stockist list this wine is widely available. It is a pity that Jansz and Starvers (below) have limited coverage but, if you can, hold a comparative head-to-head taste-off between these delicious styles, to find your favourite.

£11.99 **Pelorus, Cloudy Bay, NV**, Marlborough, New Zealand (**Adnams**, **Bot**, **Corks**, **General Wine**, **Harvey Nichols**, **S.H. Jones**, **Lay & Wheeler**, **Maj**, **James Nicholson**, **Peckham & Rye**, **Philglas**, **Selfridges**, **Wimbledon** and **WRa**). Pelorus is my favourite New Zealand fizz. I prefer this NV cuvée to the vintage wine, as it is fresher and livelier and, hee hee, cheaper. It is made by the famous Cloudy Bay team and is Chardonnay dominant with a dash (20%) of Pinot Noir to fatten up the middle palate. The packaging is ultra-chic and the taste is knockout. So join the ranks of fashion-conscious wine lovers everywhere who have a bottle of Pelorus in the fridge in case of unexpected thirst attacks.

£12.99 **Jansz, 1997**, Tasmania, Australia (**Corks**, **Selfridges** and **Vin du Van**). What a difference a year makes, or should I say a vintage. 1996 Jansz was a dreary so and so, and this was because the new owners, the Yalumba team, inherited a fair amount of old wine, and couldn't make a silk purse out of a dodgy blend. The 1997 is a complete turn around, and now that fizz supreme, Nathalie Fryar, is at the helm, the quality of this estate's wines is rising at an exponential rate. NV Jansz (£9.99, **Odd**) is a beauty, but for only three more measly pounds you can step up to this elegant, vintage thoroughbred. The focused Pinot and Chardonnay fruit is spot on, neither too rich, nor too tropical. It has a creamy, citrus theme that nods towards brioche and hazelnut, but never lapses into broad brushstrokes of flavour. The elegance is there, and so is the crucial, palate-cleansing acidity. '97 Jansz is a super drop.

£12.99 **Starvedog Lane, Chardonnay/Pinot Noir/ Pinot Meunier, 1998**, Australia (**D. Byrne** and **Inspired Wines**). This wine has only just landed, so the number of retailers is a tad limited (albeit highly respected). By the time this book is published, I would be amazed if there were not a further ten or fifteen names to add to this list. My tasting note for this wine was a brief one – 'brilliant, cheery, classy, lively, buy it'. £12.99 is a staggeringly low price to pay for this degree of finesse and elegance.

£14.99 **Knappstein Chainsaw Sparkling Shiraz, 1999**, Clare Valley, South Australia (**Odd**). Put your seatbelt on, this is gonna be a rough ride. Chainsaw is as chainsaw does and this huge, intense, bulletproof fizzy Shiraz is a palate-shredder of a wine. Someone asked me when Aussies actually drink it. They always tell me it is on the beach with a Barbie (or do they mean barbecue?). I'm not sure. I would never make it back to the shore if I went swimming after a glass of this stuff. I think you should stick to drinking it with food – preferably something meaty and rare, as the plum and black-fruit palate is so turbo-charged and glossy. Venison or wild boar would be a good match, but my all-time winner would be with a rare hunk of Brontosaurus. If you are into the Clare Valley red wine thing – and everybody should be – track down Knappstein's senior reds, Enterprise Cabernet and Enterprise Shiraz, made by Andrew (the Ox) Hardy. They are real collector's items and are sold in limited quantities in the UK. The 1998s are nearly finished and are incredible. The more elegant (by comparison!) and restrained 1999s arrive in November (£13.99, **OFW** and **Roberts & Speight**).

£16.99 **Pierre Gimonnet et Fils, Gastronome, 1997, Cuis 1er Cru, Blanc de Blancs**, Champagne, France (**Odd**). This 100% Chardonnay wine comes from a well-situated, premier cru-rated village on the Côte des Blancs. The Gimonnet's vintage brew is only two pounds more expensive than their NV, so it is well worth trading up. You can taste the minerality of the raspingly fresh Chardonnay grapes in this lean, foody sparkler. It is a canapé party dream date as the clean, rich fruit and teeth-tingling acidity would waltz through a cornucopia of culinary delights. We all too often save fizz for celebrations and special occasions. Wrong. There are many different styles of sparkling wine and this one is foody through and through. Drink it with a *plateau de fruits de mer* and you'll see that one bottle of this is worth two Sancerres any day.

£18.95 **Pirie, 1997**, Tasmania, Australia (**deFINE**, **Harvey Nichols**, **Noble Rot**, **Roberson**, **Sommelier Wine Co.** and **Wines of Interest**). For me, the 1996 Pirie was a landmark wine. It made my 2002 Top 250. So the first thing I did when I got off the plane in Melbourne this year was track down a bottle of the 1997, hoping it was up to scratch. After several bottles (just to confirm my thoughts, honest!) I am delighted to pronounce it is the greatest fizz that winemaker Dr Andrew Pirie has ever made. It is, you may have guessed, a classic blend of Pinot Noir and Chardonnay. He first made it as an experiment in 1993, to see whether Tasmania had the correct climate for making sparkling wine. Nowadays everyone heads down to Tazzy for their sparkling wine grapes and I'm sure it won't be too long before the Champenois are spotted off the coastline in a canoe. Pirie '97 is a monumental wine. Track it down – it is a microscopic price to pay for such excellence. For goodness sake, it's cheaper than a bottle of Mumm Cordon Rouge!!

£23.99 **Pol Roger, White Foil, NV**, Champagne, France (**Berry Bros.**, **Direct Wines**, **Lay & Wheeler**, **Maj**, **Odd** and **Wine Society**). I recently conducted a blind Champagne tasting for a group of keen wine enthusiasts and included all of my favourite labels. I will not list the wines that White Foil beat, but I can assure you it was a roll call of the greats. The reason, according to the panel, was that it was neither too assertive, nor too easy and relaxed, but somewhere in the middle. That is my definition of a crowd-pleaser, so well done Pol Roger for coming top of the pops.

£24.95 Louis Roederer, Brut Premier, NV, Champagne, France (**Bot**, **Harrods**, **Harvey Nichols**, **Odd**, **Saf**, **Tes**, **Unw**, **Wai** and **WRa**). Louis Roederer is a superb Champagne house – they are the team responsible for the uber-cuvée Cristal. The great thing about these guys is they invariably turn out one of the most consistently delicious NVs around. I have never had a 'green' bottle of Brut Premier, and that is something I cannot say about most of the other famous names from this legendary region. So, if you are on your way out to dinner; need to buy a birthday gift; are entertaining clients; or are blinded by a roll call of Champagnes on a restaurant wine list – Roederer is a safe haven, guaranteed to perk up your palate and turn an occasion into a celebration.

£27.99 Bollinger, Special Cuvée, NV, Champagne, France (**Asd**, **Berry Bros.**, **Bot**, **Rodney Densem**, **Fortnum Mason**, **Harrods**, **Harvey Nichols**, **Lay & Wheeler**, **Maj**, **Odd**, **Saf**, **Sai**, **Selfridges**, **Som**, **Tanners**, **Tes**, **Thr**, **Wai** and **WRa**). In addition to the stockists above, I'm sure this wine is available virtually everywhere. The Bolly legend strides on and yet very few people really know just how characterful this Champagne is. It is a big wine that even in NV form needs bottle age. Buy some, lay it down then try it out. Two-year-old NV Bolly is sublime. This is a wine drinker's Champagne house, so if you want fluffy, spritzy fruit and fresh summery flavours, go elsewhere. Bollinger is rich, masterful and decadent, with oaky nuances, full fruit and considerable weight.

£32.99 **Billecart-Salmon, Blanc de Blancs, NV**, Champagne, France (**Berry Bros.**, **Fortnum & Mason** and **Odd**). I am delighted to report that the first new style of Champagne in years from Billecart has gone straight into my Top 250. This Blanc de Blancs, as the name suggests, is white wine made from white grapes, and, in the case of Champagne, that means 100% Chardonnay. I opened a sneak preview of this wine for fifty experienced wine tasters and they were unanimously amazed. The creamy, smooth fruit is juicy and positively uplifting. They guessed at the price and overshot the mark by miles. If you love Champagne, you are guaranteed to love this wine.

£32.99 **Billecart-Salmon, Brut Rosé, NV**, Champagne, France (**Bentalls**, **Berry Bros.**, **deFINE**, **Ben Ellis**, **Fortnum & Mason**, **Harvey Nichols**, **Lay & Wheeler**, **Lea & Sandeman**, **Luvians**, **James Nicholson**, **Odd**, **Peckham & Rye**, **Philglas**, **Portland**, **Roberson**, **Selfridges**, **Uncorked**, **Valvona & Crolla** and **Noel Young**). This is, and always has been, my favourite rosé Champagne. It is not as powerful and richly rosy as Laurent-Perrier (or as expensive). It is, however, refined, relaxed, stylish, calm and self-confident. Just one sniff and sip and you'll fall under this wine's spell immediately. Thank goodness we are all leaving that 'rosé for Valentine's Day' hang-up behind. Rosé Champagne is a mood wine. How are you feeling? Do you fancy a bracing glass of NV Brut Réserve to wash away the day and kick off an evening's merriment, or are you after a mellow, elegant, unruffled glass of Brut Rosé? The choice is yours.

£34.99 **Taittinger, Brut 1996**, Champagne, France (**Luvians**, **Maj**, **Odd** and **Wimbledon**). They have cracked it in '96 after a few years in the wilderness. Well done Tatty for making a '96 with rich, toasty, floral fruit and no austere characteristics whatsoever. Celebratory fizz for a celebratory achievement.

£37.99 **Billecart-Salmon, Cuvée Nicolas-François Billecart, 1997**, Champagne, France (**Fortnum & Mason**, **Harrods**, **James Nicholson**, **Odd**, **Portland**, **Roberson**, **Selfridges** and **Uncorked**). Once again François Roland-Billecart can do no wrong. In his wisdom, he has decided to release his forward 1997 vintage before the firm, age-worthy 1996. This is a masterstroke, as while everybody else asks you to glug tight, hard, muscular wines, we in the know can relax and enjoy this smooth, harmonious brew. When the rest of the pack move on to the light, fresh '97s, Billecart '96 will have had that extra year of bottle age, softening it up and making it taste all the more sexy. Remember, this is £35 cheaper than Dom Pérignon and £60 cheaper than Cristal, so get with the beat – this wine is not only a bargain, it is an icon, and the intelligent, well-read (!) wine connoisseur's favourite secret weapon.

£45.99 **Bollinger, Grande Année, 1996**, Champagne, France (**Asd**, **Berry Bros.**, **Bot**, **Rodney Densem**, **Fortnum & Mason**, **Harrods**, **Harvey Nichols**, **Lay & Wheeler**, **Lea & Sandeman**, **Maj**, **Odd**, **Playford Ros**, **Sai**, **Selfridges**, **Tanners**, **Tes**, **Thr** and **WRa**). Bollinger make magnificent vintage wine. Recently they have made the best 1992, one of the top three

1995s and now this sensational 1996. These three vintages are all sublime efforts, with immense charm, complexity, style and age-worthiness. However, the 1996 is the most backward of the last three releases, so buy some, but try to exercise restraint and hold off for as long as possible before uncorking it. It is glorious now, but could happily live for a decade. As usual, the Pinot Noir-dominant recipe results in a rich, yeasty, biscuity, sweet kindling and almond croissant nose, which opens out to a full, mouth-filling, savoury, somewhat flamboyant palate. Bollinger is an unapologetically heavyweight style, but it is not all brawn; as the minutes-long finish melts away, you can pick up tender moments and delicate flavours like wild strawberry and shiny red cherry.

●●●●●●●●●●●●●●●●●●●●●●●●

£2.99 **Matra Springs, 2001**, Northern Hungary (**Wai**). There must be a mattress springs joke, but I can't think of it. This budget Hungarian white is made from Pinot Gris, Riesling, Muscat and Irsai Oliver. The first two varieties command 85% of the blend and lead the way on the palate. It is an assertively herbal wine, with fresh, clean, zingy fruit. Buy it as a party wine and most palates will love it. It is bone dry and squeaky clean. But you could also serve it with seafood, salads and goat's cheese. I rarely find anything I like under the dreaded three-pound barrier; in fact I haven't recommended a sub-three quid white wine for over a year. Avoid the 2000 vintage, as it is a little tired, and wait for this superb '01 to arrive in the autumn.

£3.65 **Le Pujalet, 2001**, Vin de Pays du Gers, France (**Wai**). Made from three weird but not that wonderful varieties – Ugni Blanc, Colombard and Listan – this superb white is a real surprise and a must for party or apéritif glugging. It is fresh-as-daisies, with crisp, citrusy fruit and a lively, perky finish. Le Pujalet is a glorious, pinpoint-accurate, refreshingly fruity wine and it is inexpensive to boot – hurrah.

£3.75 half bottle, **Tesco Finest Chablis, Vaucher, 2001**, France (**Tes**). This dinky little half of Chablis is quite superb. The classic hallmarks are all there and it is so nice to see an affordable half bottle on the shelves. Perfect for a glass and a half at lunchtime for two wine lovers.

£3.99 **Flagstone Noon Gun, 2001**, Coastal Region, South Africa (**Odd**). It was a close run thing, but this cheeky little number nearly got left by the wayside. I love the cool label, the microscopic price tag and the producers, Flagstone, but my first sniff and sip were a little below par. I dragged it into my kitchen to have another go alongside a simple salad – what a revelation. Noon Gun is a blend of Sauvignon Blanc, Chardonnay, Chenin Blanc and Riesling, with a teeny amount of barrel-fermented fruit to broaden the mid-palate. This oaked element gives the palate a slight grainy feel that deadens some of the fresh pineapple and grapefruit message. I think it's a bit of an error, because it makes Noon Gun a food-only proposition. Whatever you match this wine to, it will rise to the challenge. Just make sure you're eating when you are sipping, and you will be delighted with the result.

£3.99 **Lunaran Sauvignon Blanc, 2001**, Rueda, Spain
(**M&S**). £3.99, unoaked Sauvignon Blanc from Rueda in Spain.
Excited? No, I didn't think so, but I promise you this wine
is a stunner. Last year's 2000 vintage was a joy, and the
star of an eighty-wine M&S line up – sales went ballistic.
The new 2001 is a worthy successor; in fact, Telmo Rodriguez,
the gifted winemaker behind Lunaran, has made it even
more captivating. It can be used for all occasions, with zippy,
crunchy pear and apple-scented Sauvignon fruit, perfect as
an apéritif, but also with enough weight for food. You can
drink this with everything from salads and starters via fish
dishes to Asian food and goat's cheese. The stunning flavours
on show are quince, fresh herbs, lemon zest, greengage
jelly, honey and lemon curd. Lunaran is unmissable.

£3.99 **Malambo Chenin Blanc/Chardonnay, 2002**,
Mendoza, Argentina (**Sai**). Malambo is a new creation, which
launched with the 2001 vintage. This wine sold out in seconds
(I went bonkers about it). The 2002 was rushed on to the
shelves and it is even finer. The skilful team at Malambo are
also responsible for the highly acclaimed, best-selling Argento
wines. The cool thing about this blend is that it is even
cheaper (one pound) than its stablemate. The cunning combo
of zesty, pineapple-scented Chenin Blanc and smooth, cool,
pear-and-honey Chardonnay makes this irresistible. It is one
of the finest sub-four-pound whites I have ever tasted.
Fresh, clean, dry and juicy, Malambo is the perfect apéritif
or light lunchtime wine – it looks the part, tastes great and
is destined to be a star.

£4.79 **Domaine Spiropoulos, Mantinia, 2001,**
Peloponnese, Greece (**Odd**). This super-clean, organic grown
fruit is humming with vibrant, summery flavours. The zingy,
lemony acidity makes it remarkably thirst-quenching, and
the herbal, pear and apple fruit means it is the perfect
accompaniment to salads and starters.

£4.98 **Baron de Ley Blanco, 2001,** Rioja, Spain (**Asd**).
The Spanish Revolution is still being waged in wineries
throughout Spain. Old school bodegas favour woody whites
that age forever and smell like hospital disinfectant. New-
wave producers leave oak barrels to the reds (where they
belong) and let the feisty Viura grape express itself fully.
This gloriously fresh wine has clean, zesty pear fruit, with a
touch of honey and an energetic finish. At two pence (Asda
prices?!) under the fiver, this is a fabulous antidote to the
gallons of international grape varieties that we merrily
slosh down. And remember, if you feel like tapas, there is
only one white to drink.

£4.99 **Goats do Roam White, Fairview Estate,**
2002, Paarl, South Africa (**Sai** and **Som**). The 2002 takes
over from the sublime 2001 and no changes have been made
to the perfect recipe behind this wine. It is made from the
classic southern Rhône grapes Grenache Blanc, Clairette,
Viognier and Muscat (hence the cheeky play-on-words
name). Goats is tremendous, with elegance and complexity,
class and beguiling fruit. The white peach and fresh flower
theme is enhanced with nuances of nutmeg, vanilla, lemon

tart and Comice pear. The weight of the mid-palate is a little heavier than expected, so it can be drunk as either an apéritif or with food. The price tag is teeny, compared to the amount of finesse that the wine exudes. If you wanted to experience this taste from anywhere else in the world, you'd certainly be in the Rhône Valley, but goodness knows where – and you'd have to throw a tenner at a bottle.

£4.99 **Las Mulas Verdejo, 2001**, Rueda, Spain (**M&S**). A tremendous little wine, made from the underrated Verdejo variety. Telmo Rodriguez is the palate and mind behind this beauty and he has worked some amazing magic. The smooth stone-fruit flavours and impeccable balance are dreamy. It is mildly tropical, bitingly refreshing and gloriously cheap.

£4.99 **Norton Torrontes, 2002**, Mendoza, Argentina (**Bot, Mor, Odd** and **WRa**). Weird, yes, but this inexpensive wine will put a smile on your face. Torrontes, the grape responsible for this fruit explosion, makes a perky, sour-lemon-and-cool-melon-cube wine with a zesty, spritzy finish.

£4.99 **Oxford Landing Sauvignon Blanc, 2002**, South Eastern Australia (**Coo, Maj, Odd, Saf, Sai, Som, Tes, Unw** and **Wai**). I tasted this wine while it was still fermenting in Australia and was flabbergasted. 2002 was a spectacular vintage in Oz and this wine, usually a simple, budget glugger, is in a completely different league. This is Oxford Landing's best ever Sauv, loaded with citrus and pineapple. There are 75,000 cases, so there is no need to panic.

joyous fruit

£4.99 **Tatachilla Breakneck Creek Chardonnay, 2001**, South Australia (**Maj**, **Saf** and **Sai**). This clean, crisp Chardonnay is grapefruity, lively and ever so refreshing. What a relief it is to find an inexpensive Aussie Chardonnay that isn't trying too hard. There is no lumpy alcohol, no raw sawmill oak and no sickly overripe flavours, just uninterrupted, no nonsense, joyous fruit.

£4.99 **Villa Bianchi Verdicchio Classico, 2001**, Marche, Italy (**Sai** and **Valvona & Crolla**). It was at Vinitaly, the huge annual Italian wine fair, that I tasted a sneak preview of the 2001 whites from Umani Ronchi. I believe that they are the best wines this outstanding company has ever made. Villa Bianchi is their baby Verdicchio and I swear it is nearly as impressive as Casal di Serra, their more expensive, multi-award-winning, single vineyard Verdicchio. The trademark floral nose and bone-dry finish are simply stunning. Add to this the intensity of mid-palate, smooth, creamy, apple and honey fruit and the result is breathtaking. The real trick is how they do all of this for under a fiver.

£5.49 **Domaine Lafage Blanc, 2000**, Côtes du Roussillon, France (**Odd**). This classy Rhône blend offers intellectual drinking at an affordable price. The fruit is multi-layered, creamy and peachy, with fairly firm acidity, which makes it very much a foody wine. You have to be a fan of funky southern French blends to get your palate around this beauty, but once you're in the zone, I'm sure you will order a few more bottles to impress your friends.

LIGHT, DRY AND UNOAKED

£5.49 **Jacob's Creek Dry Riesling, 2001**, South Eastern Australia (**Tes**). Wine giant Orlando has come up trumps with this stunning crowd-pleaser. It is smartly packaged and sealed with a screwcap, thus guaranteeing it is in perfect condition when you drink it. One twist and you will be rewarded with crisp, lemony, smooth, tropical, summery flavours. This is the best Jacob's Riesling ever made, and this is entirely down to the method of closure. The screwcap works brilliantly, cork would only flatten this wine. I know because I've tasted this exact wine in both closures.

£5.49 **Lugana Villa Flora, Zenato, 2001**, Italy (**Wai**). This wine must spend most of its life being matched to Italian dishes, and no wonder, as it is such a slick little mover. Villa Flora has superb pear and apple fruit, a juicy texture and keen acidity, and these qualities make it a gorgeous accompaniment to food. If you like Soave, then this is made in the same style, but possesses a tad more fleshy fruit thanks to its fully ripe, juicy Trebbiano grapes.

£5.49 **Peter Lehmann Sémillon, 2001**, Barossa Valley, South Australia (**Asd**, **Boo**, **Odd**, **Saf**, **Sai** and **Unw**). There is an annual slot free for this wine. As long as PL keeps delivering the goods, I'll write it up. There is nothing that this outfit doesn't know about Sémillon, and year after year they encourage their vines to perform to the highest standards. Style-wise, this brew is three wines in one. We tend to drink it very young, when it is all gangly lemon and lime. All you have to do is just chill it down and let it go.

Throw any grub in its path – no problem. But what many of us don't know is that after a year or two this bottle will enter awkward adolescence. Aged three or four, it will start to sprout honeyed notes, and zesty lemon becomes lanolin and candle wax as it puts on a little weight. Aged five to eight this puppy fat blossoms into lemon meringue pie, honey and pistachio. The 1994 is about at its peak now! So, next time you are out and about, grab a few bottles of this awesome-value Grand Vin, drink a few and stick the rest in the cellar.

£5.99 **Houghton Classic Dry White HWB, 2001**, Western Australia (**Wai** and **Wine Society**). This is one of the oldest, most famous white wine brands in Australia. HWB stands for Houghton's White Burgundy. But you can't write that on a label these days, because WA is an awfully long way from central France. HWB is a complicated blend of Chenin Blanc, Sauvignon Blanc, Sémillon, Chardonnay and Verdelho, with a whisper of American oak thrown in. It is a stunning wine that borrows all of the best elements from the different varieties and ends up being ripe, fruit-driven, smooth, honeyed, and vaguely tropical, but with a long, dry, harmonious finish. This is one of the definitive all-purpose white wines. At this price you should buy a few and use them for emergency food and wine matching.

£5.99 **Ken Forrester Chenin Blanc, 2001**, Stellenbosch, South Africa (**Odd**). Ken Forrester is a restaurateur/winemaker who makes seriously stunning Chenin Blancs at refreshingly low prices. He has two of these beauties currently on the shelves

– a super little dry, tangy, tropical glugger called Petit Chenin at £3.99 (**Odd**), and its upmarket sibling, which I have chosen for my Top 250. This wine sees a small amount of oak to complement the pineapple and plump lime fruit. The palate is smooth and sexy and it is all topped off with a healthy dollop of racy acidity. I suspect that Ken's passion for food and wine has driven him to create this wine, and it is perhaps no surprise that it is one of the most multi-talented foody white wines available today. The '02 arrives in the New Year and is a worthy successor to the sublime 2001.

£6.99 **Banwell Farm Sémillon, 1999**, Barossa Valley, South Australia (**M&S**). This isn't light, but it is dry and unoaked, and if you are willing to let me squeeze this wine in here I'd be grateful. Despite being difficult to pigeonhole, this is one of the finest Aussie Sémillons I think I have ever tasted. I know that's weird at only seven quid, but this wine was made at St Hallett and they are a switched-on team. The honeyed, nutty, oily intensity of pineapple, mango and guava fruit is stunning. Match this to creamy main course dishes and you'll be gobsmacked.

£6.99 **Château Tahbilk Marsanne, 2000**, Victoria, Australia (**Boo**, **Dunnells**, **Harvey Nichols**, **Love Saves the Day**, **Mills Whitcombe**, **Springfield**, **Vin du Van** and **Wai**). Tahbilk is a famous old name in the wine world. It has historically made fat, blowsy, somewhat stewed Marsannes that need five or six years to shed their jaw-aching acidity. This fresh, clean '00 is the third vintage of the new regime.

And the change in style is welcome indeed. The flavour is broad, creamy and unoaked, with rich, appley, honeyed fruit, and the acidity is perky and refreshing. It is drinking well now despite its youth. In the past I struggled to understand the appeal of Tahbilk's Marsanne, but I've finally fallen in love with this awkward grape.

£6.99 **Domaine de L'Hospitalet Summum Blanc, 2001**, La Clape, South of France (**Odd**). This estate has made a couple of crackers of late and Summum is their inexpensive, superbly elegant baby white wine. It comes from the unfashionable appellation, La Clape, on the Mediterranean coast and is made from some pretty odd grapes – Grenache Blanc, Roussanne, Bourboulenc and Rolle. The result is a herbal, smooth, peachy elixir that sets the palate racing. I was bowled over on my very first sniff. This estate's wines are snapped up by three-Michelin-star restaurants all over France, so get in quick and treat yourself to some star treatment.

£6.99 **Mission Hill Private Reserve Pinot Blanc, 2001**, Okanagan Valley, British Columbia, Canada (**Maj** and **Wai**). I am happy to offer an extended visa to Mission Hill's classy Pinot Blanc. These guys continue to dominate the international Pinot Blanc Richter scale, and this new vintage is a star. I know that PB is not that serious a grape. But given the number of nobby, boutique Italian estates which struggle to make wine as yummy as this, I would say this bottle is a remarkable achievement. The fruit and acidity is in perfect balance, making it so delicious to drink – and it is a step up on the impressive 2000. Mission Hill is expanding its portfolio in the UK with a couple of near-miss reds, whose intensity and varietal appeal should be there or thereabouts in a few years. The fiendishly expensive Icewine is an icon, albeit with a limited wealthy audience (£19.95, half bottle, **Wai**).

£6.99 **Pinot Grigio, Puiattino, Puiatti, 2001**, Friuli, Italy (**Italian Continental Stores of Maidenhead** tel. 01628 770110 and **Red or White of Trowbridge** tel. 01225 781666). Two trailblazing retail specialists have snapped up Giovanni Puiatti's terrific PG, and I'm sure an avalanche of stockists will follow. This wine is one of the few Pinot Grigios on the market that actually has richness and true varietal character. It is lively, so much so it practically leaps out of the glass. The tangy, zesty, tart apple and juicy pear fruit is keen, spicy and gloriously thirst quenching. As Martini-loving, basketball-dunking, dandy around town, Giovanni would say 'Save a tree and drink Puiatti', in reference to the unoaked nature of his beloved wines.

£6.99 **Pinot Grigio, San Angelo, Castello Banfi, 2001**, Tuscany, Italy (**Maj**). This single vineyard San Angelo Pinot Grigio is amazing. For a start, PG is usually grown in chilly northern Italy, where, more often than not, the grapes yield lean fruit with raw acidity. Such a hollow style of Pinot Grigio is fresh and clean, but hardly anything to get excited about. But if you move south the weather warms up a bit, and the Tuscan climate has been kind to the

LIGHT, DRY AND UNOAKED

San Angelo vineyard, allowing the fruit to ripen fully. The winemaker's trick is to capture as much flavour as possible in these ripe grapes, whilst retaining a degree of crisp, refreshing acidity. Banfi have achieved this balance perfectly.

£6.99 **Simon Gilbert Card Series Verdelho, 2002**, New South Wales, Australia (**Amps**, **Bot**, **deFINE**, **Philglas** and **WRa**). The 2001 version of this funky wine made it into my Top 250 last year and it sold like wildfire. Perhaps the message is finally getting through – Verdelho is an epic variety for apéritifs, starters and, importantly, Asian food. The spectacular 2002 doesn't divert from the crunchy-pineapple-chunk-theme and is dotted with exotic fruit moments but never slips into full-on fruit salad, as the acidity is so perky, nervy and refreshing it keeps the wine on an even keel. The bottle looks smart and the price tag is mercifully low. Due into the shops in November, impress your friends – drag Simon Gilbert home for dinner.

£7.05 **Mâcon-Montbellet, Domaine Paul Talmard, 2001**, Burgundy, France (**Goedhuis**). This juicy, fruit-driven, unoaked Chardonnay is so gluggable, you'll have polished off half the bottle before you know it. It must be one of the most crowd-pleasing Mâconnais wines of all time. I couldn't put the glass down the first time I tasted it as the floral, mild, honey and pear fruit glides over the palate with ease. If you find Chablis a little tight and mineral, then this wine is for you. It is the perfect apéritif, but could easily step up to a roast poussin without missing a beat.

£7.99 **Nether Hill Unwooded Chardonnay, Chain of Ponds, 2001**, Adelaide Hills, South Australia (**Bibendum** and **Philglas**). Purple Patch Riesling, Square Cut Sémillon and this wine are all new releases from the ever-brilliant COP. They are all vibrant, varietally precise and fantastically well priced. The future is already here.

£7.99 **Lawson's Dry Hill Sauvignon Blanc, 2002,** Marlborough, New Zealand (**Bacchanalia**, D. Byrne, **Cairns & Hickey**, Lay & Wheeler, Maj, **Philglas**, Tes, **Valvona & Crolla** and **Noel Young**). This spectacular Sauvignon Blanc is one of the first 2002s to hit our shores from New Zealand. It sports a spanking new 'Stelvin' screwcap and it is a seriously delicious wine. So shout 'pop' when you twist and you will find a dry, lean, zesty, refreshing, passion fruit, asparagus, lime and mango concoction desperate to impress.

£7.99 **St-Véran Louis Jadot, 2000,** Burgundy, France (**Wai** and **Wimbledon**). Made from Chardonnay, this white Burgundy, from the Chalonnais region, is dry, ripe and refreshing. The classy fruit is generous, with hints of apple, pear and hazelnut and the finish – long and harmonious. Burgundy, the spiritual home of Chardonnay, churns out some of the greatest dry white wines on the planet. But you usually have to pay a fortune for good kit, and this wine is very grown up, but eminently affordable. If you love fit, toned, invigorating Chardonnay, unencumbered by the taste and aroma of pungent oak barrels, this is the wine for you.

£7.99 **Terrunyo Sauvignon Blanc, Concha y Toro, 2001**, Casablanca Valley, Chile (**Bot**, **Odd**, **Wine Society** and **WRa**). Terrunyo is a superb-looking thoroughbred, bottled in inch-thick glass and sporting an asymmetrical arty label. You may need two hands to pour it, but once safely in your glass you only need one second for the terrific herbal, citrusy aroma to infiltrate your olfactory system. This wine is made by Ignacio Recabarren, one of the two wizards at the helm of the Concha y Toro empire. He set out to make Chile's finest Sauvignon Blanc and on this showing, he has done it. There are only two other wines of this quality in Chile (Floresta and Pirque) and, surprise surprise, they are in this list, too. This wine is gorgeously ripe, yet impeccably balanced, and if you have tasted Chilean Sauv before, then you will be familiar with the classic, green-pepper-and-lime-juice theme. But what sets this wine apart from the masses is its intensity and length of flavour. Terrunyo is totally impressive and it will walk over all but the finest Kiwi Sauvignons and Sancerres. Also keep your eyes peeled for a small parcel of 2001 Terrunyo Pinot Noir (£12.99, **Odd**) coming onto our shelves in the autumn – it's a stonker.

£7.99 **Wither Hills Sauvignon Blanc, 2002**, Marlborough, New Zealand (**Great Western(c)**, **Jeroboams & Laytons(c)**, **Odd(s)**, **Edward Sheldon(c)**, **T & W(c)**, **Wai(s)** and **Wine Society(s)**). Brent Marris has done it again. Every year, he raises the quality bar, and every year he manages to sail over. Once again, I was first to sample the '02 with

LIGHT, DRY AND UNOAKED

Brent in May, and it is even more pungent and fruit-driven than the delightful '01. There is less exotic fruit and more steely, nervy acidity than last year, and this makes Wither Hills more refreshing and piercingly attractive than ever before. You'll note that each of the stockists has either a 'c' or an 's' next to them. This code details which retailer has taken the cork-sealed bottles and which the Stelvin (screwcap). In my experience the cork-sealed bottles tend to be more aromatic early on and after a few month the screwcaps catch up. Conversely the screwcaps keep the bottle fresher and zingier for longer, and have the added bonus of never being 'corked'. Given the choice, I would always plump for the screwcaps for out-and-out flavour and safety.

LIGHT, DRY AND UNOAKED

£8.30 **Chablis, Domaine Daniel Dampt, 2001**, Burgundy, France (**Haynes, Hanson & Clark**). Dampt racks up two years on the trot as my chosen Chablis geezer – good effort, as this slot is fiercely contested. I am forever comparing fine, balanced, sensitively oaked New World Chardonnays with the elegance and breeding found in top-flight Chablis. I accept that this is misleading, as nobody other than the lucky people in this AC could ever make the energetic, mineral, chiselled Chardonnay that these guys do. It is the soil, water, folds in the hills and sun, or lack of, which imbues the grapes with the attitude and edginess for which they are famous. For perfect, unspoilt, unoaked, stylish Chardonnay, taste this wine – it is a really invigorating experience.

£8.49 **Springfield Special Cuvée Sauvignon Blanc, 2002**, Robertson, South Africa (**Bibendum**, **Bot**, **Wai** and **WRa**). This Sauvignon is very serious indeed. It is bursting with lime juice and passion fruit flavours and has a huge amount of vitality and freshness. Buy this over its 'Life from Stone' brother, (£7.99, **M&S**), as it has more oomph. My favourite part of the wine is its glacially cool acidity and uninterrupted, minutes-long finish.

£8.80 **Sancerre, Etienne Daulny, 2001**, Loire, France (**Haynes, Hanson & Clark**). Burgundy specialists Haynes, Hanson & Clark have a terrific, well-chosen Loire selection, and this is one of the stars. I have chosen it above all of the Sancerre's I have tasted this year because it is gloriously forward, honest and juicy. In a tricky vintage like 2001, I don't want to have to hang around for months waiting for the brutal acidity and lean fruit to soften. Daulny's wines always drink well from the off, capturing Sauvignon Blanc's hallmark grassy, asparagus and lemon flavours and zippy, thirst-quenching finish. And, if you like top-flight Sauvignon, then grab some of Rouzé's '01 Quincy (£7.40, **HH&C**); it is a glorious brew that reinforces his status as best winemaker in the village. Six of each please guv'.

£8.95 **San Vincenzo, Roberto Anselmi, 2001**, Veneto, Italy (**Roberson** and **Wimbledon**). Roberto Anselmi's '01s are fleshy, ripe, smooth and luxurious wines that redefine Soave. The honeyed, floral aroma coupled with the nutty, lingering finish is otherworldly and positively revolutionary.

LIGHT, DRY AND UNOAKED

£8.99 Chapel Down, Curious Grape, Bacchus Reserve, 2001, England (Jeroboams & Laytons, Philglas and **Tenterden Vineyards** tel. 01580 763033). This is the finest English wine I have ever tasted. The price tag may be a little steep, but don't let that deter you from hunting down a bottle and relaxing in its nettle, herb quince and lime scent and edgy, crisp, steely finish. Bacchus Reserve is the perfect foody wine as the leggy fruit and vital acidity are so good at cutting through creamy sauces, spicy ingredients and fatty recipes. You can test this wine with challenging dishes and it will come up trumps. Top marks to Chapel Down for two in the Top 250, and if that's not enough, you could also uncork their 2001 Curious Grape Aromatic (£4.99, **Saf**).

£8.99 Floresta Sauvignon Blanc, Santa Rita, 2001, Casablanca Valley, Chile (**Bot** and **WRa**). I have been waiting an eternity for this icicle-sharp, lean, mean, citrus, passion fruit and herb Sauv to turn up. Thank goodness it's here, I am dying of thirst.

£8.99 Jackson Estate Sauvignon Blanc, 2002, Marlborough, New Zealand (**Adnams**, **Beaminster**, **Boo**, **Bottleneck**, **D. Byrne**, **Cairns & Hickey**, **Dartmouth**, **Garland**, **General Wine**, **Peter Graham**, **Grog Blossom**, **Hedley Wright**, **Charles Hennings**, **Jolly Vintner**, **S.H. Jones**, **Maj**, **Odd**, **Oxford Wine**, **Christopher Piper**, **Terry Platt**, **Portland**, **Charles Steevenson**, **Tanners**, **Tes**, **T & W**, **Wai**, **Weavers** and **Wright**). Epic. There's no need for anything else. Just look at the support this wine has from the trade!

£8.99 **Vernaccia di San Gimignano, Panizzi, 2001**,
Panizzi, Tuscany, Italy (**Valvona & Crolla** and **Wimbledon**).
It is no surprise to me that both eagle-eyed Philip Contini,
from V&C, and trend-spotting Andrew Pavli from WW,
stock this wine. These guys don't mess around, and when
a good Vernaccia di San Jimmy comes along, you can
guarantee they'll spot it. Unfortunately, this style of wine is
one of the most overrated in Italy, with ten quid versions,
stuffed with sad, lean, soulless fruit being sold in trendy
bars in Milan by the truckload. But Panizzi is different. His
2000 was a tour de force, and this 2001 is surely a once-in-
a-lifetime experience. It is bone dry, witha meadow flower
aroma and a smooth, creamy palate, punctuated with pear
and apple moments. The finish is crisp and refreshing. This
Vernaccia is head and shoulders above any wine I have ever
tasted, and if you want to eclipse even this stunning effort,
ask Andrew or Philip if they can get you any of Panizzi's
rare '99 Reserva!

£9.95 **Menetou-Salon, Clos des Blanchais,
Domaine Henry Pellé, 2000**, Loire, France
(**Jeroboams & Laytons**). This is categorically the best Menetou
I have ever tasted. In fact, in the realms of Loire Sauvignon
Blanc, there have only been a few bonkers, old Chavignol
Sancerres from Cotat that really stick in my mind as being
significantly more impressive. Pellé is a great footballer,
sorry winemaker, whose forty-year-old Sauvignon vines
have played a blinder – magnificent structure, purity and
length (and, of course, price).

LIGHT, DRY AND UNOAKED

£4.99 **Accademia del Sole Vioca, Calatrasi, 2001**, Sicily, Italy (**Saf**). This brilliant bottle of wine tastes miles more expensive than its sub-fiver price tag. It is made predominately from Cattarato, a funky, if often dull, Italian grape variety. The genius ingredient is the addition of 15% Viognier, which adds a sensational nose of peach and honey and a gloriously smooth, long palate. In addition, a small proportion of this wine sees oak barrels, a clever little tweak that adds complexity to the overall package. So how did this all come about? The answer is Linda Domas, the alchemist Aussie winemaker who makes this beauty. If you have ever tasted Viognier and enjoyed it, you must make it your duty to find Accademia del Sole Vioca. It will blow you away. If you haven't you are in for a treat.

£4.99 **Domaine de Boulas, Côtes-du-Rhône Blanc, 2001**, France (**M&S**). It may be a little unfashionable to drink white Rhône, as chunky reds dominate the region and the few whites that filter on to our shelves tend to be dull and lacklustre. But fear not, this wine is absolutely tremendous, and is a measly five quid. The mature Grenache Blanc vines that make up 80% of this wine are at the top of their game. The fresh, fuzzy-peach-skin nose is swiftly followed by a silky smooth Galia melon, honeycomb and white flower palate. The finish is ripe and long and, as there is no oak used in the production of this beauty, it trumpets just one message – aromatic, unctuous, uninterrupted fruit flavours.

AROMATIC

100   white

£5.45 **Mas Carlot Marsanne/Roussanne, Vin de Pays D'Oc, 2001**, France (**Jeroboams & Laytons**). I am a dedicated follower of Marsanne/Roussanne blends. Some of the most profound Rhône Valley whites use these two underrated grapes to great effect. It is, however, incredible that this inexpensive French Country blend captures the mood and carries the weight of expectation perfectly. The fruit is rich and peachy, with honeyed notes and considerable depth of flavour. This exuberance is underpinned by thirst-quenching acidity and a lively, youthful, fresh feeling throughout. It is, quite simply, a delicious wine. J & L are in the process of revamping their entire wine list and if you are serious about wine, you should be on their mailing list.

£5.49 **Dürkheimer Michelsberg, Riesling, Helmut Darting, 2001**, Pfalz, Germany (**M&S**). Helmut Darting has an impressive CV. He used to work for respected Riesling experts, Müller-Cattoir (see Gazetteer). He has managed to stuff this cheeky little Riesling with an enormous amount of smooth fruit-salad flavours and top it off with a juicy, but crisp finish. This style of wine is faithful to the German classic Riesling model, but zesty enough to appeal to modern palates. Dunk it in an ice bucket and serve as a stunning apéritif.

£5.99 **Torres Viña Esmeralda, 2001**, Penedès, Spain (**Boo**, **Bot**, **Odd**, **Thr**, **Unw** and **WRa**). This is a perennial favourite of mine. In fact, the 2000 made my Top 250 last year. It is a 85% Muscat/15% Gewürztraminer blend that cunningly uses the Gewürz element for the perfumed, floral nose and the Muscat for the sleek body. It is an aromatic wine with tropical nuances and a creamy palate, but the finish is much drier than expected and the wonderful, zesty acidity cleanses the palate after each sip. Esmeralda is a superb apéro-style or salad/lunchtime favourite, but it is also the perfect Thai, Indian or Chinese food wine.

£5.99 **Trio Viognier, 2002**, Casablanca Valley, Chile (**Odd**). I tasted a tank sample of this first crop Viognier and it is terrific. The '01 is on stream now and is a worthy scene-setter. But just wait for this gorgeous, aromatic, honeyed, peachy '02. Oddbins estimate they will swap over around December. Keep your eyes peeled, because it is a stunning, brilliant-value wine.

£6.49 **Houghton Verdelho, 2001**, Western Australia (**Mill Hill** and **Mitchells**). Fresh, vibrant, clean and pineappley, this is a cracking Verdelho at a brilliant price. Uncork, pour, chill out and dream.

£6.99 **Santa Julia Reserve Viognier, 2001**, Mendoza, Argentina (**Wai**). In 2001, Santa Julia effortlessly managed to keep control of pole position on the Argentinian Viognier grid. The clever 20% oaked slice of this wine props up the busty fruit and allows the peach, melon, vanilla and hazelnut ingredients to tango together in style – great value.

AROMATIC

£6.99 Wilkie Estate Organic Verdelho, 2001, Adelaide Plains, South Australia (**Wai**). Wilkie Verdelho is broad, tropical and luscious, oozing pineapple, sherbet and mango flavours. It is marvellously decadent and almost brazen on the palate, but watch out for the finish, as it tightens up to a glorious acidic kick. The Adelaide Plains are not considered to be prime vine-growing turf, but a few geniuses manage to turn grapes from this flat land into nectar, and Bernard Wilkie is one of them.

£7.35 Mas des Aveylans Viognier, 2001, Vin de Pays du Gard, France (**Jeroboams & Laytons**). In the absence of Condrieu – the terrifyingly expensive, tiny production, ultra-famous Viognier incarnation from the Northern Rhône – I have tracked down this superb expression of the beguiling grape for a third of the price. Aveylans captures all of the perfumed peachiness and weight you'd expect and packages it very smartly indeed. This estate also makes a desperately impressive, classic Rhône blend red (£5.95).

£7.49 Armand, Riesling Kabinett, Reichsrat von Buhl, 2001, Pfalz, Germany (**Odd**). This exciting Riesling is practically fizzing, it is so anxious to get out of the bottle. The pervading aromas and flavours of elderflower and lemon balm are absolutely amazing. This lovely, dry wine perks you up and cleans your palate, and is the sort of wine you pray is waiting in the fridge for you at home after a grotty day in the office.

AROMATIC

£7.49 **Chapel Hill Verdelho, 2001**, McLaren Vale, South Australia (**Wai**). I am stacking up the Verdelhos this year, as it is such a wonderful variety, but don't, for a second, think they are all the same. On a recent trip to McLaren Vale, I tasted this wine and declared that it was a landmark creation. I also had the pleasure of sampling an old bottle of 1997. The newly arrived 2001 takes over from the superb '00 and sadly the 1997 is long gone, but it showed just how sensational this grape variety can be at all ages of its life. The epic 2001 is loaded with lime juice, pineapple, green apple and stone fruit. It is more linear and less flamboyant than Wilkie, and more complex and studied than Simon Gilbert. If Gilbert is a lithe, explosive sixty-metre sprinter and Wilkie is a hundred-metre runner, all lycra and lunch box, then Chapel Hill is a golden mile specialist with flappy shorts, tousled hair, rock-hard stamina and sinewy, taut fruit. Pam Dunsford is the winemaker at Chapel Hill and she is one of the finest exponents of this grape variety on the planet. The piercingly fresh, neon green fruit and bracing acidity mean that this wine can cut through any dish loaded with spice or chilli, and it is also a firm favourite with fish.

£7.49 **Tim Adams Riesling, 2002**, Clare Valley, South Australia (**Australian Wine Club**, **Harvey Nichols** and **Tes**). If you pick up this book in early October, the 2002 may not yet be on the shelves, so grab yourself a bottle of the chiselled, stern, toned 2001. It is lean and mean – think Brad Pitt in *Fight Club*. But what a difference a year makes. The 2002 is the same muscular Hollywood hero, but this time he is in relaxed, cool-dude mood, perhaps more *Ocean's Eleven*-style. Tim's Riesling is not normally an aromatic, succulent beast. It usually possesses a stripped-down mineral core of fruit which often needs five or more years to express itself. But in '02 he had been forced by perfect weather conditions into making an ethereal work of art. It is perfumed, plump, exotic and luscious. Don't, however, think that this wine is a fruity, cocktail-lounge-lizard-pushover. The trademark Adams focused, zesty, firm acidity and edgy citrus, herb and pear fruit are there, but they are just hovering behind the gloriously, sexy, glossy flesh. This wine is undoubtedly gorgeous now, but try to keep a few bottles aside, as it has barely begun its odyssey. This year, Tim has wisely sealed the bottle with a Stelvin (screwcap) closure to preserve the perfect flavours and allow it to age forever. This is a model example of a wine that will gradually emerge from its chrysalis over the next few years, if given the chance. One of the finest wines of the year.

£7.99 **Burgans Albariño, 2001**, Rías Baixas, Galicia, Spain (**Odd**). I love Albariño. It is Spain's finest and quirkiest indigenous white grape, and when on top form, it can be transformed into one of the zaniest brews around. The tropical nose and tangy fruit in this wine are extremely thirst quenching, and the final lick of acidity is almost nerve tingling. The whole point of this grape is to capture as much aroma and flavour as possible, but also to follow it up with bracing acidity and freshness on the finish. Burgans manages this with style and you'll find pink grapefruit,

AROMATIC

apricot, pineapple and lime here. Watch out for plastic corks appearing soon in this wine. This is a superb idea, as Burgans Albariño is all about freshness, and with a plastic stopper none of the aromatic qualities will be leeched out of the bottle – you'll be able to drink it safe in the knowledge that it is in tip-top condition. Who knows, next year they may even make the quantum leap to screwcaps.

£7.99 **Redbank Sunday Morning Pinot Gris, 2001**, Pyrenees, Victoria, Australia (**Charles Hennings** and **Selfridges**). Its official, you are now allowed to uncork before midday on a Sunday – it says so on the label. This terrific Pinot Gris is clean, tangy, refreshing and appley, and the 20% oaked fruit gives the mid-palate a depth of flavour and style that sets it apart from its competitors. Food-wise, this wine handles it all, and is particularly accurate with Asian-fusion cuisine and, of course, corn flakes.

£7.99 **Tokay-Pinot Gris, Heimbourg, Turckheim, 2000**, Alsace, France (**Bacchanalia**, **D. Byrne**, **Halifax**, **Luckins** and **Mill Hill**). This T-PG is light years away from its sibling variety Pinot Grigio. The only characteristic that these two wines share is their love of thirst-quenching acidity. Otherwise this wine's palate meanders through a veritable Horn of Plenty of fruit and spice flavours before the finish kicks in. Italian PG, on the other hand, has only one message, zippy fru— and it's over before you've bothered to listen. The baby '01 T-PG from Turckheim is sold through Oddbins for £6.29, if you want to get your

AROMATIC

palate in the zone. But once you have sniffed and slurped this introductory wine, you'll crave more and the Heimbourg is the place to go. The spicy, edgy, tropical richness on the nose, and honeyed, pear and citrus palate craves the company of food and wine lovers.

£8.49 **Gewürztraminer Vieilles Vignes, Turckheim, 2001**, Alsace, France (**Corks**, **The Vineyard** and **Wine Society**). When Alsace Gewürz is good, it is usually very good and very expensive. But this one is superb and it's well under a tenner. The minerality in this wine cuts through some of the more flamboyant flavours usually associated with this variety. It is made from 35-year-old vines and the quality of rose petal, lychee and rhubarb fruit is sublime. The finish is clean, dry and very long – a classy wine.

£8.60 **Forrest Estate Gewürztraminer, 2002**, Marlborough, New Zealand (**Adnams**). A breathtakingly well-balanced wine. It is easy to be heavy-handed with Gewürz, loading the wine with oily, mouth-coating, heady fruit. However, the skill is to balance the explosive, tropical fruit with refreshing, palate-cleansing acidity. F.E. Gewürz is exotic, but prettily so, not soaked in gaggy scent. It has a medium-weight palate, with moments of lychee and rose petal, interrupted by pear, peach and papaya, and is one of my favourite aromatic Kiwi wines. It is expected to arrive in October, so keep your eyes peeled. Drink this heavenly brew with Asian food and you'll find it difficult to wipe the grin off your face.

AROMATIC

dead sexy *(if a little tarty)* —

£8.75 **d'Arenberg The Hermit Crab Marsanne/ Viognier, 2001**, McLaren Vale, South Australia (**Bibendum**, **Philglas** and **Wine Society**). A serious, aromatic, yet zesty, dry wine that follows a southern Rhône model, but is made in the idyllic McLaren Vale region of South Australia. The great thing about this wine is that it loves tricky food, such as spicy, chilli-laden, Mexican, Indian and fishy dishes. The honey, apricot (Viognier, doing its job well), lime and spearmint flavours combine beautifully and wash over the smooth, oily palate. The keenly acidic finish hoovers up the fat Marsanne fruit and you are left with a zippy, citrus tang – yum.

£8.99 **Fairview Viognier, 2002**, Paarl, South Africa (**Great Western**, **Odd**, **Sai** and **Wai**). Deep joy, Charles Back's '02 Viognier is a stunning creation. This is a dead sexy (if a little tarty) wine, with a hypnotic aroma and sassy chassis. The oak barrels used to enhance its allure tend to add pneumatic appeal to an already dishy model. The showy peach and praline fruit, coupled with the rich, buxom, bouncing palate is sheer perfection. This succulent offering is guaranteed to tickle your fancy.

£8.99 **Ürziger Würzgarten, Riesling, Ernst Loosen, 2001**, Mosel, Germany (**M&S**). This is a corker, with spectacular balance and symmetrical tropical fruit and acidity. It is hard to know how German Riesling can be better. It is only nine pounds and I gave it 18/20. It's the perfect apéritif wine – please try it, you'll be hooked.

AROMATIC

£9.99 **Pazo de Barrantes Albariño, 2001**, Rías Baixas, Galicia, Spain (**Fortnum & Mason**, **Peckham & Rye**, **Philglas**, **Tes** and **Wimbledon**). This Albariño is dreamy, tropical and luscious and, just when you don't expect it, a crisp, zesty finish snaps the palate shut and you are driven to take a sip and kick start the luxurious feeling once more. It is more decadent and fleshy than Burgans and while not typical Albariño, I think the way this estate is changing our perception of this terrific grape is commendable. Bathe your palate in this delicious wine – it is organoleptic aromatherapy. For a world first, search for the rare 2001 Pazo de Barrantes Late Picked Albariño. Try asking the merchants above and don't blanch when they inform you that a 50cl bottle will set you back £16. It is a dizzyingly brilliant piece of work.

£9.99 **Petaluma Riesling, Clare Valley, 2002**, South Australia (**Fortnum & Mason**, **Harvey Nichols**, **Odd**, **Peckham & Rye**, **Portland** and **Noel Young**). In order to stay focused on the job in hand, i.e. reducing 26,000 tasting notes down to a list of 250 supreme champions, I have to take each vintage of Petaluma Riesling and subject it to the same scrutiny as an unknown bottle of Cuvée Peint-Strippeur. I am, however, pretty confident that it will always come up trumps, as this wine is one of the finest Riesling incarnations in the world. But this year a strange thing happened – an act of God no less. The 2002 vintage in Clare is, as winemaker Brian Croser puts it, probably the best Riesling he has ever made. Brian knows a thing or two about wine (there is not much he doesn't know). So if you

AROMATIC

are happily glugging through the delicious 2001, stop. Put the rest in the cellar. It will age like clockwork for a decade or more. Get out your prayer mat and await the coming of the 2002 vintage. Christmas is when this wine appears (it had to be, didn't it). No tasting notes here, just reverential silence. I will see you in the queue. I'll be the bloke with the forklift.

£9.99 Pipers Brook Gewürztraminer, 2001,

Tasmania, Australia (**Halifax**, **Hoults**, **Martinez**, **Noble Rot** and **Sommelier Wine Co.**). Notching up a second year in a row in my Top 250, this is not only the best Aussie Gewürz, it is also one of my favourite versions of this esoteric grape variety in the whole world. The reason? The nose, palate and finish are in perfect balance, with none of the sickly, heady, dizzy-Body-Shop-scent and oily, blowsy texture too often associated with Gewürz. The restrained, yet hypnotic nose of rose water, lychee and papaya will get your pulse racing, the palate is clean and crisp, but also multi-layered, with fresh tropical fruit and zesty palate-invigorating acidity. I find this level of complexity and sheer palate enjoyment absolutely mind-blowing. Pipers Brook also make a sensational Pinot Gris.

£9.99 Renwood Sierra Series Viognier, 2000,

California (**Odd**). Gosh. The nose on this beauty is peach and nutmeg crumble with a honey and apricot sauce topping. This is decadent stuff, but it is beautifully balanced on the palate and the finish is minutes long.

£12.00 **Pinot Gris, Les Princes Abbés, Schlumberger, 1999**, Alsace, France (**Maj** and **Selfridges**). This wine has great intensity, spice and tropical fruit. The texture is oily and rich and the exotic fruit flavours keep on going to the epic, dry finish. Turn the volume knob up to eleven and try 1998 Pinot Gris Spiegel (£17.00, **Wimbledon**).

£12.99 **Craigow Riesling, 2001**, Tasmania, Australia (**Bibendum**). After spending three full days at the London Wine Trade Fair and tasting over 700 wines, this Tazzy Riesling was my Wine of the Fair. It is difficult for me to restrain myself on the superlative front when describing this wine, but I'll have a go. Craigow counterpoints Riesling's heavenly tropical-fruit-coulis intensity with a statuesque backbone, a luxurious, decadent texture and an elegant, glacially cool finish. The length of flavour on the back palate is simply cosmic, running on and on for minutes. I think that'll do!

£17.95 **Yalumba, The Virgilius Viognier, 2001**, Eden Valley, Australia (**Fortnum & Mason**, **Harrods**, **Roberson** and **Selfridges**). Yalumba are passionate about Viognier, and so am I. But, I was disappointed by the first few vintages of The Virgilius. The oak was a little too ponderous and the fruit lacking in varietal complexity. But, wow, the team has nailed it in the 2001 vintage. The nose and flavour are totally focused and it is clear the twenty-year-old vines have at last bedded-in comfortably. This is a peach, apricot, nutmeg, honeysuckle and lime concoction, with praline, oak nuances and a never-ending finish.

AROMATIC

£6.99 **Argento Reserve Chardonnay, 2001**, Mendoza, Argentina (**Sai**). Alamos is dead, long live Argento Reserve. Last year's 2000 vintage Alamos label has been reborn in 2001 and it now is more closely related to its diminutive £4.99 stablemate Argento. As marketing, streamlining and corporate product positioning go, this is a solid decision as the wines in the range are tremendous and you now have a good reason to trade up the extra two pounds with confidence. The main difference between A and AR is the posh oak barrels and the quality of silky smooth Chardonnay fruit. Once again these guys have modelled this wine on a Californian Chardonnay, but cleverly made it half the price of the North American version. You may notice there are precious few USA wines in my Top 250. This is because wines like Argento Reserve Chard are destroying any chances they have. There is a '01 Cabernet Reserve (£6.99, **Sai**) coming on stream soon that is also stupendous. One of each, please.

£7.50 **Pirque Estate Sauvignon Blanc, 2002**, Maipo Valley, Chile (**M&S**). Hold on, what's a Sauvignon doing in the oaked section – call the cops. This variety doesn't like being mucked about with, so why has this gross injustice been allowed to take place? Well, the answer is that you don't argue with legendary Chilean winemaker Alvaro Espinoza (see Antiyal in the blockbuster section). Alvaro decided to augment his Sauvignon Blanc with a touch of sensitive oak treatment. It is like a kind of therapy for confused, high acid, highly strung, citrus-fruit-driven grape

OAKED

varieties. He cleverly ages about a third of this wine in American oak barrels for a few months. This can't have much of an effect, surely? Well it does, but don't worry, it is just enough to add an extra dimension of power and praline, honey and nut fruit to the lime juice, mineral and fresh herb flavours. The result is one of the dreamiest Chilean Sauvignons ever made – cue fanfare.

£7.99 **Kangarilla Road Chardonnay, 2001**, McLaren Vale, South Australia (**Maj**). This wine is beautifully balanced and gloriously harmonious. The creamy, honeyed, mildly tropical Chardonnay is so sensitively oaked it is a joy to behold. Only 30% of Kangarilla is fermented in new French oak barrels, with the balance seeing stainless steel tanks. The tanks preserve the smooth, luscious fruit flavours while the oaked portion adds depth and nutty, vanilla nuances. Style-wise, this wine has Chablis-esque qualities, but has the edge on its Gallic cousin, as the grapes are ripened by the Aussie sun and tempered by maritime McLaren breezes and cool night-time temperatures. This recipe is near perfect, as this wine will show. Majestic have the UK exclusivity on Kangarilla, so while you're tracking this wine down, grab a few bottles of Kangarilla's sappy, plummy, peppery 2000 Shiraz and the briary, elegant 2000 Cabernet (both £8.99).

£7.99 **Tim Adams Sémillon, 2000**, Clare Valley, South Australia (**Australian Wine Club**, **Harvey Nichols**, **Maj** and **Tes**). I know that the 1999 will still be dotted around the shelves for a few more weeks, and it is a beauty, but this write up focuses on the 2000, due in before Christmas. I am in awe of this tremendous wine. Tim is the Midas of the Sémillon world. The golden colour is hypnotic and it radiates from the glass wherein intense honey and lime fruit dwells. These wines mature like clockwork, but don't wait too long to enjoy this truly magnificent achievement. Also, track down 1999 The Fergus, Tim's magical Grenache (£9.99, **Australian Wine Club**, **Maj**, and **Harvey Nichols**) – it is the definition of the variety.

£8.70 **Saint-Véran, Bernard Morey, 2000,** Burgundy, France (**Domaine Direct**). I must apologise that this wine is 28 pence more expensive than last year's 1999. Why Bernard Morey, the scrupulously efficient, mightily talented, perennial overachiever-owner of this estate, thinks that this wine is worth only a fraction more than his superb 1999 is beyond me. The 2000 is twice the wine, with sensational, glossy fruit and flashes of sweet, smoky oak. What does he think he is doing, trying to upset everybody, showing off his unlimited talents in such a flagrant fashion? Irony aside, in a world of greedy winemakers, Bernard has shown remarkable restraint and loyalty to his customers with his 2000 prices. This model white Burgundy is Chardonnay at its best. It is ready to drink, under a tenner and simply stunning.

OAKED

£8.99 **Neil Ellis Chardonnay, 2001**, Stellenbosch, South Africa (**Tes**). There are a number of good SA Chardonnays at this price point – Jordan, Thelema, Vergelegen and

Warwick spring to mind – but my pick of the bunch this year is Neil Ellis's pristine lemon-and-grapefruit-themed wine. It is lean and athletic, with taut acidity and firm, tangy fruit. There is no unwanted oaky, honeyed flab as the racy, steely core of nervy acidity hurries the flavours along the linear palate and it ends in a refreshing salvo of pineapple and lime.

£8.99 **Trebbiano d'Abruzzo Altare, Marramiero, 2001**, Italy (**Odd**). Goodness me, this wine is a surprise. Marramiero is a small outfit in Abruzzo producing a monster Montepulciano called Inferi (£10.99, **Odd**). It is one of the best wines of the area, and despite needing a few years in a cellar to soften out its raucous tannins, it is a mightily impressive red. What a joy it was to acquaint myself with its sister white wine, Altare. Made from Trebbiano and fermented and aged in top quality oak barrels, it is a very serious offering indeed. The smooth, honeyed, tropical fruit flavours are well judged and beautifully seasoned with vanilla and roasted almond notes. This is an awful lot of wine for the money and is a must for trailblazing wine lovers wanting to broaden their Italian knowledge. It is in short supply, so get on the case.

£8.99 **Wither Hills Chardonnay, 2001**, Marlborough, New Zealand (**Great Western Wine**, **Lay & Wheeler**, **Odd**, **Edward Sheldon**, **T & W**, **Wai** and **Wine Society**). Wither Hills Chardonnay is a magnificent wine. The estate is renowned for its delicious Sauvignon Blanc (see Light,

OAKED

Dry and Unoaked), but pound for pound this Chardonnay must be among the world's finest. Each year I am lucky enough to be among the first people in the UK to get an early sneak preview taste of Brent Marris's creations, and this 2001 Chardonnay is the finest he has ever made. The nose alone is layered with subtle nuances of pear, orange, hazelnut and honey. The palate has waves of fruit and spice, starting with aniseed, macadamia, warm brioche and wild acacia honey and finishing with restrained peach blossom and juicy, almost-sweet lime zest.

£9.75 **Penley Estate Chardonnay, 2000**, Coonawarra, South Australia (**Bentalls**, **El Vino**, **Lay & Wheeler**, **Reid** and **Noel Young**). This unusual Chardonnay (Coonawarra is predominantly a red wine area) has spearmint and herbal notes wound around a honey, nut and lime juice core. It has an unbelievably long finish that never wavers, and the acidity and oak elements are superb. This is real class from the perfectionists at Penley.

£9.79 **Roero Arneis, Sito dei Fossili, Bric Cenciurio, 2001**, Piedmont, Italy (**Bibendum**). Last year I recommended Bric Cenciurio's 2000 Roero Arneis, saying that it was the best version of this quirky grape I had ever tasted. I am delighted to report that the 2001 is even better and it is available from Bibendum Wine (£8.13). This year's Top 250 features a different wine within the Bric Cenciurio cellar. 2001 is a stunning vintage and their super-cuvée, Sito dei Fossili, is a work of art. It comes from a specific fossil-strewn

OAKED

section of the vineyard, hence the name. The sublime Arneis fruit is given a short spell in French oak barrels and the result is a jaw-dropping wine. The balance, depth and intensity of rich greengage, pear and quince fruit is simply mind-blowing. This is one of the finest Italian white wines I have ever tasted.

£9.99 **Bonterra Vineyards Roussanne, 2001**, Mendocino, California (**Odd**). This is my favourite version of New World Roussanne. It is ripe, full and has beautiful, measured moments of peach, honey and apricot, all rounded off with a superb long, fine finish. Banish those Chardonnay blues with this classy wine.

£9.99 **Bourgogne Blanc, Clos de Loyse, Château des Jacques, Louis Jadot, 2000**, Burgundy, France (**Wimbledon**). This is the best-ever vintage of Clos de Loyse. It is basically Beaujolais Blanc that has been subjected to some tricky, smarty-pants oak treatment. The result is a stunning achievement. It easily held its own during a line-up of Pulignys and Chassagnes costing twice the price. I think this is because the balance between the luscious apple and pear-scented Chardonnay fruit and the vanilla and brioche oak is seamless.

£9.99 **Catena Agrelo Chardonnay, 2001**, Mendoza, Argentina (**Wai**). The 2000 vintage will, more than likely, still be relaxing on shelves around the country when this book is published, and what a beauty it is, too. But when it

OAKED

runs out, as all great wines tend to do, you can happily move onto the 2001. Ten quid may seem like a lot of money for a bottle of Argentinian white wine. Maybe so, but it's not a lot for a sexy, buxom, glossy, pneumatic Chardonnay, brimming with style and panache. Catena makes Chardonnay that tastes like top-flight, micro-boutique, thirty quid Californian wine. So, go on, you know you love it. The aroma, texture and finish are all top dollar, and it is like drinking a montage of highlights of every other great New World Chardonnay in the world. The professional palate is made up of honey, vanilla, hazelnut, wild flower, orange zest, honey, creamy lime, caramel, fig and more honey.

£9.99 **Errázuriz Wild Ferment Chardonnay, 2001**, Casablanca Valley, Chile (**Berry Bros.**, **Luvians**, **Odd**, **Sai** and **Wimbledon**). This is the Chardy to beat from Chile. The 'Wild' name still whips people up into an inexplicable frenzy. Not sure why, but I suppose 'Non-inoculated Ferment' wouldn't have such sexy connotations. This stunning wine is classy and soaked in sweet ripe pear, vanilla and butterscotch flavours.

£9.99 **Vasse Felix Sémillon, 2001**, Margaret River, Western Australia (**Inverarity**, **Philglas**, **Christopher Piper** and **Tanners**). The fruit in this wine is so accurate it literally buzzes with electric-green energy. The intense lime juice and melon fruit is so dry and tangy it is nerve jangling. The oaked element is carefully woven in and is never obvious. I suspect you'd only notice it if it wasn't there. These guys lead the pack in WA Sémillon.

OAKED

gorgeous, eclectic bottle

£10.99 **Châteauneuf-du-Pape Blanc, Domaine des Sénéchaux, 2001**, Southern Rhône, France (**M&S**). This is a gorgeous, eclectic bottle of wine, made from Roussanne, Clairette, Grenache Blanc and Bourboulenc. The 30% Roussanne proportion was fermented and then aged in oak barrels for a brief two months. This touch of oak adds a lovely nutty feel to the stylish, composed, floral, peachy fruit. Lay out the best cutlery and crockery and drink this elegant wine with sea bass or turbot.

£11.16 **Montagny, 1er Cru, Jean-Marc Boillot, 2000**, Burgundy, France (**Domaine Direct**). Jean-Marc has an artist's touch with oak barrels. He knows how to enhance a wine's appeal, without drowning the Chardonnay fruit in sappy, resinous wood. This bright, full Chardonnay is already drinking well, with cool, mineral elements balancing the glossy, lime and honey fruit. It is a great bottle of white Burgundy and one that reminds the New World that Burgundy is still king of the castle.

£11.99 **Boekenhoutskloof Sémillon, 2001**, Franschhoek, South Africa (**Laytons**, **Martinez**, **OFW** and **SWIG**). Marc Kent continues to blaze a white-hot trail in the wine world. This brand new Sémillon is one of my world-favourite incarnations of the grape. I find it hard to think of a white Graves (Bordeaux) with the presence, structure, intensity and, crucially, freshness that this wine engenders. Made from one hundred-year-old-vines, the greengage, honey,

OAKED

balmy beech forest, lemon crumb cake, fresh palmier and jagged lime flavours are astounding. Do you keep it or drink it? Don't ask me. Crack on, I suppose, although my own '99 Sémillon looks awesome. You had better decide. Also in the Boekenhoutskloof stable is a Cabernet and a Shiraz. If you spot either, buy them – they are the stuff of dreams. If author Michael Marshall Smith made wine, these would be they.

£11.99 **Vouvray Le Mont Sec, Huet, 2001**, Loire, France (**Wai**). I have been familiar with the wines from this estate for over fifteen years and have drunk many ancient vintages. I can wholeheartedly say that this is the classiest Le Mont Sec I have ever tasted and it is in line for the best dry Loire Chenin Blanc I have ever come across. The balance of classy floral, honey and lemon balm fruit and the brief two months spent in oak, bolstering the texture and the mid-palate is jaw-droppingly precise. I am in awe of the beauty that this wine projects. Drink it with very smart fish main courses.

£12.99 **Vavasour Single Vineyard Sauvignon Blanc, 2001**, Marlborough, New Zealand (**Martinez**, **OFW** and **Stokes**). This wine is not the most commercial style in my list. You kinda ought to fill in a questionnaire before being allowed to buy it, for fear that it might leave you with bouts of malignant vinous confusion. But let me fill you in. Glen Thomas is a studious sort, with a talent for Sauvignon Blanc. This fruit comes from one of the oldest vineyards in Marlborough, and it is very special produce indeed. What

OAKED

Glen does is take a chunk of Sauv and ages it in new French oak barrels for four months. During this time it picks up extra-terrestrial weight and texture. Interestingly, Alvaro at Pirque does the same thing (see page 112), but he pads out the middle of the wine with this technique, whereas Glen radically alters the framework, layers of fruit and shell of his creation. It usually needs a year to eighteen months to settle down, and then emerges from its capsule as one of the most beguiling and underrated wines from NZ. 2001 was a spectacular vintage, the wine arrives in November and there is limited stock, so you get on your bike. If you can handle this wine, you can handle anything. If not, run.

£13.00 **Houghton Pemberton Chardonnay, 2001**, Western Australia (**Maj**, **Wine Society** and **Noel Young**). I had the pleasure of meeting Larry Cherubino, winemaker at Houghton, recently and I knew immediately that I was going to enjoy his new releases. He has an encyclopaedic knowledge of the world's great wines, and has set about making a few of his own. This cool-climate, sensitively oaked, honey, citrus and hazelnut Chardonnay is nothing short of a stroke of genius. I am well versed in WA Chardonnays and this terrifically well-balanced wine has gone straight in at number one. I mean, even Elvis couldn't do that these days, could he?! The big Aussie names like Giaconda, Leeuwin and Yattarna have a new name to think about and, while we're at it, Larry's 2000 Margaret River Cabernet (£15.00, **Wine Society**) is a masterpiece as well. It looks like a storm is brewing.

OAKED

£14.99 **Ken Forrester FM Chenin Blanc, 2001**, Stellenbosch, South Africa (UK agents – **Thierry's** tel. 01794 507100). I have put this wine in my Top 250 despite it not yet securing a retail stockist or confirmed price (I have estimated the price and I believe Waitrose are justifiably very keen). It is one of my out-and-out wines of the year. Ken is a terrific bloke, with a bear-paw handshake and a permanent air of mischief, and when he told me he had a special project Chenin on the go I was all ears (eyes, nose and mouth, obviously!). He let me taste a sneak preview barrel sample, and I could barely talk, I was grinning so much. It is a ballistic wine, with every layer of fruit imaginable. I'll stop there, and you can decide whether or not to pursue this life-changing wine. Phone the agents, Thierry's, for stockist information and bathe in the glory that is FM. Forrester's Magic Chenin, or something like that...

£14.99 **Petaluma Chardonnay, 2000**, Piccadilly Valley, Adelaide Hills, South Australia (**Amps**, **Harvey Nichols**, **Odd**, **Portland**, **Roberson**, **Sai** and **Wai**). Keep your feelers out for the 2000 vintage arriving into the shops. It is definitely one of the best-ever vintages from the Brian Croser stable. The lean, honey and citrus fruit is so beautifully balanced with the French oak it is a dream. This wine will age well, and it certainly needs a year or two to fatten out. But once there, it will be clear to see why the Piccadilly Valley has been justly compared to the Côte de Beaune in Burgundy.

OAKED

£14.99 Ravenswood Lane Beginning Chardonnay, 2000, Adelaide Hills, South Australia (**Amps**, **D. Byrne**, **Jeroboams & Laytons**, **Luckins** and **Saf**). I wrote in The Wine List 2002 that this wine is 'Australian Meursault', and I have seen the expression used a number of times over the past year. The 2000 vintage is even finer than the excellent 1999. Beginning is becoming a force to be reckoned with.

£19.99 Meursault, 2000, Domaine Vincent Bouzereau, Burgundy, France (**Wai**). If you want to drink a slice of heaven, head for this wine. I have thrown caution to the wind to recommend one of the finest and best value white Burgundies I have tasted in years. This Meursault is a luxurious example of finely balanced pear, peach and honey Chardonnay fruit and creamy, vanilla and lightly toasted brioche oak. It is drinking beautifully now, despite its youth, and is guaranteed to impress even the most discerning wine lover. Vincent Bouzereau is a young, talented winemaker and he shows remarkable skill and a sensitive touch, balancing pristine fruit with first class oak barrels. He accurately seasons the wine as opposed to dominating it with oak, and allows the epic fruit from this world famous village to sing. If you are thinking of buying this wine, go the whole hog and grab a lobster for starters and roast a chicken for the main course – oh, how glorious.

£29.95 Vintage Tunina, Vinnaioli Jermann, 2000, Farra d'Isonzo, Italy (**Jeroboams & Laytons**). This wine was awarded the prestigious Tre Bicchieri award by the Gambero

OAKED

Rosso, and I feel it is Jermann's best-ever Tunina. It is a weird blend of Chardonnay, Sauvignon, Picolit and other grapes, given a touch of oak, and the result is an elegance and complexity hitherto unknown in Italian whites. I can't wait to taste the 2001 when it arrives at Christmas.

● ●

£4.60 **Les Grès Rosé, 2001**, Coteaux du Languedoc, France (**Jeroboams & Laytons**). This is the best-value, sub-fiver rosé I have tasted in ages. I tasted fifty or so of the new crop of rosés and they really are a dreary lot. There is only a handful in my Top 250 and I reckon that is a pretty pathetic performance. So, if you are a rosé fan, don't waste any time going through bottle after bottle of off-dry, confected rubbish. Track this or one of my other rosés down. Les Grès is made from a blend of Grenache and Syrah, and is stuffed with ripe cherry and mulberry flavours. This super core of fruit is punctuated with spicy notes and topped with a gloriously dry, refreshing finish. It is head and shoulders above the rest of the sub-fiver brigade and can be drunk as an apéritif or with virtually any dish, especially Indian food. By the way Les Grès makes a fab Syrah and a flash Viognier – top trio.

£4.99 **Goats do Roam Rosé, Fairview Estate, 2002**, Paarl, South Africa (**Odd**, **Tes** and **Wai**). Made with Rhôney varieties, this super rosé is rich, red fruit-stuffed, spicy and dry. It has more fruit than Grès and Sours and less than Santa Digna – so there.

OAKED

£5.49 **Torres Santa Digna Cabernet Sauvignon Rosé, 2001**, Curicó Valley, Chile (**Ameys**, **Amps**, **Corney & Barrow**, **Oxford Wine**, **Portland**, **Selfridges**, **Tanners** and **Noel Young**). Rosés made from Cabernet Sauvignon can be austere and often need a good dose of heat to ripen fully. Luckily the Curicó Valley has the perfect climate for these Cab grapes. This spectacular rosé is nearly a red wine in terms of colour, nose and flavour. It is so rich, full, juicy and blackcurranty. The palate is superb, smooth and there is a surprise echo of fruit on the finish as the sweetness returns for an unexpected encore. This is a truly amazing brew and one of the few wines that I would ever use the term 'fruit-bomb' for.

£6.99 **Château de Sours Rosé, 2001**, Bordeaux, France (**Corney & Barrow**, **Goedhuis**, **Maj**, **Sai** and **Tanners**). Made by stalwart Scot, Esme Johnstone, this is my favourite-ever Sours rosé. It is made from juicy, plump Merlot grapes exuding ripe raspberry and cranberry fruit and a clean, crisp finish. Sours is the perfect apéritif wine as it is light and pure, with good freshness and acidity. If you want to match it to food, then sea trout or a salmon fillet would be sublime, as would a rare roast beef salad.

● ●

£2.89 **Cuvée de Richard, 2001**, Vin de Pays de l'Aude, Southern France (**Maj**). This is the cheapest wine in the book and despite its lowly price tag it is an energetic, fresh,

LIGHT AND FRUITY

light red made predominately from Grenache. It is not the greatest wine in the world, but what do you expect for £2.89? In fact, this is a good point. This wine tastes way better than any sub-three pound expectations, and for that reason I'm delighted to recommend it to you.

£3.99 **Tesco Claret Reserve, 2000**, Bordeaux, France (**Tes**). A one-off wine that proves that miracles do happen, just not very often. Cheap claret is invariably pretty filthy, but Tesco have sourced this super little Cabernet/Merlot blend and it is a cracker. The fruit is vibrant, blackcurranty, smooth and fresh. There is little or no tannin, so it is ready to go. *Une bouteille, s'il vous plaît.*

£3.99 **Viña Fuerte Garnacha, 2001**, Calatayud, Spain (**Wai**). This meaty little fellow is spicy and juicy with a curiously attractive air de Glastonbury herbal nose. Garnacha is the same grape as Grenache in France, where it is responsible for juicy Côtes-du-Rhône-style wines. It always manages to bundle sweet red-fruit flavours and funky, fresh herb nuances together, and often is subjected to a dunk in an oak barrel, bringing an unusually medicinal feel to the finished wine. This example, however, avoids oak and is much bouncier and happier for it. Drink it with stews and meaty or tomato-sauce dishes.

£4.65 **Almuvedre, 2001**, Alicante, Spain (**Adnams**). I expect the cracking little 2000 to give way to my sturdy, spicy 2001 in the late autumn. Both wines are a joy and are

LIGHT AND FRUITY

made from old Monastrell vines. The 2001 has a bright, blueberry fruit-driven message and is superbly packaged in a designer bottle, looking every bit a ten-pound wine. This is another wine made by Spanish wine wizard Telmo Rodriguez (see Lunaran in Dry, Light and Unoaked). The balance and length are spot on, the fruit full and smooth. All in all it is a winner.

£4.99 **Bardolino, 2001 Cavalchina**, Veneto, Italy (**Maj**). If you like fresh, light, chillable reds, then this wine is spot on. It is ripe, blueberry, raspberry and cranberry flavoured and has lovely refreshing acidity. It is one of the few reds in this book that can be drunk happily without food – perfect for a party.

£7.75 **Chiroubles, Domaine de la Grosse Pierre, 2001**, Beaujolais, France (**Haynes**, **Hanson & Clark**). A perfect example of the Gamay grape variety in full song. The bright, vivid red colour, explosive red fruit nose and fleshy palate tail off to a dry, peppery finish. This is the decathlete of the red wine world when it comes to food and wine matching.

£8.49 **Ninth Island Pinot Noir, Pipers Brook, 2001**, Tasmania, Australia (**Boo**, **Harvey Nichols**, **Noble Rot**, **Roberson**, **Tes** and **Wai**). This is one of the finest value Pinot Noirs I have tasted this year. It has every classic Pinot hallmark, with none of the soupy fruit and lumpy alcohol so often associated with New World Pinot. If Dr Andrew Pirie keeps this up, Tasmania will seriously challenge Burgundy's lock out on Pinot supremacy. I am so bowled over with this wine I have decided to fly to Australia in early 2003 to see the Tazzy wine industry for myself. The pure, strawberry, cherry and redcurrant aroma is wonderfully alluring. The texture is ripe and smooth and the finish long and savoury. If you like this wine, you may want to track down its big brother – 2000 Pipers Brook Reserve Pinot Noir (£16.49, **Amps**, **Harvey Nichols**, **Luckins**, **Noble Rot** and **Roberson**). It has the full bells and whistles treatment – epic.

£9.99 **Moulin-à-Vent, Château des Jacques, Louis Jadot, 2000**, Beaujolais, France (**Wai** and **Wimbledon**). Ever wanted to know what grown-up Beaujolais is all about? Then look no further than this exemplary wine. There is none of the bubblegum, banana and headaches associated with the hideous sham that is Beaujolais Nouveau. This wine is gorgeous, flamboyant Gamay at the top of its game. The wild red fruit flavours are tamed by a year spent in oak barrels. The superb, luscious aroma and texture are captivating and you'll find that it goes with almost everything in the larder. Mine's a roast chicken, Jeeves.

● ●

£2.99 **Domaine de la Bastide, 2001**, Vin de Pays d'Hauterive, France (**Boo**). The 2000 vintage of this wine completely knocked me sideways when I tasted it at an E.H. Booth wine tasting. I had to check my tasting notes, the

LIGHT AND FRUITY/MEDIUM WEIGHT

bottle and the price to be sure that everything was in order. It is a superb, chunky, meaty, black-fruit-driven, southern French red. It is every bit a fiver's worth of wine, and puts a ton of cheap French Country wines to shame. But when I asked how much stock they had left, it transpired that there was only enough of the '00 to last until the end of the summer. One Fed-Exed bottle from France later and I am delighted to tell you that the '01 is another stormer. It is a superb party wine or everyday, failsafe glugger.

£3.97 **Château Haut Pradot, 2001**, Bordeaux, France (**Asd**). Asda's baby claret is a jolly fellow, with a jaunty air. There is none of the old-fashioned, stewed fruit and manky barrel flavours, so often associated with inexpensive red Bordeaux. This is a clean, chunky, black-fruit and leather style that wouldn't look out of place on a table set for Sunday lunch. Full marks.

£3.99 **Viña Borgia, Garnacha, Bodegas Borsao, 2001**, Campo de Borja, Spain (**Bibendum** and **Boo**). Made from fabulous young Garnacha vines, this is one of the finest value blackberry, leather and tangy herb wines made in Spain. The quality of fruit and length on the palate is staggering for a sub-four-pound wine.

£4.49 **Hardys Varietal Range Cabernet Sauvignon, 2002**, South Eastern Australia (**Tes**). Equal billing must be given to the Merlot (£4.49, **Tes**) brother of this feisty Cab. They are both sealed with a screwcap and this keeps every

MEDIUM WEIGHT

ounce of fantastic, fully ripe, cheeky cherry '02 fruit in the bottle. This is set to be house wine at Jukesy Towers when it arrives in the UK in late '02. The Hardys team report that this is a 'once in a generation' vintage – cor!

£4.99 **Château Vaugélas, Cuvée Préstige, 2000**, Corbières, France (**Saf**). Watch out for a £3.99 promotion on this chunky little beauty in October. It is packed with meaty, berry fruit and is a bargain at a fiver let alone four quid. Drink this with wintry stews and hotpot.

£4.99 **Natural State Montepulciano, 2001**, Marche, Italy (**Wai**). There has been a rash of Montepulcianos this year, as people search for an inexpensive alternative to Chianti. Well, this wine punches way above its weight (and knocks out the local competition) and would put half the ten-pound Chianti's on the shelves to shame. The slightly 'socks and sandals' name is because the fruit is sourced from fifteen-year-old organically farmed vines. Half the wine is aged in smart French oak for seven months. The finished wine is dark, intense, black-fruit-driven. There is a classic whiff of thyme, rosemary and Aston Martin upholstery, followed by a wave of black cherry and berry fruit. This is a stunning example of the Monte variety at its best. Drink with full-on Italiano fare.

£4.99 **Santa Julia Tempranillo, La Agricola, 2001**, Mendoza, Argentina (**Som**). Santa Julia is a fabulous operation, and they have loads of wines out there. My pick of the bunch is this compact red, which, despite being so young, is already firing on all cylinders. This is not a big, hefty wine, despite being made from the Rioja grape variety, Tempranillo, and being dunked into oak barrels. It is a compact, juicy red, with mulberry, blackberry and vanilla notes as well as a touch of spice, wood smoke and liquorice on the finish. Excuse me; a chargrilled steak is calling.

£5.49 **Accademia del Sole Carignan, Calatrasi, 2001**, Tunisia (**Bibendum** and **Sai**). The 2000 vintage of this wine was the best Tunisian wine I had ever tasted. But, shock horror, the 2001 is mind-blowing, and leagues ahead of its predecessor. The balance between sexy, earthy, pumped-up, bramble fruit and the sweet, pungent oak component is terrific. Carignan is a funny old bugger that bumbles along in the Languedoc, making up the numbers in blends. But on its hols, it works wonders. To date the best work is done in Sardinia, but this wine shows that Tunisia is in with a shout as well. Believe it or not, there is an 'Estate Selection' version of this wine as well called Selian (£6.99, **Maj**). Wait for Majestic to move to the glorious 2001 vintage and wallow in the turbo blackberry and tricked-up wood.

£5.49 **Château de Nardon, 2000**, Bordeaux, France (**Maj**). This brilliant, inexpensive claret is spicy and rich and needs a few months to soften, but it is a bargain price. Shove it in a decanter and the firm finish will melt away, and you can enjoy it with roast beef and Yorkshire pud.

MEDIUM WEIGHT

£5.99 **Allora Negroamaro, 2001**, Puglia, Italy (**Sai**). This wine is rich and chewy, but it hasn't got a trace of abrasive tannin, so you can happily glug it without getting that uncomfortable rasping feeling on the back of the throat. Negroamaro is a fabulous red grape, bursting with coffee, herb and plum aromas. The palate is soaked in dark chocolate, liquorice, black cherry and more plum fruit. This version is packaged beautifully and looks more than a fiver's-worth of wine. Drink it with all things meaty and Italian.

£5.99 **Bidoli Cabernet, Briccolo, 2000**, Friuli, Italy (**Wai**). This wine has rich, juicy blackcurrant fruit, with dusty tannins and a lovely, smooth texture. Is this a fifteen-pound bottle of claret? No it's a whisper over a fiver and comes from the white wine country in Northern Italy. Whack it in a decanter and fool your boring Bordeaux-fixated pals. This wine is mightily impressive.

£5.99 **DFJ, Touriga Nacional/Touriga Franca, 2000**, Estremadura, Portugal (**Tes**). The porty grapes make very good red wines in the right hands, and José Neiva is one of the best winemakers around. The texture and flavour of this wine are lively and juicy with bright purple, plummy fruit and a smooth, long, spicy finish. Super stuff, great balance.

£5.99 **Neonato, Marqués de Murrieta, 2000**, Rioja, Spain (**Saf**). Rioja experts Murrieta rarely venture into this sort of territory, as their Riojas usually sell for upwards of

MEDIUM WEIGHT

fifteen pounds a bottle. I am certain, however, that they will make an awful lot of friends with this trendy-looking, eminently gluggable wine. The bright, ripe Tempranillo grapes come from vineyards close to the famous Ygay estate and this wine spends six months in new American oak barrels. It is a stunning little fellow, with a red cherry scent and a smooth, spicy, toasty oak, strawberry, mulberry and plum flavour.

£5.99 **Penfolds Rawson's Retreat Cabernet Sauvignon, 2002**, Australia (**Tes**). The 2001 vintage of this wine is a star and will be on the shelves when this book is released in October. But, believe it or not, the 2002 is even better than the 16/20 I gave the '01. It is soft, supple, concentrated and juicy, with a long, even, blackcurrant and black-cherry finish. It actually tastes more like a tenner than a fiver. Peter Gago at Penfolds reports that '02 is one of the best vintages in living memory.

£6.69 **Dominio Los Pinos, Crianza, 1999**, Valencia, Spain (**Wai**). This new-wave Cabernet/Merlot/Monastrell blend has ripe, smooth, juicy black fruit and a delicious, Spanish twang of spice and herbs on the finish.

£6.99 **Château Gallais Bellevue, Médoc, 1999**, Bordeaux, France (**M&S**). I can't believe this wine is only seven pounds. It is a classic, blackcurrant, pencil shavings, cigar box claret, and would impress even the stuffiest Bordeaux-phile. The fruit and tannin are in stunning balance. I have to admit, even as a confirmed Burgundy lover, I really like this wine.

£6.99 **Nepenthe Tryst, 2001**, Adelaide Hills, South Australia (**Odd** and **Wai**). This wine arrives into the country in September, so it should make the shelves in early October – perfect timing. If you tasted this wine blind, I would bet you couldn't guess the blend. It is a zany car crash of Cabernet (Nepenthe's reliable base for all off-piste activity), Tempranillo (what?) and Pinot Noir (why?). So Bordeaux meets Rioja and Burgundy, jets off to impossibly-cool AH and gets on down. This groundbreaking blend works and the style is forward, juicy, tangy, super-ripe and dead sexy. It is a bargain price and will move off the shelves at light speed, so I bet if you're reading this tasting note in December, the stock will already have disappeared – sorry.

£6.99 **Porcupine Ridge Merlot, 2001**, Coastal Region, South Africa (**Odd**). My regular readers will be familiar with Boekenhoutskloof wines, as I never shut up about their outstanding, palate-expanding qualities. But sadly the Syrah and Cabernet are now north of twenty bangers a bottle, so I have been praying for some of their magic to rub off on the second label from this venerable estate, Porcupine Ridge. Guess what? My dream has come true. The 2000 Porky Pie vintage was a stonker and all of the red varietals performed well. The wines are still out there, as the 2001 will only take over around Christmas time. But would winemaker, Marc Kent, sit back and relax, satisfied with his 2000s? Not on your nelly – the 2001s are a further notch up the ladder of excellence. They could even be classified as a triumph, as two wines from this estate have made this year's Top 250. This Merlot is dense and plummy, crammed with rich black cherry fruit and has a gorgeous dusting of spice and earth on the finish – hurrah.

£6.99 Rosso Conero, San Lorenzo, Umani Ronchi, 1999, Marche, Italy (**Valvona & Crolla** and **Wimbledon**). Supple fruit and brilliant balance make this the greatest San Lorenzo to date. Some 30% of the Montepulciano fruit went into old barrels to bolster the complexity and it has worked like a dream. The intense black fruit and liquorice flavours are smooth and ever so satisfying.

£7.99 Barbera d'Alba, Vigna Fontanelle, Ascheri, 2001, Piedmont, Italy (**Sai**). I am gambling a little here, as you'll have to be broadminded, or at least broad-palated, to go for this wine. Fling everything into the pan, to counter the terrific purity and fruit expression in this wine. Serve the bottle cool, not cold, and the purple, plummy, peppery, juicy fruit will dance around your palate, charming the food and impressing your taste buds at the same time. The terrific '00 should give way to my '01 around Christmas.

£7.99 Barco Reale di Carmignano, Tenuta di Capezzana, 2001, Tuscany, Italy (**Sai**). Capezzana (see Gazetteer), is a very senior estate, but I can't help thinking that this wine is so forward and gluggable it doesn't really fit with their old-school image. It is a Chianti-style wine, but is dead relaxed and open, with cranberry and blackberry fruit and a soft, spicy twist on the finish. Pizza wine.

£7.99 **Glen Carlou, Tortoise Hill, 2000**, Paarl, South Africa (**Odd**). Tortoise Hill is an odd blend of Merlot, Shiraz, Touriga Nacional and Zinfandel. This inspired alchemy is the zany equivalent of red Bordeaux, Côtes-du-Rhone, port and a chunky Californian red being chucked into the same goblet. The remarkable thing is that Tortoise Hill works and is nowhere near as big and scary as it sounds. In fact, this is one of the silkiest, black fruit smoothies I have seen for a while. If you like velvety, lugubrious reds, then this bottle is a banker. I still have yet to find out where it got its name from – it can't be that obvious, can it?

£7.99 **La Segreta Rosso, Planeta, 2001**, Sicily, Italy (**Valvona & Crolla**). Planeta's baby red and white (La Segreta Bianco, £7.99) duo is the best this estate has ever made. The Rosso is stuffed with black berry fruit and mocha and liquorice notes, the Bianco is floral, totally thirst quenching and tangy.

£7.99 **Rasteau, Perrin, 2000**, Côtes-du-Rhône Villages, Southern Rhône, France (**M&S**). This terrific, meaty Rasteau is made just up the road from Châteauneuf-du-Pape and encapsulates everything that is great about Rhône reds. This wine uses exactly the same grape varieties and methods of production as its more famous neighbour. And despite

MEDIUM WEIGHT

being only eight quid I would choose this over any of the ten- to twelve-pound Châteauneufs I have tasted recently. The blackberry- and plum-soaked, leather- and herb-scented fruit is so smooth and harmonious it is a joy. This is not surprising when you read the small print and come across the mighty Perrin name on the label. These guys are arguably the greatest producers of top-flight Châteauneuf, and some of their skill has inevitably rubbed off here.

£7.99 **Swan Bay Pinot Noir, 2001**, Geelong, Victoria, Australia (**Sai** and **Wine Society**). This is the second label of Scotchmans Hill and it is a brilliant, brilliant wine. It is up there with Ninth Island as one of the best value Pinots in the world. You should never have to worry about getting a decent sub-tenner Pinot fix again. Swan Bay PN will satisfy even the staunchest Burgundy lover.

£7.99 **Tesco Finest Gigondas, Château des Ramières, 2001**, Southern Rhône, France (**Tes**). While sitting in the £7.99 slot in this book, I have it on very good authority that this wine will go on promotion at Tesco for a teeny tiny £5.99. This is a wicked price for such pepper, game, truffle, rosemary and blackberry giggle-juice.

£7.99 **Yalumba Bush Vine Grenache, 2000**, South Australia (**Odd**). This wonderful wine comes from the old school of Aussie winemaking. It is honest, ripe, berry-drenched, chunky, plummy, spicy, chocolatey and very long on the palate. Old Barossa Valley Grenache vines

MEDIUM WEIGHT

really show the full potential of this much-maligned grape variety. Grenache is the main constituent in many Côtes-du-Rhônes, where it is chucked into a blend with loads of other varieties and often loses its chance to impress, as more forceful grapes like Syrah hog the limelight. In Rioja, Tempranillo grabs the plaudits, while Garnacha (Grenache) works quietly away in the background. So it is with great pleasure that I am able to introduce you to this superb grape variety, flying solo, in a very special bottle of wine.

£8.49 **Ravenswood Zinfandel, 1999**, Amador County, California (**Bot** and **WRa**). A top-flight Californian Zin for under a tenner, is this a typo? Nope, just a rare opportunity to wallow in this superbly suave grape variety and not have to break the bank. When on top form, Zin is crammed with super-smooth ripe plum fruit, luxurious dark chocolate nuances, heady spice and plump, juicy raisin flavours. Guess what? They are all here. Just tick the boxes as this gentle giant goes walkabout on your palate.

£8.99 **Basilica Caffagio, Chianti Classico, 2000**, Tuscany, Italy (**M&S**). I didn't realise this, but M&S have known the team at Caffagio for years and because of this special relationship, they get first choice when blending their Chianti. 2000 is a superb vintage in Tuscany and this wine shows why. The intense black fruit is smooth and supple, and while it possesses the classic herbal twang, leathery scent and bitter cherry finish, there is none of the raw acidity and tannin so often associated with the

Sangiovese variety. This wine is a must for Chianti lovers and is extremely good value, as well.

£8.99 **Chianti Classico, Badia a Coltibuono, 1999**, Tuscany, Italy (**Tes**). The bright cherry and plum flavours here signal the winds of change blowing through Coltibuono. This is an excellent Chianti, with clean, juicy fruit and a few old-fashioned tangy, spicy, leathery notes dotted around to add complexity.

£8.99 **Goat-Roti, Fairview Estate, 2001**, Paarl, South Africa (**Odd**). Ho ho, top name. This bottle will surely attract the attention of the French authorities as Charles Back has already fired a warning salvo with Goats do Roam (Côtes-du-Rhône), and this piss-take of France's national Syrah hero (Côte-Rôtie) will surely incur the wrath of Khan. Good job it's a spectacular bottle of earth, briar, coal sack and peppercorn. Maybe they'll forgive him because it is such a stunning tribute.

£8.99 **Hawequas, Mont du Toit, 2001**, Wellington, South Africa (**Corney & Barrow**). Mont du Toit is a producer of cult, mega-reds from the Cape and Hawequas, their second wine, is mightily impressive. Despite being doubly difficult to pronounce (careful), this wine should be tripping off the tongue of all wanabee wine aficionados soon. The reason? Hawequas is a superb, sleek, sensuous offering. It is apparently made for easy drinking, but I can assure you that this wine is anything but simple. It is

MEDIUM WEIGHT

basically a Bordeaux blend of Cabernet Sauvignon, Merlot and a whisper of Cabernet Franc and is intense, stuffed full of ripe black fruit. It can be drunk now, but could easily slumber in the cellar for a year.

£8.99 **Southern Right Pinotage, 2001**, Western Cape, South Africa (**Averys** and **Odd**). This wine is made under the Hamilton Russell umbrella and is probably their best vintage to date. It will not be in the stores until Christmas, but carry on with the fine 2000 in the meantime. The fruit is even, with none of the earthy, forced nature that marks so many SA Pinotages. The sleek, blackberry fruit is supple, long, slightly spicy and fully ripe.

£9.95 **Bourgogne Rouge, Domaine Barthod, 2000**, Burgundy, France (**Berry Bros.**). The 2000 vintage in Burgundy was a measured success. In general, the wines are pure, fruit-driven and forward, with lower acidity than the '99s. Most inexpensive reds are already drinking but, as usual in Burgundy, you must search out the very best domaines to find the top wines (see my Gazetteer for details). Nestling in the Côte de Nuits, in the charming village of Chambolle-Musigny, Ghislaine Barthod makes tremendous wine. She is rapidly becoming the name to follow, as she is a perfectionist winemaker, responsible for some of the most beautiful Pinot I have ever tasted. Her baby red is a bargain at ten quid, and if you are a fan of the beguiling Pinot Noir grape, then you should buy yourself a case immediately.

MEDIUM WEIGHT

£9.99 **Avila Pinot Noir, 2000**, San Luis Obispo County, California (**Berry Bros** and **Odd**). This sexy, super-smooth PN heralds the welcome arrival of Avila in the UK. They are a fine set up specialising in pure, honest, accurate wines that retail for around a tenner. This is usually tricky territory for the Americans, as the majority of boutique gear sells for nearer the twenty mark. Avila's Pinot is liquid velvet, with a plum and cherry palate and a typically sultry, pouty, mellifluous, Pinot finish. Phone Berry Bros. if you fancy a pop at the superb '00 Avila Zinfandel (£10.50).

£10.49 **Cape Mentelle Cabernet/Merlot, 2000**, Margaret River, Western Australia (**Adnams**, **D. Byrne**, **S. H. Jones**, **Maj**, **James Nicholson**, **Philglas**, **Terry Platt**, **Roberson** and **Wimbledon**). Class and control from one of the trailblazers of the region. The elegance and restraint in this blackcurrant and creamily oaked wine is remarkable. This should be the claret-drinker's first stop-off point when getting to know the finest vineyards Down Under.

£10.99 **Crozes-Hermitage, Guigal, 2000**, Northern Rhône, France (**Wine Society**). This is the first time Marcel Guigal has made a Crozes and it is a fabulous effort. His famous Côte-Rôtie now sits up around the £28 mark, so for less than half the price you can enjoy this fantastic, spicy, smooth Syrah. It is classic Crozes, medium-weight, brooding and savoury and deliciously peppery. The fruit is blackberry-dominant and it is ready to go, as the tannins are balanced and soft. A great wine – you read about it here first.

MEDIUM WEIGHT

gentleman's claret —

£10.99 **Jackson Estate Pinot Noir, 2001**, Marlborough, New Zealand (**Grog Blossom**, **Hedley Wright**, **Maj**, **Oxford Wine** and **Christopher Piper**). These guys are far more famous for their Sauvignon, but this is all set to change, as they have now made a blinder of a Pinot. Just wait for the snowball effect to take. The pure strawberry and red cherry fruit in this wine is outstanding. You must stay ahead of the pack, so get in quick.

£11.57 **Château de Lamarque, 1999,** Cru Bourgeois, Haut-Médoc, Bordeaux, France (**Corney & Barrow**). The owners of Château de Lamarque are Pierre-Gilles and Marie-Hélène Gromand d'Evry. They are the epitome of elegance, refinement and Gallic charm and their wines are made in the same mould. I recently tasted 130 '99 Cru Bourgeois clarets, and was desperately disappointed by the wines. On the whole, '99 was a pretty good vintage, but the majority of châteaux showed green, unripe fruit and horrible levels of raw, sappy oak. The current vogue of bashing relatively cool-climate grapes with new, pungent, stinky, palate-stripping oak barrels is beyond me. There were only about ten wines that I thought were balanced, and thankfully Lamarque was one of them. This wine is what I would call gentleman's claret. It is forward and juicy, with black and red currant fruit and a touch of cedar and new leather (sensitive oak seasoning) on the nose and palate. The finish is mellow, long and smooth, and you are left with a feeling of immense satisfaction and calm – bravo.

MEDIUM WEIGHT

£12.97 **Château La Croix Bonis, 1996**, St-Estèphe, Bordeaux, France (**Asd**). This claret is approaching its peak and is showing all of the classic St-Estèphe hallmarks. The Cabernet blackcurrant fruit grippiness and structure is all here. The fine tannins and leathery aromas are present too. It needs decanting, but opens out beautifully. I know, because I have road-tested it to the bottom of the bottle. This would make a great Christmas present, after my book, of course.

£13.00 **Yarra Burn Pinot Noir, 2000**, Yarra Valley, Victoria, Australia (**M&S**). Serious fruit + new French oak barrels for twelve months = superb, harmonious, stunning wine.

£14.00 **Wither Hills Pinot Noir, 2001**, Marlborough, New Zealand (**Great Western**, **Jeroboams & Laytons**, **Odd**, **Edward Sheldon**, **T & W**, **Wai** and **Wine Society**). Wither Hills has three wines in the Top 250 – a remarkable achievement. In each discipline, whether it be Sauv, Chard or Pinot, Brent Marris makes globally important wines. Usually the very top New World Pinots have the juice (sunshine) and texture that makes me think of the wines made in riper Côte de Beaune vintages. However, Wither Hills has darker fruit and cooler, focused intensity, without resorting to flashy oak and excessive alcohol. Brent has recently invested in new tanks and a basket press, and this attention to detail is here to see in this stunning wine. I scored it eighteen plus out of twenty – which, if compared to red Burgundy, would mean the wine came from one of

MEDIUM WEIGHT

about five or six wineries and was certainly a Premier or Grand Cru level, with a correspondingly astronomical price tag. The wine arrives in late September, so if you buy this book on its publication day, you are easily in with a shout of buying a bottle or twelve.

£16.45 **Chassagne-Montrachet, 1er Cru Clos St Jean, Domaine Bernard Morey, 2000**, Burgundy, France (**Domaine Direct**). Morey lives in Chassagne, a village famous for its serious white wines. But not many people know that this picturesque hamlet actually makes as much red as white. This Pinot Noir is juicy, broad and very, very classy. In contrast to the Volnay below, it is fresher and more red-fruit-driven. The tannins should melt away fairly swiftly and a glorious wine will emerge. This is a real Jukesy wine.

£17.99 **Hamilton Russell Pinot Noir, 2001**, Walker Bay, South Africa (**Averys**, **Odd** and **Wai**). It will be a few months after publication before this '01 arrives, but it is a landmark wine. Mega quality, superb texture, oak and fruit in perfect harmony, with a long crescendo of flavour on the palate and a long diminuendo of fruit on the finish.

£18.45 **Volnay, Vieilles Vignes, Nicolas Potel, 2000**, Burgundy, France (**Berry Bros.**). Made from a blend of grapes from twelve different Volnay sites, this is one of my favourites in Potel's portfolio. It is stylish, smooth, intense, pure and black-cherry-driven. And, despite its youth, it is

MEDIUM WEIGHT

showing well already. The balance is spot on and it will improve like clockwork for a decade. If you are lucky, you may be able to track down some glorious half bottles, just ask Berry Bros.

● ●

£4.99 **Casillero del Diablo Cabernet Sauvignon, Concha y Toro, 2001**, Maipo Valley, Chile (**Bot**, **Odd**, **Sai**, **Saf**, **Thr** and **WRa**). The Concha y Toro devil has some pretty good wine in his cellar. The entire range of Devil's Cellar (Casillero del Diablo) wines is mightily impressive and is priced at a remarkably competitive £4.99. The Sauvignon Blanc (**Bot**, **Thr** and **WRa**) is zippy, green and lemony, the Shiraz is spicy, earthy and blackberry-infused and the Merlot is smooth, supple and deeply plummy (both reds – **Bot**, **Odd**, **Thr** and **WRa**). My chosen wine, the meaty Cabernet, is a model for all other sub-fiver Cabs to follow. Perfectionist winemaker Marcelo Papa manages to capture spicy, dense, smoky, briary fruit in his chunky little wine. There is masses of flavour and power in the glass and any meaty dish, especially stews or steaks, would be delighted to be romanced by this superb brew.

£4.99 **Grenache Noir Old Vines, 2000**, Vin de Pays Catalan, France (**M&S**). This wine is absolutely spectacular, and I can't understand how it can be under five pounds, but I'm not complaining. Not only is it one of the chunkiest, most intensely spicy, briary, black-fruit-soaked offerings of the year, but it also looks gorgeous in a heavy bottle, sporting a chic label to boot. It is a touch young, but as long as you drink it with a robust, meaty dish or with cheese, you'll be fine.

£5.97 **Xanadu, Secession Shiraz/Cabernet, 2001**, Western Australia (**Asd**, **Odd** and **Som**). This is a colossal creation, with a black/purple colour, a stunning, pure, Ribena and spice nose and a classy, long, plum-infested finish. Secession seems to up the ante every year and this massive '01 is an awful lot of wine for six pounds. By the way, it looks dead smart, too.

£5.99 **A Mano Primitivo, 2001**, Puglia, Italy (**Ameys**, **Boo**, **Connollys**, **Dunnells**, **Inspired Wines**, **Michael Jobling**, **Luvians**, **Martinez**, **Mills Whitcombe**, **Philglas**, **Sommelier Wine**, **Frank Stainton** and **Villeneuve**). A Mano '01 is a great bottle of wine. The intensity and complexity of raisin, plum, liquorice and blackberry fruit is right up there. It is a big fella, so make sure you attack it with a plateful of hearty food.

£5.99 **Angove's Stonegate Petit Verdot, 2001**, South Australia (**Wai**). Mellowing by the day, this was a beast when it was first released, but what do you expect from PV? The full-speed-ahead, blackberry and tar-frenzy nature of this variety can be a little daunting, but match it to a hunk of chargrilled beef, preferably marinated in soy, spring onions, ginger, garlic and honey, and you have a perfect match.

BLOCKBUSTER

£5.99 **Emporio Barrel Aged Syrah, 2000**, Sicily, Italy (**Wai**). Syrah really works in Sicily. It must love the baking climate, because this wine is firing on all cylinders, accelerating away from the blocks with huge amounts of purple and black-fruit power. There is a classic dusting of de rigueur spice and pepper and a pretty fiery finish. Drink this with a meaty dish, as it definitely needs something to get its teeth into.

£5.99 **Lot 32 Malbec, Concha y Toro, 2001**, Chile (**Odd**). Concha y Toro and Oddbins have got together to create five brand-new, small-batch wines. They are, without a doubt, the finest young Chilean reds I have tasted. You must make it your mission to find them as each and every one is a triumph of intensity, texture, balance and sweet-and-sour berry fruit. They are all 2001 vintage and are arriving in the autumn. The roll call is as follows – Lot 57 Merlot (£7.99), Lot 3 Syrah (£6.99), Perro Negro Carmènere (£8.99), Los Perros Cabernet (£9.99) – Los Perros means 'the dogs'… and it is. I marked each of these wines between 17 plus and 18 plus out of twenty and wrote 'outstanding' three times, 'stunner' twice, 'serious' three times and 'magnificent' twice!

£6.49 **Vega de Castilla, 1999**, Ribera del Duero, Spain (**Wai**). Ribera del Duero is frighteningly expensive real estate, so it's a treat to find an affordable top-flight Tempranillo. The trick here is that they don't over-oak the wine; it is only kept in American oak barrels for a brief six months.

The 25-year-old vines used for this wine yield spectacular grapes, packed with black fruit flavours and pokey tannins. This is a big wine and you'll need to decant it. But when you do, you'll be rewarded with a sleek, thoroughbred, dark chocolate and berry fruit.

£6.99 **Diemersfontein, 1st Release Pinotage, 2002**, Wellington, South Africa (**Wai**). Oh my goodness me, they have done it again. Diemersfontein know how to make wine, and my early glance at the 2002s was a revelation. This wine is a blindingly serious bottle. Of course, you'll have to hurry, as last year the entire UK allocation sold out in two weeks after I made it 'Wine of the Week' in the *Mail*. You are guaranteed to be caught in a stampede when this bottle hits the shelf. So camp outside your local Waitrose and make sure you are in line for a bottle. The only tip I can offer is that it is due into the country in November. Good luck. But why is this wine sooooo good? Like I said last year, it is as smooth as Simon Templar, as rich as Bill Gates, as luxurious as an Aston Martin and as chunky as Phil Greening (did I blow it at the end?). At this price, Pinotage never usually tastes as blackberry-soaked, chargrilled, coffee-spiced and super-velvety as this.

£6.99 **Peter Lehmann Clancy's Red, 2000**, South Australia (**Asd**, **Boo**, **Dunnells**, **Mills Whitcombe**, **Odd**, **Sai**, **Unw** and **Wai**). The new 2000 vintage of Clancy's is a tremendous wine, made from a blend of Shiraz, Cabernet Sauvignon, Merlot and Cabernet Franc. This inspired grape combo is rarely practised outside Australia and it's a bit like sending Mr. Bordeaux and Miss Rhône on a Caribbean holiday with a kilo of Viagra. Not surprisingly, it is a result with smiles all round. Sixty per cent of the grapes used come from PL's beloved home turf in the Barossa Valley. The warm spice and herb nuances overlay a dense body of crushed, macerated red- and black-fruit flavours. There is a lot of depth here, but this is not a heavy wine, just intense, rich and gloriously smooth. The incredible thing about Clancy's is its price tag. Tasted blind, it could easily pass for twice the price. Open it, splosh into a decanter or jug and let it slowly unravel its full array of aromas and flavours. I have a feeling this wine will blow you away – *vive la différence*.

£6.99 **Porcupine Ridge Syrah, 2001**, Coastal Region, South Africa (**Wai**). My second Porky Pie wine is an awesomely self-assured Syrah, bursting with spice, black fruit and pepper. The 2000 will be around when this book goes on sale in October and this '01 will come on stream towards the end of the year. Both bottles are crammed to the brim with those fit Ribena berries from the advert. This Syrah is a seriously intense creation and the lowly price tag makes it a wine that is up there, challenging for best value Syrah of the year. The '01 Cab is also available (**Sai** and **Som**) and it's BIG – Ree-spect.

£6.99 **Wakefield Shiraz, 2001**, Clare Valley, South Australia (**Bacchanalia**, **Ells**, **Odd**, **Terry Platt**, **Scatchard**, **Unw**, **WineTime** and **Noel Young**). This is a Shrek of a wine

BLOCKBUSTER

– scary on the outside, but with a squelchy, soft centre. The colour is black, the nose TNT, the palate chunky-monkey, but the finish is actually quite cool and black-pastille flavoured. Delish. Are you brave enough?

£7.35 **Domaine Gardiès, Les Millères, 2000**, Côtes du Roussillon, France (**Jeroboams & Laytons**). What a serious wine this is. The blend is classic, 50% Syrah, 30% Grenache and 20% Mourvèdre, with half aged in new barrels and half in old vats. It has tremendous presence and style, with lashings of smooth, black fruit and spice, and virtually no spiky tannins. This is a tremendous coup at an inviting price.

£7.45 **Château Meunier St Louis, A Capella, 1999**, Corbières, France (**Jeroboams & Laytons**). Corbières has the same street cred as Bulgarian Cabernet in my eyes. These wicked brews bring back horrid hangover memories from the mid-eighties. Unlike Bulgaria, Corbières seems to have made quantum leaps forward since those giddy days and this estate is at the forefront of the renaissance. This wine is funky, earthy, intense, hugely impressive and packed with briary fruit. Put your goggles on.

£7.49 **Clos Petite Bellane, Valréas, 2000**, Southern Rhône, France (**Odd**). This Côtes-du-Rhône is meaty, spicy and densely fruity, crammed with wild blackberries and ground pepper. The texture is luxurious and there are intriguing nuances of freshly cut timber, bonfire night and rolling tobacco popping in and out of the heroic finish.

BLOCKBUSTER

£7.99 **Peter Lehmann Shiraz, 2000**, Barossa Valley, South Australia (**Dunnells**, **Odd**, **Sai**, **Saf** and **Wai**). Hurrah, another frenzy of blueberry, mulberry, cinnamon, clove, cracked pepper, purple ink, fat black plum and spanking clean tack room – all in one glass. This wine is top value and it sings from the rafters at the top of its voice, 'grab a corkscrew and let's get jiggy'. If you fall head over heels for this suave beast then spare a thought for the monumental 1998 Peter Lehmann Eight Songs Shiraz (£22.99, **Mills Whitcombe**, **Vin du Van**). I wrote 'a mind-blowing smorgasbord of spice, pepper, meat, juice and berries' and 'stonker'. And 1996 Peter Lehmann Stonewell Shiraz (£29.99, **Bibendum**, **Dunnells**, **Jeroboams & Laytons**, **Mills Whitcombe**, **Odd**, **Vin du Van** and **Wai**) which winemaker Andrew Wigan described as tasting like 'crunched up tractors'! Great wines all.

£8.99 **Banwell Farm Shiraz, 1999**, Barossa Valley, South Australia (**M&S**). The first-class team at St Hallett made this wine in conjunction with the wily buyers at M&S. I reckon the quality and style of Banwell is up there with Old Block, St Hallett's own top-of-the-line label. Old Block, however, sells for twice the price, so get in quick with Banwell and you'll be treated to wave after wave of stunning, briary black fruit, liquorice and smoky oak. This wine has a velvety smooth texture, with outstanding depth and a minutes-long finish. Aussie Shiraz fans must taste this wine. (I gave it a very rare 19/20!)

£8.99 **Fairview Primo Pinotage, 2001**, Paarl, South
Africa (**Great Western Wine**). This wine is heroic in every
way. The colour is inky, the nose colossal and the intensity
and length of flavour, simply jaw-dropping. Fairview is one
of those estates that can do no wrong. Pinotage is a brute of
a grape, with earthy, wild, gamey characteristics that often
mask the purity of fruit hidden within. This wine is turbo-
charged, dangerously sexy and stunningly polished. The
sheer opulence of the glossy, explosive nose is staggering.
The core of blackberry, plum and damson fruit is wickedly
hypnotic, and sweet oak, tobacco and spice elements buzz
in and out of the velvety palate with metronomic precision.
Despite being only a year or so old, it is already drinking well.
I am sure that we are meant to put a few bottles down to
see how it ages, but I suspect you will not be disciplined
enough to do this once you have tasted a glass. It is
monumentally impressive. Phew.

£8.99 **The Rogue, Nepenthe, 2001**, Adelaide Hills, South
Australia (**Ells**, **Hoults**, **Odd**, **Playford Ros**, **Raeburn** and **Wai**).
For those of you who have tasted (and loved) The Fugue,
Nepenthe's cult, flagship Cabernet blend, The Rogue is a more
approachable and more affordable alternative. It follows
The Fugue's main theme, as it is Cabernet dominant, but
Rogue's variation comes in the shape of dollops of Merlot for
texture, Syrah for mid-palate spiciness and a teeny dribble
of Pinot Noir for the gorgeously fruity nose. This wine has
all of the class of its bigger brother, but doesn't need a few
years to develop in the cellar – you can drink it today.

BLOCKBUSTER

Marvel in the red berry, dark chocolate and sweet, spicy palate – and enjoy your change from a tenner. The lighter, more fragrant 2000 is due to change over to my chosen 2001 in the autumn.

£8.99 **Vacqueyras, Perrin, 2000**, Southern Rhône, France (**Tes**). Chunky, spicy, rich and earthy, this is classic youthful Vacqueyras and is a model example of a harmonious partnership between Grenache and Syrah. There is depth here, with a whiff of garrigue, a touch of baked plum and a swish of sweet leather. This is another wine that proves that Châteauneuf-du-Pape is not the only famous village in the Southern Rhône. It is perfect for roast lamb with rosemary and garlic.

£8.99 **Viñas de Gain, Crianza Artadi, 1998**, Rioja, Spain (**Boo**). This is a very serious wine indeed. Sally Holloway, wine buyer for Booths supermarkets, cleverly bought large stocks of it before Rioja prices went crazy and Artadi became recognised as one of Rioja's emerging superstar estates. If you went out on to the market and asked a wine broker to locate a bottle of this wine, it would cost a minimum of £12, and probably more like £15. Booths are based in and around the North West of England and if you are not a local then you can order through their wine website, www.everywine.co.uk. So what does it taste like? My notes said – 'spectacular fruit, stunning!!!, amazing intensity, ripe, dusty tannins, intense (again), stunningly proportioned.' If this makes sense to you, make it your mission to find this wine.

BLOCKBUSTER

£9.99 **Chianti Classico, Brolio, 2000**, Tuscany, Italy (**Sai**, **Valvona & Crolla** and **Wimbledon**). Apart from the small fact that this estate won 'Winery of the Year 2002' in the Gambero Rosso Wine Guide, it has been business as usual at Brolio. This means they have just released their new vintage of Chianti, and it is a masterpiece. This Chianti is, I think, the best they have ever made, and it was released after the judges gave them the aforementioned award. Barone Ricasole has orchestrated a remarkable turnaround at this property and it is now a leading light in Tuscany. If you are into Italian wine, you must taste this formidable wine. It is everything that Chianti should be, and loads more besides.

£9.99 **Diemersfontein, Carpe Diem Pinotage, 2001**, Wellington, South Africa (**Tes**). Tesco are lining up to take this wine, but the deal was not rubber-stamped when this copy went to print, so I am hoping everything went to plan. If not, phone Thierry's the agents (tel. 01794 507100) and they can tell you where to find it. But what does this wine taste like? Multiply the intensity of the '02 1st Release Diemers Pinotage, a few pages back, by 10^4. Helloooo, scary beast, is it me you're looking for? This wine has just won 'Best in Show' Pinotage in South Africa! It is truly sensational. Diemers also make a spectacular Carpe Diem Merlot and Cabernet!

£9.99 **Errázuriz Merlot Max Reserva, 2000**, Aconcagua Valley, Chile (**Odd**, **Saf** and **Wimbledon**). This is a serious mega-Merlot effort from expert estate Errázuriz.

The intensity of supple, plummy fruit and swanky, toasty oak is delightful. The complexity and length are first class and this wine will age extremely well.

£10.19 **d'Arenberg Laughing Magpie, 2001**, McLaren Vale, South Australia (**Bibendum** and **Philglas**). This Shiraz/ Viognier (6%) blend copies the tried and adored recipe for celestial Côte-Rôtie and cracks it with oodles of style. Blinding wine, brilliant price – hurry, before it is all gone. You won't believe the super-smooth, creamy blackberry fruit.

£10.58 **Laurona, 2000**, Tarragona – Falset, Spain (**Georges Barbier**). Georges doesn't really sell to the public, preferring to stick to the trade, but he has a stunning list of rare beauties, so ring him up and pester him. You would have to order by the case, so get a few mates ready. This wine is one of the many reasons why GB should be a household name. The Garnacha/Cariñena blend is souped up with a dose of 20% Merlot, Syrah and Cab. The winemaker is René Barbier, of the monstrous Clos Mogador (see Gazetteer), and he has made a silky-smooth, sensational, creamy, blackberry and plum wine.

£11.99 **Montes Alpha Syrah, 2000**, Colchagua, Chile (**Adnams**, **Hedley Wright**, **Maj**, **Mor** and **Selfridges**). Only the second vintage of this Syrah and it is already hitting the high notes. The rich, chocolate and black-fruit flavours are captivating and the pepper and spice seasoning is deliciously mouth-watering.

£12.99 **Chapel Hill, The Vicar, 1998**, McLaren Vale,
South Australia (**Harvey Nichols** and **Wai**). The Vicar is
made exclusively from McLaren Vale grapes – 60%
Shiraz/40% Cabernet. This is one of Pam Dunsford's
greatest wines – spectacular intensity of first class '98
fruit, but, crucially, without ever slipping into being an
ogre of a wine. How does she do it? She is guaranteed
a record congregation for this heavenly wine. *Gaudent
in Coelis*.

£12.99 **Starvedog Lane Shiraz, 1999**, Adelaide Hills,
South Australia (**D. Byrne**, **Inspired Wines** and **Jeroboams
& Laytons**). In '98, Starvers Cab was the guv'nor, but in
'99, the baton has passed to the awesome, classy, howler
of a Shiraz. This wine is liquid naughtiness. The nose
alone is awash with hoisin, warm tar and impossibly
fat plums. The palate glides around in all directions,
enveloping anything in its path. Don't for a second think
that this is a heavy wine. It is not. It is just that resistance
is futile with such a palate-expanding substance, and it
is the intensity that hits you, not the brawn. I urge you
to put a few bottles of this wine away, because I would
place a small wager that in three or so years, it will be
extraordinary. If you want a further slice of this level of
skill, but given a firm twist of the Côte-Rôties, then try
Starvers' top Shiraz, the '99 Ravenswood Lane Reunion
(£19.99, **Amps**, **D. Byrne**, **Hoults**, **Jeroboams & Laytons**).
It is the deluxe model, with restraint, composure, a nod
to the Old World and less hectic rock-and-roll fruit.

£14.00 **Bowen Cabernet Sauvignon, 2000**,
Coonawarra, South Australia (**Harvey Nichols**). Doug
Bowen has cracked it in 2000. Both this and his superb
Shiraz, also £14.00 from HN, are on mind-blowing form.
This wine is classic Coonawarra, with an extra dimension
of velvety cassis and plum fruit. It is phenomenally serious,
and perhaps his greatest wine to date.

£16.50 **Barbera d'Asti Ca' di Pian, La Spinetta, 2000**,
Piedmont, Italy (**Harvey Nichols** and **Noel Young**). Giorgio
Rivetti, winemaker at La Spinetta, is an impossibly cool dude.
He also makes some of Italy's greatest wines. This spectacular
Barbera is the cheapest wine he releases! It is crammed
full of plum, black cherry, truffles, blackcurrants, violet,
liquorice and sweet leather. For a slice of *Piemontese*
brilliance, taste this wine.

£16.95 **Antiyal, Alvaro Espinoza, 2000**, Maipo Valley,
Chile (**Adnams**). As far as Chilean super cuvées are
concerned, this is one of the few that actually live up to the
'super' moniker. Luckily this wine has, until now, flown
under the radar, and on the whole avoided attracting
attention from wine brokers and critics. This blissful state
will not last, so grab your bottles while you can. Adnams
have only 250 six-packs of Antiyal 2000 and it will evaporate
quickly. What do you want to know about this wine? That
Alvaro is a genius winemaker, with a ruthless manner when
selecting the best fruit and barrels? That the nose and palate
of this wine is profound, with stealthy flavour attacks of

BLOCKBUSTER

black cherry, dried currants, plums, black pepper, fresh bouquet garni, damp peaty earth and chocolate truffles? That Antiyal is a wondrous blend of Cabernet, Merlot, Carmenère and Syrah? That the finish is as uplifting as the Sydney Harbour Bridge Millennium fireworks? No, you don't need to know any of this. I'm sure your curiosity will get the better of you, and before you know it you'll be booking a weekend at the Crown in Southwold.

£17.95 **Planeta Santa Cecilia, 1999,** Sicily, Italy (**Harvey Nichols**, **Jeroboams & Laytons**, **Luvians**, **Thomas Panton**, **Valvona & Crolla** and **Wimbledon**). Planeta make spectacular wines. The Santa Cecilia is 100% Nero d'Avola and it is a velvety smooth mélange of cavorting blackberries, smouldering bonfire, espresso coffee bean and dark, sweet plums. This winery could have seven wines in the Top 250, but there is not the space. Their '01 Chardonnay and '99s Merlot, Syrah and Cabernet (Burdese) all retail for around twenty pounds, and any of the above merchants can track them down for you. As portfolios go, this is one of the best in the world. I dare you to order a mixed case. By the way, their 2000 reds are epic as well.

£17.99 **MontGras Ninquén, 2000**, Colchagua Valley, Chile (**Sai**). This wine is only available in the top 24 Sainsbury's Fine Wine Stores. Ninquén is an ultra-smart Bordeaux blend, whose grapes come from a unique mountain top vineyard. It is the best Cabernet and Merlot in the formidable MontGras armoury and I reckon the folks over in Bordeaux will get a shock when they taste it. It is deliciously smooth, cultured and elegant, with powerful, lingering flavours of plum, blackcurrant, leather and classy oak. Ninquén is the pinnacle, peak and apogee of all it surveys.

£18.49 **Gravello, Librandi, 1998**, Calabria, Italy (**Valvona & Crolla** and **Noel Young**). Gravello is made from Gaglioppo and Cabernet and is one of the most amazing wines I have tasted in the last year. Despite its apparent youth, it is already into its stride, flinging liquorice, plum, balsamic, blackcurrant, leather and thyme flavours asunder. This is an awesome creation that can handle almost any rich meaty dish (see the intro to the Food and Wine section). The 1999 takes over sometime in the winter and it is a storming follow-up vintage, some say the best vintage for a decade.

£19.99 **Renwood Jack Rabbit Flat Zinfandel 1999**, Amador County, California (**OFW**). Blimey, this is a big boy. There should be some sort of warning on the label about the amount of wine inside. There is probably a barrel of intensity in this 75cl bottle. Good luck, this is the scariest, spiciest, black-cherry and plum creature around. I suspect it lives in The Black Lagoon and only comes out after dark.

£20.45 **Penley Estate Cabernet Sauvignon, 1998**, Coonawarra, South Australia (**Lay & Wheeler** and **Noel Young**). This wine has mind-blowing fruit and I would say that it is probably the best bottle of twenty-pound Cabernet on the market today. The oak control, staggering

BLOCKBUSTER

complexity of fruit and length of palate is exceptional. If you want to taste a slice of winemaker Kym Tolley's skills, but at a more affordable price, then buy the fantastic 2000 Penley Phoenix Cab (£11.95, **Lay & Wheeler**).

£22.00 **Domaine du Rempart, J.-P. Moueix, 1999**, Pomerol, Bordeaux, France (**Wimbledon**). This super-sexy 100% Merlot is just what the doctor ordered. Fleshy, ripe, and silky, with a five-star finish.

£29.99 **Penfolds St Henri Shiraz, 1998**, South Australia (**Maj**, **Odd** and **Unw**). 1998 was a monster of a vintage in South Australia and Penfolds' famous Bin number wines all performed well. Now that they have moved on to the 1999s, I have wound the clock back one year and selected one of their late-released super cuvées for you to enjoy. I had never really understood the appeal of St Henri. At thirty quid it is an expensive bottle, and always seemed to lack va-va-voom. Until, that is, I tasted the 1976, 1990, 1996 and 1998 at Penfolds HQ in Adelaide. Oh wow, each of these wines was spellbinding. The '76 was one of the greatest Aussie reds I had ever tasted. I was able to put the '98 in context and realised immediately that I had always drunk St Henri too young. Now I'm not suggesting you should wait twenty-five years before uncorking this stunning '98. But you are only going to get one chance to buy it, starting now, so grab some and put it away for three or four years. I reckon that this will be one of the most sought after Penfolds reds for years. The Shiraz fruit is dense, almost black and stuffed with inky, velvety, smooth espresso bean, blackcurrant and pepper fruit. I wrote 'heroic' and 'near perfect' in my notes. St Henri '98 is well worth trading up to, but if you want to stay in the shallow end then 1999 Bin 28 Kalimna Shiraz (£9.99, **Bot**, **Maj**, **Odd**, **Sai**, **Som**, **Tes**, **Thr**, **Unw**, **Wai**, **WCe** and **WRa**) is my pick of the current Bin number releases.

£45.00 **Eileen Hardy Shiraz, 1998**, McLaren Vale, South Australia (**Corney & Barrow**, **Fortnum & Mason**, **Maj**, **Philglas**, **Wimbledon**, **Wine Society** and **Noel Young**). This is a tour de force from winemaker Stephen Pannell – my notes read 'perfection, tannin, oak, fruit, wow, but controlled, excellent complexity, outstanding depth, stunner, 19 plus'.

£49.99 magnum, **Marqués de Murrieta 150th Anniversary Mazuelo, 2000**, Rioja, Spain (**Fortnum & Mason**, **Raeburn** and **Wimbledon**). This stratospherically brilliant magnum is from the makers of Dalmau (the 1998 is £49.50, **La Réserve**, **Raeburn**, **Wimbledon**), one of the greatest Spanish wines ever made. This magnificent mag is the ultimate present for the person who thinks they have everything.

● ●

£4.49 half bottle, **Moscato d'Asti, Nivole, Chiarlo, 2001**, Piedmont, Italy (**Averys** and **Odd**). This pocket-sized, frothy Moscato is the Disney wine in my Top 250. Can you take it seriously? Perhaps if you had a plate of dark-chocolate-dipped strawberries or a fruity tart you would understand where it is coming from; because this superb, icy, off-dry, grape-juice fizzer is one of the top wines to round off an evening's excess. It is uplifting and invigorating and will put a smile on your face. Either that, or it is just an upmarket, lower-than-normal-alcohol, adult soda pop. The decision is yours.

£5.99 **Brown Brothers Late Harvested Muscat, 2001**, Victoria, Australia (**Boo**, **Mor** and **Odd**). Metronomic in its precision year in year out, this is a full bottle of stunning, baby-soft Muscat for six quid. I call that a bargain. Drink ice-cold as a retro apéritif.

£5.99 half bottle, **Brown Brothers Orange Muscat & Flora, 2001**, Victoria, Australia (**Asd**, **Boo**, **Bot**, **Coo**, **Maj**, **Odd**, **Peckham & Rye**, **Sai**, **Tanners**, **Unw**, **Wai** and **WRa**). A half bottle and a *petit pot au chocolat* please. The nose is orange blossom scented and the palate is intricately woven mandarin, honey, caramel and tangerine. This really is a remarkable wine. Chocoholics take note.

£6.99 half bottle, **Bonterra Vineyards Muscat, 2001**, California (**Odd**, **Saf**, **Sai** and **Wai**). This is the still version of the Moscato above, with added oomph (alcohol) and the benefit of organically grown grapes. It is not too sweet – many wine lovers who can't handle sticky, sweet wines are pleasantly surprised by the clean, refreshing grapiness in this wine. It goes perfectly with fruity, creamy puddings.

£6.99 **Clairette de Die Tradition, Jaillance, NV**, Rhône, France (**Wai**). Once again the Muscat grape steps up to the plate and gets well and truly belted by this Asti-style French wine. It has lowish alcohol (7.5%) and, like Bonterra, uses organically grown grapes. The good thing about this wine is that it is drier than the Asti and a full bottle is only seven quid. You'll get six or seven good glasses out of it, so you're working on quid a pop. Not bad, hey?

£8.99 **Vin Santo Antinori NV**, Tuscany, Italy (**Wai**). What I find amazing about this wine (aside from the taste) is that it is a full bottle (75cl) but costs only £8.99. Vin Santo is never this cheap! I am assured that everything is in order, so I'll shut up and let you know that the flavour is spot on; the sweetness not cloying, just toffeed and mildly honeyed. The oaky nuances are there but not intrusive and there are glorious tropical notes balanced by a sherry tanginess. This bottle could serve ten for a dinner party – make panacotta, treacle sponge, trifle or homemade ginger biscuits. All in all I love it, but why is it so cheap (sorry to go on)?

£9.99 half bottle, **Tesco Finest Sauternes, 1999**, Bordeaux, France (**Tes**). This gorgeous little half bottle is decadent, rich and very tropical. It is much more exotic than the Doisy-Daëne opposite and the sweetness is syrupy and smooth. You can attack full-on puddings with this wine and be confident it will hold its own.

£9.99 half bottle, **d'Arenberg, Noble Sémillon, 1999**, McLaren Vale, South Australia (**Odd**). A ridiculously luxurious, brandy snap and boozy toffee elixir.

£11.99 half bottle, **Château Doisy-Daëne, 2ème Cru Classé, 2000**, Sauternes, Bordeaux, France (**Wai**). This wine is due to arrive some time in October so don't peak too soon. When it does hit the shelves, make a beeline for a bottle as it is so sexy and honeyed you'll be at a loss for words after your first sniff, let alone sip. It is hard to describe the layers and complexity of flavours. The honeyed palate is coupled with moments of crème brûlée and melon, and more restrained aromas of tropical fruit hover in the background. There is another completely different raft of creamy, almond and pastry nuances that floats into view occasionally. This is an Elysian wine.

£12.50 **Muscat de Beaumes-de-Venise, Domaine de Durban, 2001**, Southern Rhône, France (**Berry Bros.**). Durban is still the best Beaumes-de-Venise on the block and my favourite French incarnation of the Muscat grape. Note that this price is for a 75cl bottle, so it is very good value. The clean, cool, smooth grapey fruit is soothing and mellow. You can drink this instead of pud it is so satisfying.

£13.95 half bottle, **Mount Horrocks, Cordon Cut Riesling, 2001**, Clare Valley, South Australia (**Bennetts**, **Butlers**, **Andrew Chapman**, **Hedley Wright**, **Harvey Nichols**, **Martinez**, **Mills Whitcombe**, **Philglas**, **Reid**, **Vin du Van** and

Noel Young). Stephanie Toole continues to make one triumphant wine after another. This is the seventh vintage of Cordon Cut I have tasted, and it is absolutely spot on. Now I know that this tropical tincture is frighteningly expensive, but I can assure you that you only need a dribble to resurrect all of your taste buds and force them to route march around your palate singing at the top of their voices. Once again, there is a lot going on – rhubarb fool, the crunchy top of crème brûlée, candied orange peel (these are tasting notes, not orders for pudding!), a luxurious, oleaginous texture and a clean, crisp kick of acidity on the finish – altogether, oooh.

£21.99 **Billecart-Salmon, Demi-Sec, NV**, Champagne, France (**Bentalls**, **Fortnum & Mason**, **Odd** and **Uncorked**). This terrific fizz still rules the roost, as Veuve Clicquot's 'Rich' is impossible to find. Demi-Sec means 'half dry', a weird definition for a wine that is, in fact, pretty dry really. The difference between this and the 'Brut' (Dry) is that it has a much fruitier finish. This twist in the tail goes so well with tarts and mildly sweet puddings. It is also a superbly flash way to finish a feast.

● ● ● ● ● ● ● ● ● ● ● ● ● ● ● ● ● ● ● ●

£4.99 half bottle, **Magill Tawny, Penfolds, NV**, Barossa Valley, South Australia (**Bot**, **Maj**, **Saf**, **Unw** and **WRa**). This is a tawny-port-style Aussie wine made from the deviant duo Grenache and Shiraz. After fermentation and fortification, it is matured in a sherry-like fashion. Cor, talk about long-winded. But the magic that occurs during this alchemic mucking around is nothing short of David Blaine. The sweet raisin, espresso shot, homemade toffee and cough mixture nuances all weld together and result in a downright delicious drink. I'm not sure what it does to your insides, but track down a bottle and drink it with Christmas pud, or slumped on the sofa in front of an old black-and-white movie.

£5.59 **Waitrose Solera Jerezana Dry Oloroso Sherry, NV**, Jerez, Spain (**Wai**). This raisiny, yeasty, rich, smooth sherry is absolutely brilliant. It is staggering value for money, let alone a gorgeous mouthful of complex, nutty, rich, caramel-scented wine. The crucial bone-dry, long, savoury finish is there, and if you grab a few hickory-smoked almonds, you'll be in seventh heaven.

£5.59 **Waitrose Solera Jerezana Rich Cream Sherry, NV**, Jerez, Spain (**Wai**). Try not to think of this wine as a strictly sherry proposition. Think of it as a very cheap bottle of luxurious pudding wine. Serve it with coffee, fruit, choccy, ginger or almond cake. Whip up a sticky toffee pudding or get out a spotted dick. This adorable, silky-smooth, chilled sherry is rich, nutty and luxuriously sweet. I promise you it works, and no, you're not on Candid Camera.

£6.49 50cl bottle, **Henriques & Henriques Monte Seco, NV**, Madeira, Portugal (**Wai**). Cor, this is a blast from the past. Dry Madeira (Seco) was a popular apéritif at the very beginning of the twentieth century. This bottle should be served chilled and you'll discover a whisper of honey and orange zest, which fades to dry, nutty, clean-as-a-whistle, herbal flavours with a savoury, crisp finish. It is the perfect accompaniment to canapés, nuts and all manner of cheeky pre-dinner nibbles. You could also try it with hard cheeses, like Manchego and Parmesan. Groovy.

£6.99 **Dow's Midnight Port, NV**, Douro, Portugal (**hopefully widely available**). This is the smoothest baby port around. It is liquid black cherry and plums, with a lifted, fruity nose and a smooth, fruity finish. This is a very, very commercial wine, and it should clean up the sub-seven pound market this Christmas. At the time of writing, nobody had committed to listing it, but keep your eyes peeled, I expect that most of the supermarkets will fall under its spell.

£7.95 half bottle, **Vintage Mas Amiel, Maury, 2000**, Roussillon, France (**Lea & Sandeman**). Maury is a tiny area in the southwest corner of France producing a port-like wine from the noble Grenache grape. Hey, haven't we heard all this before! Yup, Magill (page 165) is the same sort of thing but, of course, as this wine is made in France I am allowing it a more reverential intro. Unlike port, Maury doesn't use the same amount of spirit in production, so the alcohol is lower and you can generally drink it younger. Mas Amiel is the estate for top-flight Maury (hence the price). You should chill this brute down and open it up before dinner as a scary Gallic-style apéritif. Your guests will either immediately order a taxi, or grin in a demonic fashion awaiting the next vinous onslaught. If, by any chance, this bottle slips down in record time, ask L&S for the 15-year-old Cuvée Réserve. It is a full bot, not half, and is only £17.50.

£7.99 **Dow's Extra Dry White Port, NV**, Douro, Portugal (**Sai**). I am not really a fan of white port, however half and half with tonic water and it makes a stunning apéritif. Add lemon or lime if you wish, but I don't think it is necessary. G 'n' T, eat your heart out.

£8.19 **Tio Pepe, Extra Dry Fino Sherry, González Byass, NV**, Jerez, Spain (**Asd**, **Bot**, **Maj**, **Mor**, **Odd**, **Saf**, **Sai**, **Som**, **Tes**, **Thr**, **Unw**, **Wai** and **WRa**). These guys rightfully rule the roost when it comes to fino sherry. The sheer volume of production of Tio Pepe is amazing, but what eclipses this is the level of quality they manage to maintain. Tio Pepe is always excellent – dry, cleansing, tangy, yeasty, ever so grown-up and terrific with canapés and pre-dinner nibblies.

£8.19 **Waitrose Late Bottled Vintage Port, NV**, Douro, Portugal (**Wai**). This LBV tastes fantastic, which is no surprise since the Symington family makes it specially. The Symingtons are the multi-award-winning team behind Graham's, Warre's and Dow's ports among others. The fruit flavours in this wine are smooth and not as fiery as some of the others I have chosen. It is a perfect style for the novice port palate as it is harmonious, plummy and silky and well balanced throughout the long, fruity finish.

£8.49 **Warre's Warrior Special Reserve Port, NV**, Douro, Portugal (**Asd**, **Bot**, **Coo**, **Mor**, **Odd**, **Sai**, **Tes**, **Thr**, **Unw**, **Wai** and **WRa**). Warrior is still the port to beat at the lower end of the price bracket. Buy it if you want a direct, plummy, heart-warming style of port, with class and complexity.

£8.95 **Pedro Ximénez, Solera Superior, Valdespino, NV**, Jerez, Spain (**Lea & Sandeman**). Nothing will prepare you for the look of this wine, let alone the flavour. Dark brown and gloopy, this potion is akin to a ridiculously intense, yet luxurious mouthful of liquidised currants, liquorice toffee and palate-jolting espresso coffee. PX, is not only a desperately suave late-night sipper, it is also every ice cream dish's dream date. Very few wines actually complement ice cream, but stick to coffee, chocolate or vanilla flavours and you won't go wrong. You could even drizzle a half glass on top – but you got this idea off that bloke on the telly, right?!

£9.99 **Taylor's LBV Port, 1997**, Douro, Portugal (**Bot**, **Maj**, **Mor**, **Odd**, **Saf**, **Sai**, **Tes**, **Thr**, **Wai** and **WRa**). Taylor's don't half make a brute of an LBV. You may see a few bottles of the excellent 1996 still hovering around, and snap them up if you do, but the 1997 is a worthy follow-up vintage. You will not be disappointed with the controlled power and brooding intensity of fruit in this bottle. It is literally black in colour and soaked in turbo plum and blackberry fruit, with a smoky oak element woven through the core. A bottle will easily do ten glasses, so it's only a quid a glass – incredible, really, for this quality of workmanship.

£9.99 50cl bottle, **Warre's Otima, 10-year-old Tawny Port, NV**, Douro, Portugal (**Asd**, **Coo**, **Odd**, **Saf**, **Sai**, **Tes** and **Wai**). This arty bottle stands out on the shelf as one of the prettiest looking wines of all. The port inside is, thankfully, also drop-dead gorgeous. The glowing amber hue is wintry and nostalgic, and the nose takes you back to Granny's toffees and sweet baked plums. The palate is dry and savoury with Dundee cake and Brazil nut moments. The finish is long and yeasty, with orange zest and honey popping in and out of view. Serve this magical wine slightly chilled.

£10.99 **Graham's LBV Port, 1996**, Douro, Portugal (**Asd**, **Mor**, **Odd**, **Sai**, **Saf**, **Som**, **Tes**, **Unw** and **Wai**). This is a mighty wine, slightly de-tuned and more family-friendly than the crusted port coming up soon. You will get hours of pleasure taking this wine through its paces.

£10.99 half bottle **Matúsalem Oloroso Dulce Muy Viejo, González Byass, NV**, Jerez, Spain (**Fortnum & Mason**, **Harrods**, **Odd**, **Sai**, **Selfridges** and **Wai**). This little bottle of sherry is the big daddy of them all. Ok, it is fiendishly expensive. But yes, you should go for it. This is a wickedly spellbinding wine, with exceptional richness, burnt honey, dried fruit, spice, prune and caramel flavours coming at you from all angles. It is thirty or so years old and has developed the most amazing raft of aromas and flavours you could ever imagine. You know that you have to taste it, don't you?

£12.99 **Blandy's 1995 Harvest Malmsey, 1995**, Madeira, Portugal (**Laithwaites**, **Maj**, **Sai** and **Wine Society**). Madeira is a forgotten gem of a wine and Malmsey is one of its most enjoyable styles. Drink this with Christmas pudding or fruitcake and whisk your palate away on a magical mystery tour. Unfashionable, but oh so impressive, and it lasts forever. You can uncork it and pour, whack the stopper back in, wait a week and the flavour will not have budged. A raisin, coffee, toffee and honeycomb palate with a dry, lip-smacking finish. You can't get more festive than this.

£12.99 **Graham's Crusted Port, 1999**, Douro, Portugal (**Harrods** and **Maj**). Are you man enough? The power and muscularity of this wine is almost shocking. It throws a mighty sediment, so decant this bruiser before tackling it. When you do, and I have lived to tell the tale, you'll be confronted by a palate not dissimilar to the England front row rucking at speed. Ooof, you'll reel from the impact. You have been warned. However, once you are battle-hardened, it is a rewarding experience playing with the big boys.

£13.00 **Ramos-Pinto LBV Port, 1997**, Douro, Portugal (**Haynes**, **Hanson & Clarke**). With the big port houses dominating the market, it is always nice to find a smaller operation making good wine. This LBV shows great flair and panache, with intense fruitcakey flavours and bright plummy notes. The structure and intensity are not overplayed nor is the spirit component forced or raw, and this port has a super, smooth, lingering aftertaste.

£14.95 **Quinta do Infantado LBV Port, 1996**, Douro, Portugal (**Bennetts**, **deFINE**, **Hedley Wright**, **Valvona & Crolla** and **Noel Young**). Infantado is a new kid on the block and they have kicked off their UK campaign with a storming portfolio of wines. My pick is this intensely muscular LBV. It not a wine for beginners, being crammed full of plump, juicy, black, prune fruit, with dark chocolate, smoke and tarry notes on the nose. It is a heroic beast, best drunk in the early hours of the morning with a square or three of dark, fruit and nut chocolate.

£15.49 **Warre's Traditional LBV Port, 1992**, Douro, Portugal (**Odd**, **Sai**, **Saf** and **Wai**). If this wine were an athlete it would be Ed Moses, as it has effortlessly won every gold medal and trophy around. And it is really no surprise why, as the complex fruit and sensational texture make this the benchmark by which all other LBVs are judged.

£20.99 **Warre's Quinta da Cavadinha Port, 1988**, Douro, Portugal (**Bot**, **Maj**, **Odd**, **Saf**, **Som**, **Wai** and **WRa**). Top-flight single quinta port, with extra stuffing, biting tannin and brooding power – decant for unbridled joy.

GAZETTEER

GRAPE VARIETIES

Before we get stuck into my roll call of favourite world wineries, I have compiled a list (with short descriptions and popular synonyms) of the most important red and white grape varieties. These tasting notes should give you an idea of the flavours of the wines mentioned in this chapter and my Top 250 (see page 71).

REDS
Cabernet Franc (Cab-er-nay Fronk)
Cabernet Franc lends a certain aromatic quality to a red wine, with good acidity, *black fruit* flavours and a *green, leafy* aroma.

Cabernet Sauvignon (Cab-er-nay So-veen-yon)
Long-lived Cabernet Sauvignon is the backbone of many sturdy red wines. Its hallmarks are a deep colour, *blackcurrant* flavour, with a *cigar-box* or *cedarwood* note and sometimes even a smooth, *dark-chocolate* texture and flavour.

Gamay (Ga-may)
Gamay is a totally underrated, early-drinking variety whose wines range in taste from summer *strawberry juice* and *red berry* lightness to wintry, robust, *black cherry*, *leather* and *pepper* concoctions.

Grenache/Garnacha (Gre-nash/Gar-natch-ah)
Grenache, usually blended – often with Syrah (Shiraz) among others – is a *meaty, earthy, red- and black-fruit*-drenched variety, often with high-ish alcohol and a garnet hue. It sometimes picks up a *herbal* scent not dissimilar to aromatic *pipe smoke*.

Malbec (Mal-beck)
This brutish grape is inevitably deep in colour and loaded with *black fruit* flavours and *earthy* spice, often enhanced by a dollop of well-seasoned *oak*.

Merlot (Mer-low)

A juicy grape, with supple, smooth, velvety, *blackberry, plum, red wine gum* and *fruitcake* flavours. It is often accompanied by a touch of sweet *wood-smoke* barrel nuances.

Mourvèdre/Monastrell/Mataro (More-veh-dr/ Mon-ah-strell/Mat-are-oh))

This rich, *plum* and *damson*-flavoured variety is often made into powerful, *earthy*, long-lived wine.

Nebbiolo (Neb-ee-olo)

An immensely tough grape that often needs five years in bottles. A great Nebbiolo can conjure up intense *plummy* flavours with *leathery, spicy, gamey* overtones and a firm, dry finish.

Pinotage (Pee-no-tahge)

Pinotage is an *earthy, spicy*, deeply coloured grape with *tobacco* and *plums* on the nose, crushed *berry fruit* on the palate and a hearty, full finish.

Pinot Noir (Pee-no Nw-ar)

When on form, the Pinot Noir nose is often reminiscent of *wild strawberries, violets* and *redcurrants*, with a *black cherry* flavour on the palate. There is usually a degree of *oakiness* apparent, depending on the style. As these wines age, they take on a slightly *farmyardy* character, and as the colour fades from dark to pale brick red, the nose can turn *leathery* and *raspberry*-like.

Sangiovese (San-geeo-vay-zee)

This grape has *red fruit* flavours (*mulberry, cherry* and *cranberry*) on the nose with a whiff of *fresh-cut herbs* and *leather*, and an acidic kick on the finish.

Syrah/Shiraz (Sirrah/Shirraz)

Syrah invokes explosive *blackberry* and *ground pepper* aromas with *vanilla, smoke* and *toasty oak* nuances. In the New World, big, inky-black Shiraz (the Syrah synonym) has high alcohol and a mouth-filling *prune, raisin* and *spice* palate.

Tempranillo (Temp-ra-nee-yo)

Ranging in flavour from *sweet vanilla* and *strawberry* to dark, brooding and *black cherry*, Tempranillo is the main variety used to make Rioja and many other Spanish red wines.

Zinfandel (Zin-fan-dell)

'Zin' tastes like a flavour collision between turbo-charged *blackberries* and *plums*, a *vanilla pod* convention and a *spice* warehouse. These wines generally have luxurious, mouth-filling texture and pretty pokey alcohol.

WHITES
Albariño/Alvarinho (Al-ba-reen-yo)

A particularly good example can have a *peachy* aroma like Viognier, and a *flowery, spicy* palate like Riesling. They always have a very dry finish, often with a touch of spritz.

Aligoté (Alee-got-ay)

Aligoté produces dry, lean apéritif styles of wine designed for drinking young.

Chardonnay (Shar-dun-ay)

From neutral and characterless to wildly exotic, you can find *honey, butter, freshly baked bread, nuts, vanilla, butterscotch, orange blossom* and fresh *meadow flowers* in a top Chardonnay.

Chenin Blanc (Shun-nan Blonk)

This makes zippy, dry apéritif wines, medium-dry, food-friendly wines and full-on *honey* and succulent *peach* sweeties dripping in unctuous, mouth-filling richness.

Gewürztraminer (Guh-vurz-tram-inner)

This has the most distinctive aroma of any grape variety. Pungent *lychee*, *spice* and *rose* petal on the nose are often accompanied by oiliness on the palate and a long, ripe finish. This grape often has the unusual knack of smelling sweet, and then surprising you by tasting bone dry.

Manseng (Man-seng)

Gros and Petit Manseng wines both have a complex nose of *quince*, *peach* and *lemon curd* and a *citrusy*, *floral* palate accompanied by a firm, crisp finish. They are also found in sweet form.

Marsanne (Marce-ann)

Plump, rich and oily, Marsanne makes rather hefty foody wines and likes to be blended with Roussanne.

Muscat (Mus-cat)

Muscat wines vary from the lightest, fizzy soda-siphon grape juice, to the deepest, darkest, headiest liqueur, like a rugby player's liniment. The common factor in all of these wines is that Muscat is the only grape variety that actually smells and tastes *grapey*.

Pinot Blanc/Pinot Bianco (Pee-no Blonk/Pee-no Be-anco)

Almost all Pinot Blanc made worldwide is unoaked, dry and relatively inexpensive, tasting vaguely *appley*, *creamy* and *nutty*.

Riesling (Rees-ling)

Riesling produces an array of wine styles, from bone-dry apéritifs, through structured and foody, via long-lived, complex and off-dry, ending up at heart-achingly-beautiful sweeties. *Rhubarb*, *petrol*, *honey*, *honeysuckle* and *spice* are there in varying degrees.

Roussanne (Roo-sann)

Generally lean and aromatic, with hints of *apricot* and *honey*. When on top form, Roussanne takes well to oak barrels and can provide a welcome change of direction for Chardonnay drinkers.

Sauvignon Blanc (So-vee-yon Blonk)

An up-front, brazen, outgoing, happy-go-lucky style, with *asparagus* and *elderflower*-scented, refreshing, zesty, dry, *citrusy* fruit.

Sémillon (Sem-ee-yon)

The dominant aromas in dry Sémillon are *honey* and *lime juice*, and sometimes creamy *vanilla* and toasty *oak*, depending on style. They are also unctuous in sweet form, tasting of *honey*, and more *honey*.

Tokay-Pinot Gris/Pinot Gris/Pinot Grigio (Tock-eye Pee-no Gree/Pee-no Gree/Pee-no Gridge-eeo)

The flavour of Tokay-Pinot Gris/Pinot Gris is somewhere between Pinot Blanc and Gewürztraminer. The distinctive nose of this grape is one of *spice*, *fruit* and *honey*. It does not have the *rose-petal-*perfumed element of Gewürz, and tends to be drier, like Pinot Blanc. Italy's Pinot Grigio is more akin to Aligoté.

Viognier (Vee-yon-yay)

In the best examples, Viognier offers a haunting perfume of *peach kernels* and *apricot blossom*, followed by an ample body with plenty of charm and a lingering aftertaste.

WINE REGIONS OF THE WORLD

In this chapter I look at the serious wine-producing regions in the world, and my favourite wineries within them. There are many additional entries since last year as I have been travelling the globe, searching out new and fascinating estates. If a much-loved winery of yours is missing, it is either because I haven't yet encountered the wines, or they sadly have not made the cut. Drop me a line to the address at the end of the book (see page 237) and I will track the wines down in time for next year's edition. I have been ruthless and pruned this section down to about half its original size. Throughout I have avoided wineries that churn out passable, average wines and any who have chanced on one-hit-wonders, instead focusing on the benchmark, top quality, talent-driven, rewarding wineries which have set my palate buzzing. You can rely on these guys when you are shopping for your cellar, dining in a restaurant, out and about on holiday, or when buying a present for a wine-loving friend. Occasionally you'll find a producer or winery whose name is in **bold**. These I deem to be outstanding estates, where their portfolio of wines is top-notch. If a producer is both in **bold** and has a **£**, it means that its wines are expensive (£25 plus). These platinum-plated names are the money-no-object, whack-'em-on-your-Christmas-list wines, for those with a no-upper-limit mentality. That doesn't mean that every wine they make is unaffordable, far from it. Their main, flagship wine may be crazily dear, but their other labels may be brilliant and significantly cheaper, so do not dismiss these wineries. Those **bold** estates without a **£** make some eminently more affordable wines (some in their range retail from £5 to £25), so keep an eye out for them.

A short list of the best recent vintages is included after some of the regions with age-worthy wines.

AUSTRALIA

Australia is rocking the boat globally. In the UK it has been reported that France's divine right to top spot on the Wine Premier League is under threat and may already have fallen to these New World assailants. It is no surprise that in a relatively short period we have all fallen in love with Australian wine. They started off with pure, if a little one-dimensional, varietal wines – cheap, accessible, fruit-driven, catchily named and attractively labelled. Just as our palates started to get bored, and we thought about switching our allegiance back to wines closer to home, the Aussies launched a second wave of more grown-up wines. These creations focused on regional diversity and accurate selection of grapes. After all, Australia is not one huge homogenous vineyard, but an infinite number of sites and microclimates, with dramatic variations in soil, temperature, altitude and rainfall. What followed for the winemakers and vineyard managers was a frantic crash course in understanding what they'd got and how best to use it. Viticultural practices and vinification techniques were mastered, and marketing skills were honed. The fashion for over-oaked wines came and, thankfully, went – and here we are today. What do you drink at home? I certainly uncork or unscrew a huge number of bottles from down under. So it follows that the country with the biggest slice of my Top 250 is Australia.

As far as I am concerned the battle with the Old World is over, and it has to be declared a draw. The Aussies are here to stay, and I'm jolly glad they are, as they are making some of the world's greatest wines at every price point – at present no other New World country is even close to offering the cornucopia of terrific wines hailing from the sunny shores of Oz.

WESTERN AUSTRALIA

The top producers are – Alkoomi, Amberley, **Brookland Valley**, **Cape Mentelle**, **Cullen**, Devil's Lair, Evans & Tate, Frankland Estate, **Houghton**, Howard Park, **Leeuwin Estate**, **Moss Wood**, Plantagenet, Picardy, **Pierro**, **Vasse Felix**, Voyager, Wignalls and Xanadu.

SOUTH AUSTRALIA

The top producers are – Tim Adams, d'Arenberg, **Ashton Hills**, Balnaves, **Barratt**, Jim Barry, Bowen, Grant Burge, **Chain of Ponds**, **Chapel Hill**, Charles Cimicky, Coriole, Crabtree, Craneford, Elderton, Fox Creek, Glaetzer, Greenock Creek, **Grosset**, **Haan**, Richard Hamilton, **BRL Hardy**, **Henschke**, **Heritage**, Hillstowe, **Hollick**, Irvine, Kangarilla Road, **Katnook**, **Kay's Amery**, Knappstein **Lenswood**, **Leasingham**, **Peter Lehmann**, Lindemans, Maglieri, **Majella**, **Charlie Melton**, Mitchell, Mountadam, **Mount Horrocks**, Neagles Rock, **Nepenthe**, Noon, Parker, **Penfolds**, Penley, Pertaringa, **Petaluma**, Pewsey Vale, Pikes, **Primo Estate**, **Ravenswood Lane**, Rockford, **Rosemount**, Seppelt, Shaw & Smith, Skillogalee, **St Hallett**, Starve Dog Lane, Tatachilla, **Torbreck**, Turkey Flat, Veritas, Wakefield (Taylors), **Geoff Weaver**, **Wendouree**, **Wirra Wirra**, Wynns and **Yalumba**.

Top South Australian red vintages – I like these wines young. Ten years old is probably the peak: 1986, 1990, 1991, 1994, 1996, 1998, 1999, 2000, 2001 – and 2002 looks promising.

NEW SOUTH WALES

The top producers are – Allandale, **Brokenwood**, **Clonakilla**, De Bortoli, **Simon Gilbert**, Lakes Folly, Lindemans, Logan Wines, Meerea Park, Mount Pleasant, **Rosemount**, Rothbury, Tower and Tyrrell's.

VICTORIA

The top producers are – Baileys, **Bannockburn**, **Bleasdale**, Brown Brothers, **Campbells**, Coldstream Hills, **Craiglee**, **Crawford River**,

Dalwhinnie, De Bortoli, **Diamond Valley Vineyards**, **Domaine Chandon (Green Point)**, Gembrook Hill, **Giaconda £**, Jasper Hill, **Mount Langi Ghiran**, Métier Wines, **Mount Mary**, Phillip Island Vineyard, Redbank, **Scotchman's Hill**, Seppelt Great Western, Tallarook, Taltarni, T'Gallant, David Traeger, Virgin Hills, Wild Duck Creek, Yeringberg, Yarra Burn and **Yarra Yering**.

TASMANIA
The top producers are – **Craigow**, **Jansz**, **Pipers Brook** and **Spring Vale**.

AUSTRIA
I probably only drink one or two bottles of Austrian wine a year, but they are always epic. Here is a short, but essential list of producers making stylish dry whites and stunning sweeties – **Weingut Bründlmayer**, Schloss Gobelsburg, **Franz Hirtzberger**, **Alois Kracher** and Willi Opitz.

CANADA
Bit by bit the Canadians are making friends in the UK market. I suspect they are set for a huge following, thanks to some great whites and wonderful sweet Icewines.
The best estates are – **Burrowing Owl**, **Cave Springs**, **Château des Charmes**, Henry of Pelham, **Inniskillin**, Daniel Lenko, **Mission Hill**, Quail's Gate, Southbrook Farms, Sumac Ridge and Tinhorn Creek.

CHILE AND ARGENTINA
Chile and Argentina seem to be getting closer to perfecting their ideal varieties and styles. Earthy, rich reds are very much the vogue

and both countries are hitting the high notes with value-for-money examples as well as some newly released super-cuvées. Most Chardonnays, though, continue to be over-oaked and sloppy, and at the bottom end there is a distinctly mass-produced feel about other white varietals. The winemakers here need to keep their eye on the ball – there is all to play for now that Aussie and Kiwi wines have crept upwards in price of late.

The best Chilean estates are – Caliterra, **Alvaro Espinoza**, Casa Lapostolle, **Concha y Toro**, Cousiño Macul, **Errázuriz, Montes**, **MontGras, Miguel Torres**, Viña San Pedro, Valdivieso and **Veramonte**.

The best Argentinian estates are – **Nicolas Catena**, Familia Zuccardi (La Agricola), Finca El Retiro, **Norton**, **Santa Julia**, Terrazas, Valentin Bianchi and Bodegas Weinert.

FRANCE
BORDEAUX

Unfortunately, the majority of decent Bordeaux reds (clarets) fall into scary price territory. They also generally have to be at least ten years old to really get going. Once again, when compiling this list I was very hard on the region and have culled a large, rambling list down to a hard core of superb châteaux. Bordeaux is where the masterful red grapes Cabernet Sauvignon, Merlot and Cabernet Franc hold court. The percentages of each in the final wine vary from château to château, but you can be sure that whatever the outcome, the brew will have spent a fair few months slumbering in oak barrels. This recipe is the benchmark for red wine around the globe. Go for it, if you are feeling flush, patient, or both.

RED WINES

Margaux d'Angludet, Cantemerle, Durfort-Vivens, d'Issan, La Lagune, Lascombes, **Margaux £**, **Palmer £** and Rausan-Ségla.
Moulis and **Listrac** Chasse-Spleen, Clarke, Fourcas Loubaney and Poujeaux.
St-Julien Clos du Marquis, **Ducru-Beaucaillou £**, Gruaud-Larose, Lagrange, **Léoville-Barton £**, **Léoville-Las-Cases £**, **Léoville-Poyferré £**, St-Pierre and Talbot.
Pauillac Batailley, Grand-Puy-Lacoste, **Haut-Bages-Libéral**, Haut-Batailley, **Lafite-Rothschild £**, **Latour £**, **Les Forts de Latour**, Lynch-Bages, **Mouton-Rothschild £**, **Pichon-Longueville Baron £**, **Pichon-Longueville-Comtesse de Lalande £** and Pontet-Canet.
St-Estèphe Beau-Site, Le Boscq, Calon-Ségur, **Cos d'Estournel £**, Haut-Marbuzet, La Haye, Lafon-Rochet, **Montrose £**, Les-Ormes-de-Pez and de Pez.
Haut-Médoc and **(Bas) Médoc Arnauld**, de Lamarque, Lamothe Bergeron, **Malescasse**, Patache d'Aux, Potensac, Rollan de By, **Sociando-Mallet**, Tour du Haut-Moulin and Villegeorge.
Graves Bahans-Haut-Brion, **Les Carmes-Haut-Brion**, Chantegrive, Domaine de Chevalier, de Fieuzal, Haut-Bailly, **Haut-Brion £**, La Louvière, **La Mission-Haut-Brion £**, Pape-Clément and Smith-Haut-Lafitte.

St-Emilion Angélus £, L'Arrosée, **Ausone £**, Canon-La-Gaffelière, Le Castelot, **Cheval Blanc £**, Clos Fourtet, Dassault, **La Dominique £**, Figeac, Larmande, Monbousquet, Le Tertre-Rôteboeuf, La Tour-du-Pin-Figeac, Troplong-Mondot and Valandraud.

Pomerol Beauregard, Bon Pasteur, Certan-Giraud, Certan-de-May, **Clinet £**, Clos de Litanies, Clos du Clocher, Clos René, **La Conseillante £**, La Croix-St Georges, Domaine de l'Eglise, l'Eglise-Clinet, l'Enclos, **l'Evangile £**, La Fleur de Gay, Le Gay, Gazin, Lafleur, La Fleur-Pétrus, Latour à Pomerol, **Pétrus £**, Le Pin, **Trotanoy £** and **Vieux-Château-Certan £**.

Lalande-de-Pomerol Bel-Air, Belles-Graves and La Fleur de Boüard.

Canon-Fronsac and **Fronsac** Canon-Moueix, Fontenil, Du Gaby, Hervé-Laroque, Mazeris, Moulin-Haut-Laroque, Rouet and La Vieille-Cure.

Côtes de Bourg and **Blaye** Haut-Sociando, Roc des Cambes and Tayac.

Top red Bordeaux vintages – The finest wines from the best châteaux can live happily for thirty or forty years, beyond that cross your fingers: 1945, 1947, 1949, 1955, 1959, 1961, 1962, 1966, 1970, 1982, 1983, 1985, 1986, 1988, 1989, 1990, 1995, 1996, 1998, 1999 and 2000.

DRY WHITE WINES

Graves Carbonnieux, **Domaine de Chevalier £**, de Fieuzal, **Haut-Brion £**, La Louvière, La Tour Martillac, **Laville-Haut-Brion £** and Smith-Haut-Lafitte.

SWEET WHITE WINES

Sauternes and **Barsac** d'Arche, Bastor-Lamontagne, Broustet, **Climens £**, Coutet, Doisy-Daëne, Doisy-Dubroca, Doisy-Védrines, de Fargues, Filhot, **Gilette £**, Guiraud, Les Justices, **Lafaurie-Peyraguey £**, Liot, de Malle, Nairac, **Rabaud-Promis £**, **Raymond-Lafon £**, Rayne-Vigneau, **Rieussec £**, **Suduiraut £**, **La Tour Blanche £** and d'Yquem £.

Top Sauternes vintages – The high sugar levels in this style of wine mean they can last for ages: 1945, 1949, 1955, 1959, 1967, 1971, 1975, 1976, 1983, 1986, 1988, 1989, 1990, 1996, 1997, 1998, 1999 and 2001.

BURGUNDY

Burgundy is, hands down, my favourite wine region. But it is a veritable minefield of tiny vineyards and artisan producers and, sadly, not everything made in these stunning vineyards is up to scratch. This is the home of the mega-famous white grape Chardonnay, and its eclectic, elegant and occasionally flamboyant red companion, Pinot Noir. The greatest Chardonnays and Pinots in the world are produced here. Everyone else can try to reach these heights of perfection, and some come close, but the turf and the brains in Burgundy, in my opinion, are still top of the pile. The funky white grape Aligoté, and much-derided red variety Gamay (Beaujolais), ably support the two aforementioned super-grapes. The Burgundy region is close to my heart, being one of the most enjoyable places to work (taste, eat, chat), but it is an ongoing battle staying up to date with its wines. This list of domaines will, I hope, get you closer to the enviable 'knowledge' that should help unlock the code to the most enigmatic region of all.

CHABLIS

Chablis (white) Billaud-Simon, A. & F. Boudin, Daniel Dampt, **René & Vincent Dauvissat**, **Jean-Paul Droin**, Jean Durup, des Genèves, Louis Michel, Laurent Tribut and **François & Jean-Marie Raveneau**. **St-Bris-le-Vineux** and **Chitry** (white) Jean-Hugues Goisot and Christian Morin.

CÔTE DE NUITS

Marsannay-la-Côte and **Fixin** (mainly red) Charles Audoin, **René Bouvier** and Bruno Clair.

Gevrey-Chambertin (red) **Claude Dugat**, **Géantet-Pansiot**, **Denis Mortet**, Joseph Roty, **Armand Rousseau** and Serafin.

Morey-St-Denis (red) des Beaumont, **Domaine des Lambrays**, Dujac, Hubert Lignier, Virgil Lignier and **Ponsot**.

Chambolle-Musigny (red) **Ghislaine Barthod**, Pierre Bertheau, **Christian Clerget**, **Comte de Vogüé** and **G. Roumier**.

Vosne-Romanée and **Flagey-Echézeaux** (red) Robert Arnoux, **de la Romanée-Conti £**, René Engel, **Jean Grivot**, **Anne-Françoise Gros**, **Leroy £**, **Méo-Camuzet**, Mongeard-Mugneret and **Emanuel Rouget**.

Nuits-St-Georges (red) Bertrand Ambroise, Jean Chauvenet, **Robert Chevillon**, Jean-Jacques Confuron, Daniel Chopin-Groffier, **Dominique Laurent**, Lécheneaut, Alain Michelot and Daniel Rion.

CÔTE DE BEAUNE

Aloxe-Corton and **Ladoix-Serrigny** (mainly red) Michel Voarick.

Pernand-Vergelesses (red and white) **Bonneau du Martray £** and Maurice Rollin.

Savigny-lès-Beaune (red and white) Chandon de Briailles, Maurice Ecard and **Jean-Marc Pavelot**.

Chorey-lès-Beaune (red) Germain and **Tollot-Beaut**.

Beaune (mainly red) Joseph Drouhin and **Louis Jadot**.

Pommard (red) Comte Armand, **Jean-Marc Boillot**, Madame de Courcel and **Hubert de Montille**.

Volnay (red) **Marquis d'Angerville**, **Michel Lafarge** and Roblet-Monnot.

Monthelie (red and white) Denis Boussey.

Auxey-Duresses (red and white) Jean-Pierre Diconne and Claude Maréchal.

St-Romain (mainly white) Christophe Buisson and d'Auvenay.

Meursault (white) **Vincent Bouzereau, Jean-François Coche-Dury £**, Vincent Dancer, Jean-Philippe Fichet, **Patrick Javillier, des Comtes Lafon £**, Marc Rougeot, **Roulot** and Michel Tessier.

Puligny-Montrachet (white) **Louis Carillon**, Chartron & Trébuchet, **Leflaive** and **Etienne Sauzet**.

Chassagne-Montrachet (white) Guy Amiot, Blain-Gagnard, Colin-Deléger, Duperrier-Adam, **Jean-Noël Gagnard**, Gagnard-Delagrange, **Bernard Morey, Michel Niellon** and **Ramonet £**.

St-Aubin (red and white) Henri Prudhon and Gérard Thomas.

Santenay (red and white) **Vincent Girardin**.

CÔTE CHALONNAISE

Rully (red and white) Vincent Dureuil-Janthial and Eric de Suremain.

Mercurey (red and white) **Michel & Laurent Juillot, Bruno Lorenzon**, J. & F. Raquillet and Antonin Rodet.

Givry (red and white) Joblot and François Lumpp.

MÂCONNAIS

(Mâcon, Pouilly-Fuissé, St-Véran, Viré-Clessé) (mainly white) Daniel Barraud, **Château de Beauregard, André Bonhomme**, Christophe Cordier, Deux Roches, Michel Forest, **Château Fuissé (Jean-Jacques Vincent)**, Goyard, Guillemot-Michel, Robert-Denogent, Talmard, Jean Thevenet and Verget (Guffens-Heynen).

BEAUJOLAIS

Producing mainly red wines, the most highly regarded sub-regions are the ten Cru Villages: St-Amour, Juliénas, Fleurie, Moulin-à-Vent, Brouilly, Côte de Brouilly, Régnié, Chénas, Chiroubles and Morgon. **The top producers are** – Aucoeur, Hélène & Denis Barbelet, Champagnon, Michel Chignard, André Cologne, **Coudert**, Georges Duboeuf (domaine-bottled wines only), **J.-L. Dutraive**, J.-F. Echallier (des Pins), **Henry Fessy**, Maurice Gaget, **Pascal Granger**, **Louis Jadot (Château des Jacques)**, **Paul Janin**, Jacky Janodet, Marcel Lapierre, Bernard Mélinand, **Alain Passot**, **Jean-Charles Pivot** and Vissoux.

Top Burgundy vintages – Pinot Noir and Chardonnay drink well up to fifteen years old, thereafter get a little bit funky: 1969, 1971, 1978, 1980, 1985, 1988, 1989, 1990, 1995, 1996, 1997, 1998, 1999 and 2000.

CHAMPAGNE

This is a strange one. In my Top 250 each year, I track down a few small Champagne houses that have made astonishing wines. They don't feature in this list of more famous names, and vice versa. The reason I have not included the smaller houses here is because I need to see a constant pedigree of year on year releases before they make this elite list. The reason not all of the wines below appear in my Top 250 is that I would quickly run out of space!

Billecart-Salmon *NV* Brut Réserve, Blanc de Blancs, Demi-Sec and Brut Rosé.

Vintage Cuvée Nicolas-François Billecart, Elisabeth Salmon Rosé, Grande Cuvée and Blanc de Blancs.

Bollinger *NV* Special Cuvée. *Vintage* Grande Année, RD and Vieilles Vignes Françaises Blanc de Noirs.

Deutz *Vintage* Blanc de Blancs and Cuvée William Deutz.
Gosset *NV* Brut Excellence and Grande Réserve Brut. *Vintage* Grande Millésime Brut.
Charles Heidsieck *Vintage* Brut Millésime.
Jacquesson *Vintage* Blanc de Blancs, Dégorgement Tardive and Signature.
Krug £ *NV* Grande Cuvée. *Vintage* Vintage and Clos du Mesnil.
Laurent-Perrier *NV* Cuvée Rosé Brut, Grand Siècle 'La Cuvée'.
Moët & Chandon *Vintage* Cuvée Dom Pérignon Brut.
Pol Roger *NV* Brut 'White Foil'. *Vintage* Brut Vintage, Brut Chardonnay, Brut Rosé and Cuvée Sir Winston Churchill.
Louis Roederer *NV* Brut Premier. *Vintage* Blanc de Blancs, Brut Millésime and Cristal, Cristal Rosé.
Ruinart *Vintage* 'R' de Ruinart Brut and Dom Ruinart Blanc de Blancs.
Salon £ *Vintage* Blanc de Blancs.
Taittinger *NV* Brut Réserve. *Vintage* Comtes de Champagne Blanc de Blancs.
Veuve Clicquot *NV* Brut 'Yellow Label' and Demi-Sec. *Vintage* Vintage Réserve, La Grande Dame Brut and La Grande Dame Rosé.

Top Champagne vintages – Surprisingly long-lived if kept in good conditions: 1964, 1966, 1971, 1975, 1976, 1979, 1982, 1983, 1985, 1988, 1989, 1990, 1995, 1996, 1997, 1998, 1999 and 2000.

ALSACE

As a nation we don't drink much Alsatian wine, but we should. This under-priced, over-performing region provides some of the best foody, apéritif, decadently sweet and casual-drinking wines in the world. These wines are usually tracked down in canny independent wine merchants. Grape varieties to seek out are Gewürztraminer, Riesling, Tokay-Pinot Gris, Muscat, Pinot Blanc and Sylvaner. Avoid the reds and fizzies.

The best producers are – Bott-Geyl, Boxler, **Marcel Deiss**, Hauller, Hugel, **Marc Kreydenweiss**, Albert Mann, **Mittnacht-Klack**, **Ostertag**, Rolly Gassmann, Schlumberger, Schoffit, André Thomas, **Trimbach**, **Weinbach** and **Zind-Humbrecht**.

Top Alsace vintages – Only Vendange Tardive and Sélection des Grains Nobles styles live for more than fifteen years: 1971, 1976, 1983, 1985, 1988, 1989, 1990, 1992, 1995, 1996, 1997, 1998, 1999 and 2000.

THE LOIRE VALLEY

My list of wines follows the Loire river inland from the Atlantic, picking out the greatest estates in this elongated, inexpensive region. Sauvignon Blanc and Chenin Blanc are the main white grapes grown here. Sauvignons are nearly always dry, whereas Chenins can be dry, medium-sweet or full-on, unctuous pudding wines. The majority of serious reds are made from Cabernet Franc, with Gamay and Pinot Noir stepping in for lighter styles.

Muscadet (white) Château de Chasseloir, **Chéreau** and Domaine de la Mortaine.

Savennières (white) **des Baumards**, **Clos de la Coulée de Serrant** and **La Roche-aux-Moines**.

Coteaux du Layon, **Coteaux de l'Aubance**, **Bonnezeaux**, **Quarts de Chaume** (white sweeties) des Baumards, **Château Pierre-Bise**, **Château de Fesles**, **Vincent Lecointre**, de Petit Val, Didier Richou and de la Roulierie.

Sparkling Saumur Bouvet-Ladubay.

Saumur and **Saumur Champigny** (red and white) **du Hureau**, **Filliatreau**, Langlois-Château and **Nerleux**.
Chinon (mainly red) **Bernard Baudry**, Couly-Dutheil and **Charles Joguet**.
St-Nicolas de Bourgueil (red) Lamé-Delille-Boucard, Jean-Paul Mabileau and **Max & Lydie Cognard-Taluau**.
Bourgueil (red) **Pierre-Jacques Druet**, de la Lande, **Lamé-Delille-Boucard** and Joël Taluau.
Vouvray (white) Bourillon-Dorléans, **Gaston Huet** and Philippe Foreau.
Sauvignon de Touraine (white) **Alain Marcadet**.
Gamay de Touraine (red) Henry Marionnet.
Jasnières (white) Joël Gigou and Jean-Baptiste Pinon.
Cheverny (white) Salvard.
Sancerre (white, rosé and red) Sylvain Bailly, Bailly-Reverdy, Philippe de Benoist, **Henri Bourgeois**, **Cotat**, Daulny, **Vincent Delaporte**, André Dézat, Alain Gueneau, Henri Natter, **Pascal & Nicolas Reverdy**, Vacheron and **André Vatan**.
Pouilly-Fumé (white) **Didier Dagueneau**, Serge Dagueneau, André Dézat (Domaine Thibault), Jean-Claude Chatelain, Château du Nozet (de Ladoucette), **Michel Redde**, Hervé Seguin and **Château de Tracy**.
Menetou-Salon (mainly white) de Chatenoy, **Henry Pellé** and Jean-Jacques Teiller.
Quincy (white) **Jacques Rouzé**.

Top Loire sweet wine vintages – With Chenin Blanc's acidity, these wines are amazingly age-worthy: 1947, 1949, 1959, 1962, 1969, 1971, 1976, 1983, 1985, 1988, 1989, 1990, 1995, 1996, 1997, 1999 and 2000.

THE RHÔNE VALLEY

This venerable region provides us with some of the best-value drinking wines around. It is here that Syrah, Grenache and Mourvèdre rule the reds. Viognier commands the whites in the north, while Roussanne and Marsanne are in charge in the south. Spend some time with these wines before comparing what has happened in the New World. You will see that Shiraz (Syrah on holiday) is cropping up all over the place, producing everything from blockbuster reds to insipid, alcoholic pretenders-to-the-throne. Then turn around, come back home to the Rhône and appreciate the great power, majesty and poise of these Old World originals.

THE NORTHERN RHÔNE
(FROM NORTH TO SOUTH)

Côte Rôtie (red) Bernard Burgaud, Chapoutier, **Clusel-Roch £**, Yves Cuilleron, **Pierre Gaillard**, **Yves Gangloff £**, Marius Gentaz-Dervieux, **E. Guigal £**, J.-P. & J.-L. Jamet and **René Rostaing £**.
Condrieu (white) **Yves Cuilleron £**, Christian Facchin, Pierre Gaillard, **E. Guigal £**, André Perret, Georges Vernay and **François Villard £**.
St-Joseph (red and white) **Jean-Louis Chave**, Yves Cuilleron, Delas, Bernard Faurie, **Pierre Gaillard**, **Pierre Gonon**, Jean-Louis Grippat, André Perret.
Hermitage (red and white) **Chapoutier £**, **Jean-Louis Chave £**, Grippat, E. Guigal, **Paul Jaboulet Aîné £**, Sorrel and **Tardieu-Laurent £**.
Crozes-Hermitage (mainly red) **Albert Belle**, Dumaine, **Alain Graillot**, Paul Jaboulet Aîné, Domaine Pochon and **Gilles Robin**.
Cornas (red) **Thierry Allemand**, **Auguste Clape**, Jean Lionnet, Robert Michel, **Tunnel (Stéphane Robert)**, Noël Verset, Tardieu-Laurent and Alain Voge.

Top northern Rhône vintages – I prefer these Syrahs fairly young, although they can happily live up to twenty years: 1978, 1979, 1983, 1985, 1988, 1989, 1990, 1991, 1995, 1996, 1997, 1998, 1999 and 2000.

THE SOUTHERN RHÔNE

Côtes-du-Rhône (and **-Villages**) (red) **Clos Petite Bellane**, **Coudoulet de Beaucastel**, des Espiers, Domaine Gramenon, E. Guigal, Piaugier, Rayas (Fonsalette), **Marcel Richaud**, **Tardieu-Laurent** and Château du Trignon.

Lirac, **Rasteau** and **Vacqueyras** (red) **Château des Tours**, A. & R. Maby, **de la Mordorée** and **Trapadis**.

Gigondas (red) Font-Sane, R. & J.-P. Meffre (Saint-Gayan), Piaugier, **Saint-Cosme**, **Santa-Duc** and Château du Trignon.

Châteauneuf-du-Pape (red and white) **de Beaucastel**, Chapoutier, Charvin, **Clos du Caillou**, **Clos des Papes**, Fortia, **de la Janasse**, Marcoux, **de la Mordorée**, **du Pégaü**, **Rayas**, Tardieu-Laurent, Versino and Vieux Donjon.

Muscat de Beaumes-de-Venise (sweet white) Chapoutier, **Domaine de Durban** and Paul Jaboulet Aîné.

Top southern Rhône vintages – I prefer these wines on the young side, but the best examples can last for up to twenty-five years: 1978, 1979, 1981, 1983, 1985, 1988, 1989, 1990, 1994, 1995, 1996, 1998, 1999 and 2000.

FRENCH COUNTRY

A clumsy, catch-all term for the huge, sprawling area that scoops together the rest of France's southerly wine regions. I have picked out my favourite dry white, sweet white, red and fortified estates.

SOUTHWEST FRANCE

Bergerac (red and white) de la Jaubertie, **Moulin des Dames** and **La Tour des Gendres**.

Cahors (reds) **Châteaux du Cédre**, Lagrezette and **Clos Triguedina**.

Jurançon (dry and sweet whites) Bellegarde, **Cauhapé**, Clos Guirouilh, Clos Lapeyre, Clos Uroulat and Charles Hours.

Madiran (reds) **d'Aydie, Bouscassé (Montus)** and Domaine Pichard.

Monbazillac (sweet white) de l'Ancienne Cure, la Borderie and **Tirecul La Gravière**.

Saussignac (sweet white) Château Richard and Clos d'Yvigne.

LANGUEDOC-ROUSSILLON

Banyuls (fortified) and **Collioure** (red) **de la Casa Blanca**, Château de Jau, **du Mas Blanc** and de la Rectoire.

La Clape (red and white) **Camplazens l'Hermitage**, **de l'Hospitalet** and Pech-Redon.

Corbières (mainly red) **La Baronne**, Etang des Colombes, de Lastours, Meunier St. Louis, Château les Palais, Pech-Latt and Château Vaugélas.

Costières de Nîmes (red, white and rosé) de Belle-Coste, **Grande-Cassagne**, des Aveylans, Mourgues-du-Grès and **de Nages**.

Coteaux du Languedoc (red and white) **Les Aurelles**, **de Font Caude**, Mas Jullien, Puech-Haut, La Sauvagéonne and Abbaye de Valmagne.

Faugères (mainly red) **Alquier**, des Estanilles and Moulin de Ciffre.

Minervois (red and white) **Borie de Maurel**, **Le Cazal**, **Clos Centeilles**, Fabas, de Gourgazaud and d'Oupia.

Pic St-Loup (mainly red) Mas Bruguière, Cazeneuve, Ermitage du Pic St-Loup, **l'Hortus**, de Lascaux, Lascours and **Mas Mortiès**.

St-Chinian (red and white) Cazal-Viel, Coujan, des Jougla and Mas Champart.

Miscellaneous estates of excellence (and where to find them): **Domaine Gardiès** – Côtes de Roussillon; **de l'Aigle** – Limoux; **Mas Amiel** – Maury; **Domaine de Baruel** – Cévennes; **Cazes** – Muscat de Rivesaltes; **Mas de Daumas Gassac** – L'Hérault; **Granges des Pères** – L'Hérault; **Domaine de Ravanès** – Coteaux de Murveil; and **Elian da Ros** – Côtes du Marmandais.

PROVENCE
Bandol (red) Pradeaux, **de la Bégude**, Château Jean-Pierre Gaussen, **Lafran-Veyrolles**, **Tempier**, de Pibarnon, **Mas de la Rouvière** and La Suffrène.
Les Baux-de-Provence (mainly red) Hauvette, des Terres Blanches and **de Trévallon £**.
Bellet (red, white and rosé) Château de Crémat.
Cassis (mainly white) Clos Ste-Madeleine.
Côtes de Provence (mainly red) de Rimauresq, Gavoty, de St-Baillon and **de la Courtade**.
Palette (red, white and rosé) **Château Simone**.

GERMANY
The UK still drinks copious quantities of shockingly poor German wine and seems reluctant to trade up to the country's delicious wines, such as those made by the superstars listed below. Thankfully there are at least a few faithful fans out there who know just how beautiful the Riesling grape can be in all its styles, from bone dry and refreshing, to unctuous and pudding-friendly.

The best producers are – **J.B. Becker**, Dr Bürklin-Wolf, J.J. Cristoffel, **Fritz Haag**, Weingut Kerpen, **von Kesselstatt**, Koehler-Ruprecht, **Franz Künstler**, H. & R. Lingenfelder, Schloss Lieser, **Dr Loosen**, **Egon Müller**, Müller-Cattoir, **J.J. Prüm**, Schloss Reihartshausen, Willi Schaefer, **von Schubert-Maximian Grünhaus**, **Selbach-Oster**, Dr H. Thanisch and Robert Weil.

Top German vintages – Riesling loves the long haul: 1971, 1975, 1976, 1983, 1985, 1988, 1989, 1990, 1992, 1993, 1995, 1996, 1997, 1998, 1999 and 2000.

GREAT BRITAIN
This year I haven't let patriotism get the better of me, and, after intensive tasting, I have recommended only the most reliable, professional, homegrown talent. So, come on – support your local wine industry. Most of these guys have websites for you to peruse and also accept visitors at certain times of the year. Their prices are fair if you buy directly from the vineyard.
The chosen few are – **Camel Valley**, **Chapel Down**, **Davenport**, Denbies, Nyetimber, RidgeView, **Shawsgate**, Three Choirs and Valley Vineyards.

ITALY
With thousands of grape varieties, regions and styles of wine, Italy has to be the most difficult of all countries to understand. But, if you stick to the estates below, you will hit upon some celestial offerings. Italy still makes some of the best-value wines on the shelves. You will, though, have to go to independent wine merchants to find the majority of the estates listed below.

NORTHWEST
PIEDMONT
Barolo, Barbaresco and other reds – **Elio Altare**, Giacomo Ascheri, Bruno Ceretto, **Aldo Conterno**, Giacomo Conterno, **Conterno Fantino**, **Domenico Clerico**, Fontanafredda, **Angelo Gaja £**, Elio Grasso, **Armando Parusso**, E. Pira, **Bruno Rocca**, **Luciano Sandrone**, Paolo Scavino, **La Spinetta**, Aldo Vajra and **Roberto Voerzio**.
Moscato (fizzy, sweet white) **Fontanafredda** and **La Spinetta**.
Gavi (dry white) Nicola Bergaglio, **La Giustiniana** and **La Scolca**.
Arneis (dry white) **Bric Cenciurio** and Carlo Deltetto.

LOMBARDY
Red and white – Bellavista, **Ca' del Bosco**, **Ca' dei Frati** and Nino Negri.

Top Piedmont vintages – The Nebbiolo grape's structure and tannin carries these wines far: 1970, 1971, 1974, 1978, 1982, 1985, 1988, 1989, 1990, 1995, 1996, 1997, 1998 and 1999.

NORTHEAST
TRENTINO
All styles – Vigneto Dalzocchio, **Foradori**, Bossi Fedrigotti, **Ferrari**, Letrari, Pojer & Sandri and **Tenuta San Leonardo**.

ALTO ADIGE
All styles – **Colterenzio**, San Michele Appiano, Hofstätter, **Franz Haas** and Alois Lageder.

VENETO
Soave (white) **Roberto Anselmi**, **Ca' Rugate**, Gini, **Leonildo Pieropan** and Prà.
Valpolicella (red) **Allegrini**, Villa Bellini, Dal Forno, Masi and **Giuseppe Quintarelli £**.

Miscellaneous estates of excellence – (fizz) **Ruggeri**; (reds and sweeties) **Maculan**.

Top vintages for Amarone della Valpolicella – The power in Amarone makes these wines long-lived: 1970, 1971, 1974, 1976, 1979, 1983, 1985, 1988, 1990, 1993, 1995, 1997, 1998, 1999 and 2000.

FRIULI VENEZIA GIULIA
All styles – Livio Felluga, **Vinnaioli Jermann**, Miani, **Alvararo Pecorari**, **Vittorio & Giovanni Puiatti**, Ronco del Gnemiz, **Mario Schiopetto**, Tercic and Villa Russiz.

CENTRAL
TUSCANY
Chianti (red) P. Antinori, **Brolio**, Villa Caffagio, Carobbio, **Castello di Fonterutoli**, **Isole e Olena**, **Felsina Berardenga**, Fontodi, **La Massa**, Poggerino, **Querciabella** and **Selvapiana**.
Brunello di Montalcino (red) Altesino, **Argiano**, Case Basse, **Costanti**, **Fuligni**, La Gerla, Lisini, Silvio Nardi, Pietroso and Sesti.
Vino Nobile di Montepulciano (red) **Dei**, Il Macchione, **Poliziano** and Villa Sant'Anna.
Carmignano (red) Ambra and **Tenuta di Capezzana**.
Super-Tuscans (red) **Ardingo** (Calbello), Il Bosco (Manzano),

Brancaia, **Camartina £** (Querciabella), Campora (Falchini), **Il Carbonaione** (Poggio Scalette), Casalfero (Ricasoli), **Cepparello £** (Isole e Olena), Cortaccio (Villa Caffagio), Flaccianello della Pieve (Fontodi), Fontalloro (Felsina Berardenga), Ghiaie della Furba (Capezzana), **Lupicaia £** (Tenuta del Terricio), **Ornellaia £** (L. Antinori), Palazzo Altesi (Altesino), Paleo Rosso (Le Macchiole), **Saffredi £** (Le Pupille), Sammarco (Castello dei Rampolla), **Sassicaia £** (Marchesi Incisa della Rochetta), **Solaia £** (P. Antinori), **Solengo £** (Argiano), Tassinaia (Tenuta del Terriccio) and Tignanello (P. Antinori).

Vernaccia di San Gimignano (white) Montenidoli, **Panizzi**, Pietraserena and Teruzzi & Puthod.

Vin Santo (sweetie) **Isole e Olena £**, Selvapiana and Villa Branca.

Top Tuscan vintages – I usually attack these wines early (within ten years) although they seem to be able to hang on for ages: 1975, 1978, 1979, 1982, 1983, 1985, 1988, 1990, 1993, 1995, 1997, 1998, 1999 and 2000.

MARCHE

Red and white – **Coroncino**, Brunori, Saladini Pilastri, **Le Terrazze** and **Umani Ronchi**.

UMBRIA

Red and white – Bigi, **Arnaldo Caprai**, La Carraia, Castello della Sala, Lungarotti and **Palazzone**.

LAZIO

Red and white – **Castel De Paolis**, **Falesco** and Pallavincini.

ABRUZZO AND MOLISE
Red and white – Di Majo Norante and Edoardo Valentini.

SOUTHERN AND ISLANDS – All Styles
PUGLIA
Botromagno, Francesco Candido, **Tenuta Rubino** and **Cosimo Taurino**.

CAMPANIA
Colli di Lapio, Feudi di San Gregorio, **Luigi Maffini**, Mastroberardino and **Montevetrano**.

BASILICATA
D'Angelo and **Paternoster**.

CALABRIA
Librandi and San Francesco.

SICILY
De Bartoli, Calatrasi, Inycon, **Planeta** and Abbazia Santa Anastasia.

SARDINIA
Antonio Argiolas, Sella & Mosca and **Santadi**.

NEW ZEALAND
Each year I add five or six names to this list. There is no doubt New Zealand winemakers are getting it right, but it is taking a while. They must either be very deliberate people, or are just in no hurry. One thing is for certain; the average price of a bottle of New

Zealand wine sold in the UK is higher than that for a bottle from any other country, and continues to creep up every year. And the amount of wine we consume from these two fabulous islands on the other side of the world also continues to increase. So they must be getting it right. You can now expect excellent Chardonnay and Cabernet Sauvignon from New Zealand as well as the more renowned Sauvignon Blanc and Pinot Noir. Long may this country and its passionate winemakers continue their rise up the wine charts.
The top producers are – Alana Estate, **Ata Rangi**, **Cloudy Bay**, **Dry River**, **Esk Valley**, **Felton Road**, **Forrest Estate**, Giesen Estate, Goldwater Estate, Grove Mill, Hawkesbridge, **Hunter's**, **Isabel Estate**, **Jackson Estate**, Kim Crawford, **Kumeu River**, **Lawson's Dry Hills**, **Martinborough Vineyards**, **Palliser Estate**, Saint Clair, Selaks, Seresin Estate, Solstone, Stonecroft, **Stonyridge**, Te Mata, Tohu, **Unison**, **Vavasour**, Vidal, **Villa Maria** and **Wither Hills**.

Top New Zealand red vintages – Almost always drunk young, few reds would last more than ten years: 1989, 1991, 1994, 1995, 1996, 1998, 1999, 2000, 2001 and 2002 already looks good.

PORTUGAL

Portugal makes two of the finest fortified wines in the world – port and Madeira. This year, in addition to the big names, I have listed some of the smaller producers. Their wines are luscious, good value and can often compete with their more famous colleagues. I must admit that I don't drink much Portuguese wine. While the wines are getting better each year, we still don't see many of the best ones. Changes are afoot in Portugal, though, and more of the finer examples are gradually making their way over to the UK, so watch this space.

PORT
The best special-occasion port houses are – Dow, Fonseca, Graham, Quinta do Noval Nacional, Taylor and Warre.
The best everyday port houses are – Niepoort, Ramos-Pinto, Quinto do Infantado, Quinta do Portal, Quinta do Vesuvio and Senhora da Ribeira.

Top port vintages – No surprise, port is the keeper of them all: 1927, 1931, 1935, 1945, 1948, 1955, 1963, 1966, 1970, 1977, 1980, 1983, 1985, 1992, 1994, 1997 and 2000.

MADEIRA
The top producers are – Blandy's, Cossart Gordon and Henriques & Henriques.

THE REST OF PORTUGAL
Here's a short hit list of commendable winemakers in the better regions.
Alentejo Quinta do Carmo and Segada.
Bairrada Caves São João and Luis Pato.
Dão Quinta dos Roques, José-Maria da Fonseca and Conde de Santar.
Douro Niepoort, Quinta do Crasto, Quinta da Gaivosa, Quinta do Portal, Quinta de Roriz, Quinta de la Rosa and Quinta do Vale da Raposa.
Estremadura Quinta da Boavista, Quinta de Pancas and Palha Canas.
Ribatejo Bright Brothers.
Setúbal José-Maria da Fonseca.

Terras do Sado Quinta de Camarate, Pasmados, Periquita and **João Pires**.
Vinho Verde Palácio da Brejoeira and **Quinta do Ameal**.

SOUTH AFRICA

Now that South Africa has found its feet – an astonishing performance in just a few years – I have started to drink a lot more Cape wines. I also keep unearthing plum estates; there seems to be a non-stop supply of great new wine. But tread carefully, as for every bottle of top stuff there are a few more old-fashioned turkeys. Most estates are improving each year and SA should now feature in every serious wine drinker's collection. My list is growing yearly and the great thing is that none of the estates below has a wine over £25 – so there are no £! My problem has been choosing favourites, as I think they are all worthy of **bold** type. Go for any of the wines made by any of these estates and you should, I hope, be impressed at not only the taste, but also the value for money.

The top producers are – Avondale, Beaumont, Beyerskloof, **Boekenhoutskloof (Porcupine Ridge)**, **Bouchard Finlayson**, **Diemersfontein**, **Fairview**, **Ken Forrester**, Glen Carlou, Graham Beck, Grangehurst, **Hamilton Russell**, Hartenberg, Hidden Valley, Jean Daneel, **Jordan**, Kanonkop, **Klein Constantia**, Linton Park, Longridge, **Mont du Toit**, Morgenhof, Neethlingshof, **Neil Ellis**, Simonsig, **Spice Route**, Steenberg, Stellenzicht, **Thelema**, **Veenwouden**, **Vergelegen**, Villiera, **Warwick**, Waterford, **WhaleHaven** and Wildekrans.

Top South African vintages – It's rare to find older examples, and there is not much variation year on year from the best producers due to largely uniform weather conditions: 1986, 1987, 1989, 1991, 1992, 1994, 1995, 1997, 1998, 2000 and 2001.

SPAIN

I have only noted my favourite regions, and within each one, my top producers. Spain is woefully underrated at present and there is some delightful bargain drinking to be had. Almost all of the wineries below make great red wines, only a handful make whites to match.

Campo de Borja Bodegas Borsao.

Calatayud Marqués de Aragón.

Chacolí de Guetaria Txomín Etaniz.

Conca de Barberá Josep Foraster.

Jerez (sherry) González Byass, Hidalgo, **Lustau** and **Valdespino**.

Mallorca Anima Negra.

Navarra Agramont, Guelbenzu, Navasqüés, Ochoa and Principe de Viana.

Penedès Can Rafols dels Caus, Jean Léon, Puig & Roca and **Miguel Torres**.

Priorato Clos de l'Obac, L'Ermita, Clos Martinet, **Clos Mogador £** and Scala Dei.

Rías Baixas Lagar de Cervera, **Pazo de Barrantes**, Valdamor and **Valmiñor**.

Ribera del Duero Alion, **Cillar de Silos**, Pago de Carraovejas, **Pesquera**, Pingus, Tarsus and **Vega Sicilia £**.

Rioja Artadi, Barón de Ley, **CVNE**, **Contino**, Dominio de Montalvo, R. Lopez De Heredia, **Marqués de Murrieta**, Muga, Navajas, **Remelluri**, **La Rioja Alta**, Salceda, Urbina and **Marqués de Vargas**.

Rueda Bodegas Dos Victorias.

Somontano Blecua (Viñas del Vero).

Tarragona Capçanes and **Laurona**.
Terra Alta Xavier Clua and Bárbara Forés.
Toro Viña Bajoz.
Valencia Dominio Los Pinos.

Top Rioja vintages – I like to drink Riojas when they still have plenty of fruit, generally within ten years: 1978, 1981, 1982, 1985, 1987, 1989, 1990, 1991, 1994, 1995, 1996, 1998, 1999 and 2000.

USA
CALIFORNIA

An enormous industry with thousands of producers, so how can I sort it all out? Regionally doesn't really work as wineries source fruit from all over, so I have gone for grape variety. Just find your favourite grape and choose from the wineries listed below.

Cabernet Sauvignon/Merlot/Cabernet Franc Beringer, **Bryant Family £**, **Cain £**, Caymus, Clos LaChance, Corison, **Dalle Valle £**, Diamond Valley, Dominus, Etude, Flora Springs, Forman, Gallo Estate, **Harlan Estate £**, **Havens**, Paul Hobbs, Justin Vineyards, Lail Vineyards, Matanzas Creek, **Peter Michael**, Robert Mondavi, Moraga, Newton, Opus One, Pahlmeyer, **Paradigm £**, Joseph Phelps, **Quintessa £**, **Ridge £**, **Shafer £**, **Spottswoode £**, **Stag's Leap £** and **Viader £**.

Chardonnay Arrowood, **Au Bon Climat**, Beringer, Clos LaChance, Far Niente, Gallo Estate, Paul Hobbs, **Kistler £**, **Landmark**, Matanzas Creek, Peter Michael, Robert Mondavi, Sinskey and **Shafer £**.

Sauvignon Blanc Beringer, **Carmenet**, **Matanzas Creek** and Robert Mondavi.

Pinot Noir Au Bon Climat, Calera £, Etude £, Kistler £, J. Rochioli, Saintsbury and Talley Vineyards.
Rhône Rangers Alban, Au Bon Climat, Bonny Doon, **Jade Mountain**, Qupé, Sean Thackrey and **Turley £.**
Zinfandel Cline, **Elyse**, De Loach, **Doug Nalle**, Ravenswood, **Renwood**, **Ridge** and **Turley £.**

Inexpensive estates: **Avila**, Bonny Doon, Fetzer Bonterra, **J. Lohr**, Marietta Cellars, R.H. Phillips, **Ramsay** and Wente.

Top Californian vintages – These wines don't offer the longevity that you might expect, as they generally mature early: 1984, 1985, 1986, 1987, 1990, 1991, 1992, 1994, 1995, 1997, 1998, 1999 and 2000.

PACIFIC NORTHWEST
Wines from Oregon and Washington State are still hard to get hold of and are invariably dear. They tend to exist at the eclectic end of the spectrum and usually get opened when you are feeling inquisitive or have a fellow wine-lover over for dinner.
Oregon's best estates – **Adelsheim**, Bethel Heights, **Cristom**, **Domaine Drouhin**, Duck Pond, **Evesham Wood**, Ponzi and **Rex Hill**.
Washington State's best estates – L'Ecole No 41, **Château Ste-Michelle**, **Leonetti**, **Andrew Will £** and Woodward Canyon.

Top Oregon and Washington vintages: 1989, 1990, 1991, 1992, 1994, 1996, 1997, 1998, 1999 and 2000.

THE REST OF THE WORLD

A few pockets of France didn't make my list. **Jura**, **Savoie** and **Corsica** were the main omissions, but I suspect the wines from these regions are better off drunk in situ, on hols where the local colour and ambience help such unusual offerings down. **Swiss** wines have failed to pop up in any great numbers on our shelves. Why? The answer is they only export about two per cent of their production – lucky them. I am still trying to get my head around **Bulgaria**. Perhaps the problem is my mighty consumption of all of that Bulgarian Cab Sauv in the eighties... unfortunately I think I preferred the wines back then. The rest of **eastern Europe** also leaves me cold, except, that is, for the odd bottle or two. But for consistent excellence head to **Hungary** for the decadent sweet wine Tokaji. There are a few good producers and you'll discover a taste somewhere between Sauternes and a top-flight sherry. **Lebanon** has one great wine, Château Musar, and it is well worth a punt. It ages beautifully, and there is no such thing as a duff vintage. **Greek** wines are all the rage and I have tried to get to know them better over the last year. I am making headway and Greece might just be the last great discovery (after all it was probably one of the first) in the wine world.

I have little experience of **Cypriot** wine – I feel in need of a holiday – nor of **North African** wines; those from **Tunisia**, though, are increasingly seen on UK shelves. Further afield, wines from **Mexico**, **Bolivia** and **Peru** have yet to trouble my palate. Although **Uruguay** can produce good wine, there is little of it in the UK. I am not convinced that the three or four **Indian** wines I have tasted mean I need to investigate further. And the threat of wine from the former **Soviet Republic**, **China** and **Japan** may be too much to bear!

DIRECTORY
OF UK WINE
MERCHANTS

This year there are a handful of new entries in this chapter, and if your favourite wine shop is not listed, do drop me a line for next year's book. The next few pages contain the vital contact details for the merchants responsible for selling nearly all of the excellent wines in the UK. Use this directory and get dialling. There has never been a better time to shop for wine and this list has every number you need to fill your cellar. Buying wine is a glorious way to wile away the hours. Chatting, tasting, pushing back the boundaries of your knowledge and unearthing new finds. The following list of merchants is sorted alphabetically and then regionally to help you access as wide a choice of merchants as possible. I have included the main contact number and e-mail address or website, where appropriate, for each company's HQ. Remember that every outlet mentioned below delivers wine around the country. So use this service if you are pushed for time, not in the area or have placed a particularly large order. Many of these companies have newsletters (either via e-mail or post), so ask to be put on their mailing list and you will be first to hear about new releases. If you want to buy a specific bottle, one of my Top 250 perhaps, then phone before and reserve it, as some of these wines will move very swiftly indeed. Most importantly of all, if you locate an independent wine merchant near to where you live, do your best to support them. These pioneering merchants are the lifeblood of the wine trade. Supermarkets and chain stores have massive buying power and search out the best wines possible, but their orders are usually multiples of hundreds, if not thousands, of cases. Each year the supermarkets and the famous wine chains increase their selections and buy better wine. They are very skilled at this and often the place to go when buying big brand names. But the smaller outfits sniff out individual parcels, sometimes a case at a time, and you want to know about these rare gems. In the same way that your local butcher and fishmonger know your likes and dislikes, your local wine merchant will get to know your taste. Now, what could be better than that?

KEY
✪ = Jukesy-rated wine merchant worthy of particular note
C = Wine sold by the case (often mixed) of twelve bottles
M = Mail order company, usually with no retail premises
F = Fine wine sales/wine broker/good range of expensive stuff!

RECOMMENDED LARGER CHAIN STORES AND SUPERMARKETS (PLUS ABBREVIATIONS)

Asda (**Asd**) 255 stores 0500 100055 www.asda.co.uk ✪

E.H. Booth & Co., of Lancashire, Cheshire, Cumbria and Yorkshire (**Boo**) 26 stores 01772 251701 www.booths-supermarkets.co.uk ✪

Co-operative Group CWS (**Coo**) 1,100 stores 0800 068 6727 www.co-op.co.uk

First Quench – including **Bottoms Up** (**Bot**), **Thresher** (**Thr**) and **Wine Rack** (**WRa**) 2,200 stores 01707 387200 www.firstquench.co.uk ✪

Majestic Wine Warehouses (**Maj**) 100 stores 01923 298200 www.majestic.co.uk ✪C

Marks & Spencer (**M&S**) 308 stores 020 7935 4422 www.marksandspencer.co.uk ✪

Wm Morrison (**Mor**) 115 stores 01924 870000 www.morereasons.co.uk

Oddbins (**Odd**) 234 stores and **Oddbins Fine Wine shops** (**OFW**)
7 stores 020 8944 4400 www.oddbins.com ✪

Safeway (**Saf**) 477 stores 020 8848 8744 www.safeway.co.uk ✪

Sainsbury's (**Sai**) 445 stores 0800 636262 www.sainsburys.co.uk ✪

Somerfield Stores (**Som**) 550 stores 0117 935 6669
www.somerfield.co.uk

Tesco Stores (**Tes**) 696 stores 0800 505555 www.tesco.co.uk ✪

Unwins Ltd (**Unw**) 432 stores 01322 272711 www.unwins.co.uk ✪

Waitrose (**Wai**) 136 stores 01344 825232 www.waitrose.com ✪

Wine Cellar (**WCe**) 62 stores 0800 838251 www.winecellar.co.uk

RECOMMENDED INDEPENDENT RETAIL SPECIALISTS, SMALL CHAINS, WINE BROKERS AND MAIL ORDER WINE COMPANIES SORTED ALPHABETICALLY

A & A Wines, Cranleigh, Surrey 01483 274666 AAWINES@aol.com C

A & B Vintners, Brenchley, Kent 01892 724977
info@abvintners.co.uk ✪ M C

Adnams Wine Merchants, Southwold, Suffolk 01502 727222
wines@adnams.co.uk ✪

Ameys Wines, Sudbury, Suffolk 01787 377144

Amps Fine Wines of Oundle, near Peterborough, Northamptonshire
01832 273502 info@ampsfinewines.co.uk

Arkells Vintners, Swindon, Wiltshire 01793 823026
arkells@arkells.com

John Armit Wines, London 020 7908 0600 info@armit.co.uk
✪ M C F

W.J. Armstrong, East Grinstead, West Sussex 01342 321478
www.wjarmstrong.com

M = Mail order company, usually with no retail premises
F = Fine wine sales/wine broker/good range of expensive stuff!

Arnolds, Broadway, Worcestershire 01386 852427
Arriba Kettle & Co., Honeybourne, Worcestershire
01386 833024 **C**
Australian Wine Club, Hounslow, Middlesex 0800 8562004
orders@austwine.co.uk ✪ **M C**
Averys, Bristol 0117 921 4146 ✪

Bacchanalia, Cambridge 01223 576292
Bacchus Fine Wines, Warrington, Buckinghamshire 01234 711140
wine@bacchus.co.uk ✪ **C**
Ballantynes, Cowbridge, Vale of Glamorgan 01446 774840
info@ballantynes.co.uk ✪
Balls Brothers, London 020 7739 1642 info@ballsbrothers.co.uk **M C**
Georges Barbier, London 020 8852 8501 ✪ **M C**
Barrels & Bottles, Sheffield 0114 255 6611
sales@barrels&bottles.co.uk
Bat & Bottle, Knightley, Staffordshire 01785 284495
mail@batwine.com ✪
Beaconsfield Wine Cellar, Beaconsfield, Buckinghamshire
01494 675545 cellars@btinternet.com
Beaminster Fine Wines, Beaminster, Dorset 01308 862350
Bennetts Fine Wines, Chipping Campden, Gloucestershire 01386
840392 www.bennetsfinewines.com ✪
Bentalls, Kingston-upon-Thames, Surrey 020 8546 1001
Bergerac Wine Cellar, St Helier, Jersey 01534 870756
Berkmann Wine Cellars, London 020 7609 4711
info@berkmann.co.uk ✪ **M**
Berry Bros. & Rudd, London 0870 900 4300
www.bbr.com ✪ **F**

Bibendum Wine Ltd, London 020 7449 4120
  sales@bibendum-wine.co.uk ✪ M C F

Bideford Wines, Bideford, Devon 01237 470507

Booths of Stockport, Heaton Moor, Stockport 0161 432 3309
  johnbooth@lineone.net

Bordeaux Index, London 020 7278 9495
  sales@bordeauxindex.com ✪ M F

The Bottleneck, Broadstairs, Kent 01843 861095
  sales@thebottleneck.co.uk

Brinkleys Wines, London 020 7351 1683 www.brinkleys.com

F.E. Brown & Son, Hoddesdon, Hertfordshire 01992 421327 M C

Burgundy Shuttle, London 020 7341 4053 M C

Butlers Wine Cellar, Brighton, East Sussex 01273 698724 ✪

Anthony Byrne Fine Wines, Ramsey, Cambridgeshire 01487
  814555 sales@abfw.co.uk M C

D. Byrne & Co., Clitheroe, Lancashire 01200 423152 ✪

Cairns & Hickey, Bramhope, Leeds 0113 267 3746

Carley & Webb, Framlingham, Suffolk 01728 723503

Carringtons, Manchester 0161 881 0099

Castang Wine Shippers, Pelynt, Cornwall 01503 220359 M C

Les Caves du Patron, Stoneygate, Leicester 0116 221 8221
  info@lescavesdupatron.com

Cave Cru Classé, London 020 7378 8579 enquiries@ccc.co.uk M C F

Andrew Chapman Fine Wines, Abingdon, Oxfordshire
  0845 458 0707 ✪

The Charterhouse Wine Co., London 020 7587 1302
  norman@charterhousewine.co.uk

Cheshire Smokehouse, Wilmslow, Cheshire 01625 540123

Chippendale Fine Wines, Bradford, West Yorkshire 01274 582424
mikepoll@freenetname.co.uk **M C**

Church House Vintners, Newbury, Berkshire 01635 579 327
chv@saqnet.co.uk **M C**

Classic Wines, Chester, Cheshire 01244 288444

Clifton Cellars, Bristol 0117 973 0287 clifton@cellars.freeserve.co.uk

Brian Coad Fine Wines, Ivybridge, Devon 01752 896545
briancoadfinewines@lineone.net **M C**

Cochonnet Wines, Falmouth, Cornwall 01326 340332
sales@wineincornwall.co.uk

Cockburns, Leith, Edinburgh 0131 346 1113 sales@winelist.co.uk

Colombier Vins Fins, Swadlincote, Derbyshire 01283 552552 **M C**

Connollys, Birmingham 0121 236 9269 www.connollyswine.co.uk ✪

Corks, Cotham, Bristol 0117 973 1620 sales@corksof.com

Corkscrew Wines, Carlisle, Cumbria 01228 543033
corkscrewwines@aol.com

Corney & Barrow, London 020 7539 3200 wine@corbar.co.uk ✪ **F**

Croque-en-Bouche, Malvern Wells, Worcestershire
01684 565612 mail@croque-en-bouche.co.uk ✪ **M C**

Dartmouth Vintners, Dartmouth, Devon 01803 832602
bill@dartmouthvintners.fsnet.co.uk

Decorum Vintners, London 020 7589 6755 admin@decvin.com ✪ **M C**

deFINE Food and Wine, Sandiway, Cheshire 01606 882101

Rodney Densem Wines, Nantwich, Cheshire 01270 626999
sales@onestopwine.com

Direct Wine Shipments, Belfast, Northern Ireland 028 9050 8000
enquiry@directwine.co.uk ✪

Direct Wines, Windsor 0870 444 8383 www.laithwaites.co.uk **M C**

Domaine Direct, London 020 7837 1142 mail@domaindirect.co.uk ✪ C

The Dorchester Wine Centre at Eldridge Pope, Dorchester, Dorset
01305 258266 ✪

Draycott Wines, Topsham, Devon 01392 874501
enquiries@draycott.co.uk

Dunnells Ltd, St Peter Port, Guernsey 01534 736418

Du Vin, Henley-on-Thames, Oxfordshire 01491 637888
wine@duvin.co.uk

Edencroft Fine Wines, Nantwich, Cheshire 01270 629975
sales@edencroft.co.uk

Ben Ellis, Brockham, Surrey 01737 842160
sales@benelliswines.com ✪ C

Ells Fine Wines, Portadown, Northern Ireland 028 3833 2306
rrwines@hotmail.com

El Vino, London 020 7353 5384 www.elvino.co.uk

English Wine Centre, Alfriston Roundabout, East Sussex 01323
870164 bottles@englishwine.co.uk

Eton Vintners, Windsor 01753 790188
enquiries@etonvintners.co.uk M

Evertons, Ombersley, Worcestershire 01905 620282

Evingtons Wine Merchants, Leicester 0116 254 2702
evingtonwine@fsbdial.co.uk

Farr Vintners, London 020 7821 2000 sales@farr-vintners.com ✪ M F

Fine & Rare Wines, London 020 8960 1995
wine@frw.co.uk ✪ M F

Fine Cheese Co., Bath 01225 483407 sales@finecheeseco.demon.co.uk

Irma Fingal-Rock, Monmouth, Monmouthshire 01600 712372

Flagship Wines, Brentwood, Essex julia@flagshipwines.co.uk
01227 203420 **M C**

Le Fleming Wines, Harpenden, Hertfordshire 01582 760125 **M C**

La Forge Wines, Marksbury, Bath 01761 472349
kevin@laforgewines.com

Fortnum & Mason, London 020 7734 8040 ✪

Four Walls Wine Company, Chilgrove, West Sussex 01243 535360
fourwallswine@cs.com ✪ **M F**

Friarwood, London 020 7736 2628 sales@friarwood.com

Gallery Wines, Gomshall, Surrey 01483 203795

Garland Wine Cellar, Ashtead, Surrey 01372 275247
simon@garlandwines.freeserve.co.uk

Garrards, Cockermouth, Cumbria 01900 823592
admin@garrards-wine.co.uk

Gauntleys, Nottingham 0115 911 0555 rhone@gauntleywine.com ✪

General Wine Company, Liphook, Hampshire 01428 727744
www.thegeneralwine.co.uk ✪

Goedhuis & Co., London 020 7793 7900 sales@goedhuis.com ✪ **M C F**

Peter Graham Wines, Norwich, Norfolk 01603 625657
louisa@petergrahamwines.com

Great Gaddesden Wines, Harpenden, Hertfordshire 01582
760606 sales@flyingcorkscrew.com **M C**

Great Northern Wine Company, Ripon, North Yorkshire 01765
606767 info@greatnorthernwine.com **M**

Great Western Wine Company, Bath 01225 322800
post@greatwesternwine.co.uk

Peter Green, Edinburgh 0131 229 5925 petergreenwines@talk21.com

The Grog Blossom, London 020 7794 7808

Patrick Grubb Selections, Oxford 01869 340229 ✿
Gunson Fine Wines, South Godstone, Surrey 01342 843974
gunsonfinewines@aol.com ✿ **M C**

H & H Bancroft, London 0870 4441700
sales@handhbancroft.co.uk ✿ **M C**
Halifax Wine Company, Halifax, West Yorkshire 01422 256333
www.halifaxwinecompany.com
Handford – Holland Park, London 020 7221 9614
james@handford-wine.demon.co.uk ✿
Hanslope Wines, Milton Keynes, Buckinghamshire 01908 510262
charles@hanslopewines.co.uk
Roger Harris Wines, Weston Longville, Norfolk 01603 880171
sales@rogerharriswines.co.uk ✿ **M C**
Harrods, London 020 7730 1234 **F**
John Harvey & Sons, Bristol 0117 927 5006 **M C**
Harvey Nichols & Co., London 020 7201 8537
wineshop@harveynichols.co.uk ✿
Richard Harvey Wines, Wareham, Dorset 01929 481437
harvey@lds.co.uk **M C**
The Haslemere Cellar, Haslemere, Surrey 01428 645081
info@haslemerecellar.co.uk ✿
Haynes, Hanson & Clark, London 020 7259 0102
london@hhandc.co.uk and Stow-on-the-Wold, Gloucestershire
01451 870808 stow@hhandc.co.uk ✿
Hedley Wright, Bishop's Stortford, Hertfordshire 01279 465818
hedleywine@aol.com **C**
Pierre Henck, Wolverhampton, West Midlands 01902 751022 **M C**
Charles Hennings Vintners, Pulborough, West Sussex

01798 872485 sales@chv-wine.co.uk

Hicks & Don, Edington, Wiltshire 01380 831234
mailbox@hicksanddon.co.uk **M**

George Hill, Loughborough, Leicestershire 01509 212717
andrewh@gerorgehill.co.uk

Hopton Wines, Kidderminster, Worcestershire 01299 270734
chris@hoptoncourt.fsnet.co.uk **M C**

Hoults Wine Merchants, Huddersfield, West Yorkshire
01484 510700 bob@malvasia.freeserve.co.uk ✪

House of Townend, Kingston upon Hull, East Yorkshire
01482 586582 info@houseoftownend.co.uk

Ian G. Howe, Newark, Nottinghamshire 01636 704366
howe@chablis-burgundy.co.uk

Victor Hugo Wines, St Saviour, Jersey 01534 507977
sales@victor-hugo-wines.com

Inspired Wines, Cleobury Mortimer, Shropshire 01299 270064
info@inspired-wines.co.uk

Inverarity Vaults, Biggar 01899 308000
enquiries@inverarity-vaults.com

Irvine Robertson, Edinburgh 0131 553 3521 **C**

Jeroboams (incorporating **Laytons Wine Merchants**), London
020 7259 6716 sales@jeroboams.co.uk ✪

Michael Jobling, Newcastle-upon-Tyne 0191 261 5298 **M C**

The Jolly Vintner, Tiverton, Devon 01884 255644

L & F Jones, Radstock near Bath 01761 417117
buying.buying@lfjones.aclm.co.uk

S.H. Jones, Banbury, Oxfordshire 01295 251179 shjonesbanbury@aol.com

Justerini & Brooks, London 020 7484 6400 ✪ F
Just in Case Wine Merchants, Bishop's Waltham, Hampshire
01489 892969

Joseph Keegan, Holyhead, Isle of Anglesey 01407 762333
enquiries@josephkeegan.co.uk
John Kelly Wines, Boston Spa, West Yorkshire 01937 842965
john@kellywines.co.uk M C
David Kibble Wines, Fontwell, West Sussex 01243 544111
Richard Kihl, Aldeburgh, Suffolk 01728 454455
sales@richardkihl.ltd.uk ✪ F C

Laithwaites, Reading, Berkshire 0870 444 8282
orders@laithwaites.co.uk M C
Larners, Holt, Norfolk 01263 712323 ctbaker@cwcom.net
Lay & Wheeler, Colchester, Essex 01206 764446
sales@laywheeler.com ✪
Laymont & Shaw, Truro, Cornwall 01872 270545
info@laymont-shaw.co.uk M C
Lea & Sandeman, London 020 7244 5200
sales@leaandsandeman.co.uk ✪
Liberty Wines, London 020 7720 5350 info@libertywine.co.uk ✪ M C
O.W. Loeb, London 020 7928 7750 finewine@owloeb.com ✪ M C
J & H Logan, Edinburgh 0131 667 2855
Longford Wines, Lewes, East Sussex 01273 400012
longfordwines@aol.com M C
Love Saves the Day, Manchester 0161 832 0777
chris@lovesavestheday.co.uk
Luckins Wine Store, Great Dunmow, Essex 01371 872839

M = Mail order company, usually with no retail premises
F = Fine wine sales/wine broker/good range of expensive stuff!

Luvian's Bottle Shop, Cupar, Fife 01334 654820
v.fusaro@ukonline.co.uk

Martinez Fine Wines, Ilkley, West Yorkshire 01943 603241
editor@martinez.co.uk ✪
Mill Hill Wines, London 020 8959 6754
millhillwines@compuserve.com
Mills Whitcombe, Peterchurch, Herefordshire 01981 550028
info@millswhitcombe.co.uk ✪ C
Milton Sandford Wines, Knowl Hill, Berkshire 01628 829449 ✪ M C
Mitchells Wines, Sheffield 0114 274 5587
Montrachet Fine Wines, London 020 7928 1990
charles@montrachetwine.com ✪ M C
Moreno Wine, London 020 7286 0678
morenowi@dialstart.net ✪
Moriarty Vintners, Cardiff 029 2022 9996
sales@moriarty-vintners.com
Morris & Verdin, London 020 7921 5300 info@m-v.co.uk ✪ M C

James Nicholson, Crossgar, Co. Down, Northern Ireland
028 4483 0091 info@jnwine.com ✪
Nickolls & Perks, Stourbridge, West Midlands 01384 394518
sales@nickollsandperks.co.uk
Nicolas UK of London, 20+ stores 020 8964 5469
www.nicolas.co.uk
Noble Rot Wine Warehouse, Bromsgrove, Worcestershire
01527 575606 info@nrwinewarehouse.co.uk
The Nobody Inn, Doddiscombsleigh, Devon 01647 252394
info@nobodyinn.co.uk ✪

Oasis Wines, Southend-on-Sea, Essex 01702 293999

The Old Forge Wine Cellar, Storrington, West Sussex
01903 744246 chris@worldofwine.co.uk

Oxford Wine Company, Witney, Oxfordshire 01865 301144
info@oxfordwine.co.uk ✪

Thomas Panton, Tetbury, Gloucestershire 01666 503088
info@wineimporter.co.uk M

Paxton & Whitfield, London 020 7930 0259
sales@cheesemongers.co.uk

Thos Peatling, Bury St Edmunds, Suffolk 01284 714285
sales@thospeatling.co.uk

Peckham & Rye, Glasgow 0141 445 4555
johnatpeckhams@aol.com ✪

Penistone Court Wine Cellars, Penistone, Sheffield 01226 766037
pcwc@dircon.co.uk ✪ M C

Philglas & Swiggot, London 020 7924 4494
philandswig@aol.com ✪

Christopher Piper Wines, Ottery St Mary, Devon 01404 814139
sales@christopherpiperwines.co.uk ✪

Terry Platt Wine Merchants, Llandudno, Conwy 01492 874099
plattwines@clara.co.uk ✪ M C

Planet Wine, Sale, Cheshire 0161 973 1122
sales@planetwine.co.uk M C

Playford Ros, Thirsk, North Yorkshire 01845 526777
sales@playfordros.com M C

Portal, Dingwall & Norris, Emsworth, Hampshire 01243 370280

Portland Wine Co., Sale, Manchester 0161 962 8752
portwineco@aol.com

Quay West Wines, Stoke Canon, Exeter 01392 841833
quaywest@btopenworld.com **C**
Quellyn Roberts, Chester, Cheshire 01244 310455
qrwines@chesternet.co.uk

R.S. Wines, Bristol 0117 963 1780 **M C**
Arthur Rackham, Guildford, Surrey 01483 722962 **C**
Raeburn Fine Wines, Edinburgh 0131 3431159
sales@raeburnfinewines.com ✪
Ravensbourne Wine, London 020 8692 9655
sales@ravensbournewine.co.uk **C**
Reid Wines, Hallatrow, Bristol 01761 452645
reidwines@aol.com ✪ **M F**
La Réserve, London 020 7589 2020
redwine@la-reserve.co.uk ✪
Revelstoke Wines, London 020 8875 0077
sales@revelstoke.co.uk ✪ **M C**
Howard Ripley, London 020 8360 0020 and 020 8877 3065
info@howardripley.com **M C**
Roberson, London 020 7371 2121 wines@roberson.co.uk ✪
Roberts & Speight, Beverley, East Yorkshire 01482 870717
sales@robertsandspeight.co.uk
Robert Rolls, London 020 7606 1166 mail@rollswine.com ✪ **M C F**

St Martin Vintners, Brighton, East Sussex 01273 777788
sales@stmartinvintners.co.uk
Sandhams Wine Merchants, Caistor, Lincolnshire 01472 852118
sandhams@nildram.co.uk
Scatchard, Liverpool 0151 709 7073 info@scatchards.com

Seckford Wines, Woodbridge, Suffolk 01394 446622
sales@seckfordwines.co.uk ✪ M C F

Selfridges, London 020 7318 3730 and Manchester 0161 629 1234
wine.club@selfridges.co.uk ✪

Shaftesbury Fine Wines, Shaftesbury, Dorset 01747 850059

Shaws, Beaumaris, Isle of Anglesey 01248 810328
wines@shaws.sagehost.co.uk

Edward Sheldon, Shipston-on-Stour, Warwickshire 01608 661409
finewine@edward-sheldon.co.uk

Laurence Smith, Edinburgh 0131 667 3327 vintnersmith@aol.com M C

Soho Wine Supply, London 020 7636 8490 info@sohowine.co.uk

The Sommelier Wine Co., St Peter Port, Guernsey 01481 721677 ✪

Springfield Wines, near Huddersfield, West Yorkshire 01484 864929

Frank Stainton Wines, Kendal, Cumbria 01539 731886
admin@stainton-wines.co.uk

William Stedman, Caerleon, Newport 01633 430055
info@wmstedman.co.uk

Charles Steevenson, Tavistock, Devon 01822 616272
sales@steevensonwines.co.uk M C

Stevens Garnier, Oxford 01865 263303 info@stevensgarnier.co.uk

Stokes Fine Wines, London 020 8944 5979
sales@stokesfinewines.com

SWIG, London 020 7903 8311 imbibe@swig.co.uk ✪ M C

T & W Wines, Thetford, Norfolk 01842 765646
contact@tw-wines.com

Tanners, Shrewsbury, Shropshire 01743 234455
sales@tanners-wines.co.uk ✪

Totnes Wine Co., Totnes, Devon 01803 866357 info@totneswine.co.uk

Trenchermans, Sherborne, Dorset 01935 432857
steve@trenchermans.com
Turville Valley Wines, Great Missenden, Buckinghamshire 01494
868818 info@turville-valley-wines.com ✪ M C F

Uncorked, London 020 7638 5998 drink@uncorked.co.uk

Valvona & Crolla, Edinburgh 0131 556 6066
sales@valvonacrolla.co.uk ✪
Helen Verdcourt, Maidenhead, Berkshire 01628 625577 M C
La Vigneronne, London 020 7589 6113 lavig@aol.com ✪
Villeneuve Wines, Peebles, Haddington and Edinburgh
01721 722500 wines@villeneuvewines.com ✪
Vin du Van, Appledore, Kent 01233 758727 ✪ M C
Vinceremos, Leeds 0113 2440002 info@vinceremos.co.uk M C
The Vine Trail, Hotwells, Bristol 0117 921 1770
enquiries@vinetrail.co.uk ✪ M C
The Vineyard, Dorking, Surrey 01306 876828
Vino Vino, New Malden, Surrey 07703 436949
vinovino@macunlimited.net M C
The Vintage House, London 020 7437 2592
vintagehouse.co@virgin.net
Vintage Roots, Arborfield, Berkshire 0118 976 1999
info@vintageroots.co.uk M

Wadebridge Wines, Wadebridge, Cornwall 01208 812692
wadebridgewines@eclipse.co.uk
Waterloo Wine, London 020 7403 7967
sales@waterloowine.co.uk

Waters Wine Merchants, Coventry, Warwick 01926 888889
   info@waters-wine-merchants.co.uk
David J. Watt Fine Wines, Ashby-de-la-Zouch, Leicestershire
   01530 415704 shop, 01530 413953 fwatt@lineone.net **M**
Weavers, Nottingham, Nottinghamshire 0115 958 0922
   weavers@weavers.wines.com
Wessex Wines, Bridport, Dorset 01308 427177
   wessexwines@btinternet.com **C**
Whitebridge Wines, Stone, Staffordshire 01785 817229
   sales@whitebridgewines.co.uk
Whitesides, Clitheroe, Lancashire 01200 422281
Whittalls Wines, Walsall, West Midlands 01922 636161 **C**
Wilkinson Vintners, London 020 7272 1982
   wilkinson@finewine.co.uk ✪ **M C F**
James Williams, Narberth, Pembrokeshire 01834 862200
Wimbledon Wine Cellar, London 020 8540 9979
   enquiries@wimbledonwinecellar.com ✪
Winchcombe Wine Merchants, Winchcombe, Gloucestershire
   01242 604313
The Wine Cellar, Croydon, Greater London 020 8657 6936
   winecellarsnd@aol.com
Wine Society, Stevenage, Hertfordshire 01438 741177
   memberservices@thewinesociety.com ✪ **M C F**
The Wine Treasury, London 020 7793 9999
   quality@winetreasury.com ✪ **M C**
The Winery, London 020 7286 6475
   dmotion@globalnet.co.uk ✪ **F**
Wines of Interest, Ipswich, Suffolk 01473 215752
   woi@fsbdial.co.uk

The Winesmith, Peterborough, Cambridgeshire 01780 783102
cases@winesmith.co.uk
WineTime, Milnthorpe, Cumbria 01539 562030 **M C**
The Wright Wine Company, Skipton, North Yorkshire
01756 700886 ✪
Wrightson & Co. Wine Merchants, Darlington 01325 374134
ed.wrighton.wines@oxynet.co.uk **M C**
Wycombe Wines, High Wycombe, Buckinghamshire
01494 437228
Peter Wylie Fine Wines, Plymtree, Devon 01884 277555
peter@wylie-fine-wines.demon.co.uk ✪ **F**

Yapp Brothers, Mere, Wiltshire 01747 860423 sales@yapp.co.uk ✪ **M C**
Noel Young Wines, Trumpington, Cambridgeshire 01223 844744
admin@nywines.co.uk ✪

RECOMMENDED INDEPENDENT RETAIL SPECIALISTS, SMALL CHAINS, WINE BROKERS AND MAIL ORDER WINE COMPANIES SORTED REGIONALLY

(For contact details see alphabetical list)

LONDON
John Armit Wines, W11 ✪ **M C F**
Australian Wine Club, Hounslow ✪ **M C**
Balls Brothers, E2 **M C**
Georges Barbier, SE12 ✪ **M C**
Berkmann Wine Cellars, N7 ✪ **M**
Berry Bros. & Rudd, SW1 ✪ **F**

O = Jukesy-rated wine merchant worthy of particular note
C = Wine sold by the case (often mixed) of twelve bottles

Bibendum Wine Ltd, NW1 O M C F
Bordeaux Index, EC1 O M F
Brinkleys Wines, SW10
Burgundy Shuttle, SW11 M C
Cave Cru Classé, London M C F
The Charterhouse Wine Co., SE11
Corney & Barrow, EC1 O F
Decorum Vintners, SW7 O M C
Domaine Direct, N1 O C
El Vino, EC4
Farr Vintners, SW1 O M F
Fine & Rare Wines, W10 O M F
Fortnum & Mason, W1 O
Friarwood, SW6
Goedhuis & Co., SW8 O M C F
The Grog Blossom, NW6
H & H Bancroft, SW8 O M C
Handford – Holland Park, W11 O
Harrods, SW1 F
Harvey Nichols & Co., SW1 O
Haynes, Hanson & Clark, SW1 O
Jeroboams (incorporating Laytons Wine Merchants), W1 O
Justerini & Brooks, SW1 O F
Lea & Sandeman, SW10 O
Liberty Wines, SW8 O M C
O.W. Loeb, SE1 O M C
Mill Hill Wines, NW7
Montrachet Fine Wines, SE1 O M C
Moreno Wine, W9 O

Morris & Verdin, SE1 ✪ M C
Nicolas UK of London 20+ stores
Paxton & Whitfield, SW1
Philglas & Swiggot, SW11 ✪
Ravensbourne Wine, SE10 C
La Réserve, SW3 ✪
Revelstoke Wines, SW15 ✪ M C
Howard Ripley, N21 M C
Roberson, W14 ✪
Robert Rolls, EC1 ✪ M C F
Selfridges, W1 ✪
Soho Wine Supply, W1
Stokes Fine Wines, SW18
SWIG, SW6
Uncorked, EC2
La Vigneronne, SW7 ✪
The Vintage House, W1
Waterloo Wine, SE1
Wilkinson Vintners, N19 ✪ M C F
Wimbledon Wine Cellar, SW19 ✪
The Wine Cellar, Croydon
The Wine Treasury, SW8 ✪ M C
The Winery, W9 ✪ F

SOUTH EAST
A & A Wines, Cranleigh, Surrey C
A & B Vintners, Brenchley, Kent ✪ M C
W.J. Armstrong, East Grinstead, West Sussex
Bacchus Fine Wines, Warrington, Buckinghamshire ✪ C

Beaconsfield Wine Cellar, Beaconsfield, Buckinghamshire

Bentalls, Kingston-upon-Thames, Surrey

The Bottleneck, Broadstairs, Kent

F.E. Brown & Son, Hoddesdon, Hertfordshire M C

Butlers Wine Cellar, Brighton, East Sussex ✪

Church House Vintners, Newbury, Berkshire M C

Direct Wines, Windsor M C

Ben Ellis, Brockham, Surrey ✪ C

English Wine Centre, Alfriston, East Sussex

Eton Vintners, Windsor M

Le Fleming Wines, Harpenden, Hertfordshire M C

Four Walls Wine Company, Chilgrove, West Sussex ✪ M F

Gallery Wines, Gomshall, Surrey

Garland Wine Cellar, Ashtead, Surrey

General Wine Company, Liphook, Hampshire ✪

Great Gaddesden Wines, Harpenden, Hertfordshire M C

Gunson Fine Wines, South Godstone, Surrey ✪ M C

Hanslope Wines, Milton Keynes, Buckinghamshire

The Haslemere Cellar, Haslemere, Surrey ✪

Hedley Wright, Bishop's Stortford, Hertfordshire C

Charles Hennings Vintners, Pulborough, West Sussex

Just in Case Wine Merchants, Bishop's Waltham, Hampshire

David Kibble Wines, Fontwell, West Sussex

Laithwaites, Reading M C

Longford Wines, Lewes, East Sussex M C

Milton Sandford Wines, Knowl Hill, Berkshire ✪ M C

The Old Forge Wine Cellar, Storrington, West Sussex

Portal, Dingwall & Norris, Emsworth, Hampshire

Arthur Rackham, Guildford, Surrey C

St Martin Vintners, Brighton, East Sussex
Turville Valley Wines, Great Missenden, Buckinghamshire ✪ M C F
Helen Verdcourt, Maidenhead, Berkshire M C
Vin du Van, Appledore, Kent ✪ M C
The Vineyard, Dorking, Surrey
Vino Vino, New Malden, Surrey M C
Vintage Roots, Arborfield, Berkshire M
Wine Society, Stevenage, Hertfordshire ✪ M C F
Wycombe Wines, High Wycombe, Buckinghamshire

SOUTH WEST
Arkells Vintners, Swindon, Wiltshire
Averys, Bristol ✪
Beaminster Fine Wines, Beaminster, Dorset
Bideford Wines, Bideford, Devon
Castang Wine Shippers, Pelynt, Cornwall M C
Clifton Cellars, Bristol
Brian Coad Fine Wines, Ivybridge, Devon M C
Cochonnet Wines, Falmouth, Cornwall
Corks, Cotham, Bristol
Dartmouth Vintners, Dartmouth, Devon
The Dorchester Wine Centre at Eldridge Pope, Dorchester, Dorset ✪
Draycott Wines, Topsham, Devon
Fine Cheese Co., Bath
La Forge Wines, Marksbury, Bath
Great Western Wine Company, Bath
John Harvey & Sons, Bristol M C
Richard Harvey Wines, Wareham, Dorset M C
Hicks & Don, Edington, Wiltshire M

The Jolly Vintner, Tiverton, Devon
L & F Jones, Radstock near Bath
Laymont & Shaw, Truro, Cornwall M C
The Nobody Inn, Doddiscombsleigh, Devon ✪
Christopher Piper Wines, Ottery St Mary, Devon ✪
Quay West Wines, Stoke Canon, Exeter C
R.S. Wines, Bristol M C
Reid Wines, Hallatrow, Bristol ✪ M F
Shaftesbury Fine Wines, Shaftesbury, Dorset
Charles Steevenson, Tavistock, Devon M C
Totnes Wine Co., Totnes, Devon
Trenchermans, Sherborne, Dorset
The Vine Trail, Hotwells, Bristol ✪ M C
Wadebridge Wines, Wadebridge, Cornwall
Wessex Wines, Bridport, Dorset C
Woodhouse Wines, Blandford, Dorset
Peter Wylie Fine Wines, Plymtree, Devon ✪ F
Yapp Brothers, Mere, Wiltshire ✪ M C

MIDLANDS
Amps Fine Wines of Oundle, near Peterborough, Northamptonshire
Arnolds, Broadway, Worcestershire
Arriba Kettle & Co., Honeybourne, Worcestershire C
Bat & Bottle, Knightley, Staffordshire ✪
Bennetts Fine Wines, Chipping Campden, Gloucestershire ✪
Les Caves du Patron, Stoneygate, Leicester
Andrew Chapman Fine Wines, Abingdon, Oxfordshire ✪
Colombier Vins Fins, Swadlincote, Derbyshire M C
Connollys, Birmingham ✪

Croque-en-Bouche, Malvern Wells, Worcestershire ✪ M C

Du Vin, Henley-on-Thames, Oxfordshire

Evertons, Ombersley, Worcestershire

Evingtons Wine Merchants, Leicester

Gauntleys, Nottingham ✪

Patrick Grubb Selections, Oxford ✪

Haynes, Hanson & Clark, Stow-on-the-Wold, Gloucestershire ✪

Pierre Henck, Wolverhampton, West Midlands M C

George Hill, Loughborough, Leicestershire

Hopton Wines, Kidderminster, Worcestershire M C

Ian G. Howe, Newark, Nottinghamshire

Inspired Wines, Cleobury Mortimer, Shropshire

S.H. Jones, Banbury, Oxfordshire

Mills Whitcombe, Peterchurch, Herefordshire C

Nickolls & Perks, Stourbridge, West Midlands

Noble Rot Wine Warehouse, Bromsgrove, Worcestershire

Oxford Wine Company, Witney, Oxfordshire ✪

Thomas Panton, Tetbury, Gloucestershire M

Edward Sheldon, Shipston-on-Stour, Warwickshire

Stevens Garnier, Oxford

Tanners, Shrewsbury, Shropshire ✪

Waters Wine Merchants, Coventry, Warwick

David J. Watt Fine Wines, Ashby-de-la-Zouch,
    Leicestershire M

Weavers, Nottingham, Nottinghamshire

Whitebridge Wines, Stone, Staffordshire

Whittalls Wines, Walsall, West Midlands C

Winchcombe Wine Merchants, Winchcombe,
    Gloucestershire

EASTERN COUNTIES
Adnams Wine Merchants, Southwold, Suffolk ✪
Ameys Wines, Sudbury, Suffolk
Bacchanalia, Cambridge
Anthony Byrne Fine Wines, Ramsey, Cambridgeshire M C
Carley & Webb, Framlingham, Suffolk
Flagship Wines, Brentwood, Essex M C
Peter Graham Wines, Norwich, Norfolk
Roger Harris Wines, Weston Longville, Norfolk ✪ M C
Richard Kihl, Aldeburgh, Suffolk ✪ F C
Larners, Holt, Norfolk
Lay & Wheeler, Colchester, Essex ✪
Luckins Wine Store, Great Dunmow, Essex
Oasis Wines, Southend-on-Sea, Essex
Thos Peatling, Bury St Edmunds, Suffolk
Sandhams Wine Merchants, Caistor, Lincolnshire
Seckford Wines, Woodbridge, Suffolk ✪ M C F
T & W Wines, Thetford, Norfolk
Wines of Interest, Ipswich, Suffolk
The Winesmith, Peterborough, Cambridgeshire
Noel Young Wines, Trumpington, Cambridgeshire ✪

NORTH WEST
Booths of Stockport, Heaton Moor, Stockport
D. Byrne & Co., Clitheroe, Lancashire ✪
Carringtons, Manchester
Cheshire Smokehouse, Wilmslow, Cheshire
Classic Wines, Chester, Cheshire
Corkscrew Wines, Carlisle, Cumbria

deFINE Food and Wine, Sandiway, Cheshire
Rodney Densem Wines, Nantwich, Cheshire
Edencroft Fine Wines, Nantwich, Cheshire
Garrards, Cockermouth, Cumbria
Love Saves the Day, Manchester
Planet Wine, Sale, Cheshire M C
Portland Wine Co., Sale, Manchester
Quellyn Roberts, Chester, Cheshire
Scatchard, Liverpool
Selfridges, Manchester ✪
Frank Stainton Wines, Kendal, Cumbria
Whitesides, Clitheroe, Lancashire
WineTime, Milnthorpe, Cumbria M C

NORTH EAST
Barrels & Bottles, Sheffield
Cairns & Hickey, Bramhope, Leeds
Chippendale Fine Wines, Bradford, West Yorkshire M C
Great Northern Wine Company, Ripon, North Yorkshire M
Halifax Wine Company, Halifax, West Yorkshire
Hoults Wine Merchants, Huddersfield, West Yorkshire
House of Townend, Kingston upon Hull, East Yorkshire ✪
Michael Jobling, Newcastle-upon-Tyne M C
John Kelly Wines, Boston Spa, West Yorkshire M C
Martinez Fine Wines, Ilkley, West Yorkshire ✪
Mitchells Wines, Sheffield
Penistone Court, Penistone, Sheffield ✪ M C
Playford Ros, Thirsk, North Yorkshire M C
Roberts & Speight, Beverley, East Yorkshire

Springfield Wines, near Huddersfield, West Yorkshire
Vinceremos, Leeds **M C**
The Wright Wine Company, Skipton, North Yorkshire ✪
Wrightson & Co. Wine Merchants, Darlington **M C**

SCOTLAND

Cockburns, Leith, Edinburgh
Peter Green, Edinburgh
Inverarity Vaults, Biggar
Irvine Robertson, Edinburgh **C**
J & H Logan, Edinburgh
Luvian's Bottle Shop, Cupar, Fife
Peckham & Rye, Glasgow ✪
Raeburn Fine Wines, Edinburgh ✪
Laurence Smith, Edinburgh **M C**
Valvona & Crolla, Edinburgh ✪
Villeneuve Wines, Peebles, Haddington
    and Edinburgh ✪

WALES

Ballantynes, Cowbridge, Vale of Glamorgan ✪
Irma Fingal-Rock, Monmouth, Monmouthshire
Joseph Keegan, Holyhead, Isle of Anglesey
Moriarty Vintners, Cardiff
Terry Platt Wine Merchants, Llandudno, Conwy ✪ **M C**
Shaws, Beaumaris, Isle of Anglesey
William Stedman, Caerleon, Newport
James Williams, Narberth, Pembrokeshire

M = Mail order company, usually with no retail premises
F = Fine wine sales/wine broker/good range of expensive stuff!

NORTHERN IRELAND
Direct Wine Shipments, Belfast, Northern Ireland ✪
Ells Fine Wines, Portadown, Northern Ireland
James Nicholson, Crossgar, Co. Down, Northern Ireland ✪

CHANNEL ISLANDS
Bergerac Wine Cellar, St Helier, Jersey
Dunnells Ltd, St Peter Port, Guernsey
Victor Hugo Wines, St Saviour, Jersey
The Sommelier Wine Co., St Peter Port, Guernsey ✪

If you are a wine merchant in the UK and would like to be
mentioned on this list, or if your details are listed incorrectly,
the author and publisher will be happy to amend later editions.
We have tried to make The Wine List as helpful as possible but
if you have any ideas as to how we could improve it then write
to The Wine List, c/o Headline Book Publishing, 338 Euston Road,
London, NW1 3BH.

Matthew Jukes